The Furnace for Gold

The Furnace for Gold

A Teacher's Story

John A. Manicone

John Manicone
2004

VANTAGE PRESS
New York

Cover design by Susan Thomas

FIRST EDITION

Copyright © 2003 by John A. Manicone

Published by Vantage Press, Inc.
516 West 34th Street, New York, New York 10001

Manufactured in the United States of America
ISBN: 0-533-14523-6

Library of Congress Catalog Card No.: 2003090371

0 9 8 7 6 5 4 3 2 1

This work, my life as a teacher, is dedicated to my wife, Josephine. Without her support, her encouragement and her faith in me, this book would never have seen the light of day. My Josephine is my companion for life. Josephine, thank you and I love you always.

Contents

Author's Note

My journey from September 1960 to January 1991 is set down here for you. Along the way, I met some wonderful and incredibly talented people who shaped my way. One was Anne Kenny, Assistant Principal at Fashion High, and the other was John O'Connell, at J.H.S. 22M.

Ann was an excellent teacher and a gifted administrator. She died much too soon and never received the proper "chicken dinner." John taught me how to survive in the junior high school system for seven years. He was articulate, a dedicated teacher and a wonderful family man. God bless you, John.

And to the rest of the teaching staffs whom I've known and with whom I've worked, I say you made the journey too short. Those who never taught have the luxury to criticize and perhaps demean our efforts, but those who did stand in front of a classroom, every day, have the honor to reply, "With a few pieces of chalk and some lined sheets of paper I had the marvelous opportunity to stimulate minds and shape lives!"

And to my students, thank you.

January 2003

The Furnace for Gold

One

Who's in Control Here?

"Hello, Mr. Levine? Mr. Nat Levine?"

"Yes, who's this?"

"I'm Mr. Manicone, and I was told you have a job in Social Studies at 22."

"Probably. Can you handle children?"

"I have a master's in history from N.Y.U. and I have excellent references from all my mentor/teachers in the program."

"I asked if you can handle children?"

"I can handle children," I replied forcefully.

"Good, then get down here before lunch and you got a job!"

In September 1960, my brief conversation from a pay phone on Forsyth Street to Mr. Nat Levine, Assistant Principal of Social Studies at Junior High School 22 in Manhattan, started my thirty-one year adventure in the New York City school system. I possessed a substitute teaching license and I planned to get one year of teaching under by belt and then head for the golden shores of California and teach there. Little did I know that the beautiful girl I had met in June was to become Mrs. Manicone in July of 1961. J.H.S. 22M, as it turned out, was to become my mistress.

So, on a crisp September morning, I started my climb up a cement ramp to the four glass doors of the

1

junior high school I would call "home" for seven years. As I reached midway on the ramp I could see the courtyard below and it was full of children. I remembered saying to myself, "Boy, are these kids really this eager to start school? Can't be." As I started to ascend the second leg of the ramp, the entire courtyard was in view and the milling children were now screaming and running to one side. "What the hell's going on?" I asked myself. "Did Mickey Mantle just arrive?"

It's incredible that I can still recall with such clarity those events that began my teaching life. And yet, it wasn't clarity, but a sense of horror that did it for me on that beautiful September morning nearly thirty-five years ago. The "Mickey Mantle" the kids were running to in that courtyard turned out to be in reality the Cape Man and the Umbrella Man!

"I don't care what the judge said, I won't let those criminals in my building!"

As I entered the main office of Gustave Strauben-mueller Junior High School, I was witnessing the principal, Mr. Z., as he passionately tried to convince, persuade and argue his points of appeal into a small, mute phone which he held in his rather large hand. He was surrounded by his secretaries who sat in stunned silence and obedient awe. As I walked up to the counter, I was immediately stopped in my tracks when one of the seated ladies slowly shook her head from side to side and placed her right index finger to her lips.

"How do you expect me to run a normal school with those two animals loose in the building? Hm?" The principal's face was flushed with anger and he kept raising and lowering his left arm to make his points. "I'm telling you, I won't open this building to them or their friends! You should see the courtyard. It's mobbed with people. I can't control that mob. It's just not safe!"

After a few seconds, Mr. Z. appeared to relax and became calm. Then, a moment of silence, a quick "Good-bye" and he jubilantly spun around and announced to everyone in the office that "we can open now, they're going to 165."

Within one hour of actually becoming a paid member of the New York City Board of Education, I had witnessed the incredible fluid power of those-in-charge. Power could be dispensed on the phone with the same effect and authority as written instructions. Some lessons were harder to learn than others. For me, I saw power as an object; to those-in-charge power was a tool. In the hands of a ruthless practitioner, power was used to run classrooms, to control departments, effect transfers and change lives. Sometimes, it was used to run schools.

My first class was 8-19, a music class. I received this class, as it turned out, by default. Two Social Studies positions were open that morning and since I was the sub and the other was a regular appointee, she got the "better program." A week or so later, I saw that same regular run out of the building with her coat flapping over her shoulders. It was about midmorning and I was walking in the hall as she flew past me.

"Where are you going?" I asked. I was afraid something was wrong.

She screamed at the top of her voice, without dropping a step. "No one's going to call me a son-of-a-bitch and get away with it! I'm leaving!"

With that, she slammed open the front door and I never saw her again.

That first year was remarkable. I learned more from my students than I actually taught them. Besides 8-19, I had two seventh- and two eighth-grade Social Studies classes. There were a few "Barbaras" and "Susans," and a couple of "Williams" and "Roberts." But, there were also Jesus, Brunhilda, Wilfredo and Tomasino. Here and there I would find that Juanita Pabon was the daughter of Mr. And Mrs. Pabon—and yet, her sister was Carmela Sanchez. *Who was Sanchez?*

Coming from a typical middle class home, it was my belief that all children possessed the same last name as their parents. Further, all members of the same family belonged to the same race. Imagine my shock when J.J.S. 22M had its first Open School Night that term!

It was late October of 1960 when I realized that actual physical force was a necessary part of teaching. Nothing prepared me for that brief but significant episode that took place outside my classroom. It was the policy of Mr. Z. for all teachers to stand outside in the halls during the changes of classes. On this day, it was the beginning of the first period, and I was trying to impress my supervisors. I was at my station directing the student traffic. I had survived, but my next door colleague was not so fortunate. A steady parade of teachers had come and gone. Today was to be different! A tall, muscular young man was making his way toward me, walking with determination. He passed by and as he approached the classroom door, he was greeted by Brunhilda, the class brat.

"We've had sixteen teachers here and you're next!" she said proudly.

With that, this new instructor reached down and picked Brunhilda up by her ponytail and, holding her at eye level as she tried to struggle free, he announced, "I'm Mr. Seigel and I'm the last one you're going to see, dearie!"

Believe it or not, he was. Mr. Seigel completed that

4

term and the next.

As luck would have it, I had Brunhilda scheduled in Social Studies the following September. She lived up to her reputation. Now that she was an eighth-grader, she was as mean-spirited and surly as they came. For nearly two months of that term, she disrupted my class at will. I wrote her up to the Dean many times, and at long last, I received a promise that a parent would appear at the Parent-Teacher Conference scheduled in the last days of October. Well, it wasn't a parent, but her grandmother showed up. This lady told me that she was raising her grandchildren and she worked, and she apologized for not coming sooner. When I recounted all the disruptive things Brunhilda did, the woman jumped up; grabbing her granddaughter, she made the girl apologize to me. The grandmother, visibly mortified, then said, "If Brunhilda ever disrupts your class again, I will come to your room and pull her pants down and beat her backside in front of the entire class!" I told her that was not necessary. The following days and weeks turned out to be incredible. Brunhilda was as good as gold. Perhaps I should have called in the grandmother sooner!

It became quite evident that to teach in any junior high school in New York City in general (and at Junior High School 22M in particular), physical "control" was a necessary tool. It wasn't enough to "motivate" the students. Many children, with the exception of the SPE and the top four or five classes in each grade, came to school without the proper reference points. If a teacher prepared a map or chart, most students within any particular class would have difficulty reading what was in front of them. They didn't know what a key was at the bottom of a map; they could not interpret a graph correctly, even if it were the simplest bar graph; most had difficulty with a basic hand-held ruler or a pie graph; telling time or predicting a trivial time problem was a source of some of the most outlandish answers a teacher would hear. That's when "force" becomes a reality.

Faced with these frustrations, many students, especially the girls, would become silent, embarrassed and look down at their desks, playing with their pens or paper. The boys, however, were "threatened." At the risk of being called a bigot, I attributed this "threat" as part of the Latino manhood. The girls in the class were keenly observing this interplay between the teacher and the class—"The Man" and "us." It became the obligation of the boys to defend the "honor" of the class and many times, these boys would mistake prodding of a teacher struggling to get a point across and looking stupid. Believe me, nothing in the mind of a junior high school student is more important than their "image"! Being called or even inferred to as stupid is very dangerous to any unwary teacher.

It may be a simple, called-out answer, a giggle by a girl—whatever, and someone will have taken offense. A male student has assumed the mantle of "class defender" and the teacher is now confronted by an actual physical challenge. The "rule book" tells you to "disarm" the situation, but the author of this testament is not in the Lower East Side, or in Bed-Stuy at this moment. He or she is probably in Princeton, New Jersey, writing another worthwhile tome for publication so that he or she can give "expert" advise on a TV talk show. What are you to do?

Unfortunately, these "episodes" occurred too many times, both to me and to many of my colleagues. We were forced to use force. I remember one particular occasion in September of 1962 or 1963. (These confrontations always occur in the first weeks of the new term.) I was attempting to go over the instructions and regulations I had prepared for the class. Each student was given a sheet with the enumerated items listed.

As I began to go over the items listed on the fact sheet, I started to pick up an "echo." At first, it was difficult to establish its source, but as I walked up and down each aisle, I was able to determine the culprit. He was a rather good-looking Puerto Rican, tall for his age, wiry and seated next to a rather charming young lady. Hoping not to escalate the situation to any uncontrollable degree and equally hoping not to embarrass the young man in front of his lady friend, I bent over and whispered into his ear to cease and desist. I continued to review the items on my list, but still the "echo" persisted. Now, in front of the class, I identified the problem and ordered him to stop. He repeated my charge with the young lady smiling approval.

At this junction, I faced a dilemma. Problems in a junior high classroom are classified as either "in-house" or dean referrals. In order to "score" points with the administration, a subject teacher attempts to solve as many "in-house" problems as possible. Principals must rate teachers at the end of each year, and a "Satisfactory" rating each year goes a long way if one wants to remain in good stead with everyone in positions of authority.

I decided right then and there that this was an "in-house" situation. Raising my voice, I told the young man to stop. He imitated my order exactly. "I told you to cut it out!" I yelled. "I told you to cut it out!" he returned. My frustration was peaking and his smirking throughout this ordeal was not helping. I was beginning to lose control of the class because students were—of course—siding with him and all attention was narrowing on what I would do next.

I walked toward his seat sternly and when I got to his desk, I slammed my hand on it as hard as I could and yelled at loudly as my lungs were able, "Cut it out!"

He could not duplicate that, so, he jumped out of his seat and whipping off his glasses, he challenged me to fight him.

I said, "You want to take on a man, not a kid? Fine with me; but first I am going to empty the room!"

I instructed the young man to remain by his seat and commanded the rest of the class to exit the room by using both doors. As the class reluctantly left the room, I could hear them grumbling about the fact that they would not witness the fight. After the students were gone, I pulled down both shades to each door and locked them.

Now, I returned to my problem. My young nemesis stood there, by his seat, bewildered and confused. His girlfriend and the rest of his admirers were gone. The room was very quiet.

I approached him without a word, picked him up bodily, and threw him against the blackboard, all in one motion. He fell to the floor. I asked him, "Do you want any more?" He scrambled to his feet, walked to the door, and without a word, he opened the door, walked past his classmates in the hall and left the building. I never saw him again.

It's amazing! Within hours, practically everyone in the school had heard of "our fight." My colleagues and other students alike had heard how Mr. Manicone had dispatched the "problem" so efficiently and routinely. "How did I isolate the situation so quickly?;" "What made me think of dismissing the class?;" "Why did I feel I had to confront the situation alone?"—etc., and etc. I really could not give an honest or thought-filled answer on the spot. I only knew that it was the most practical and expedient action to take at the moment. I later was to learn that the "higher-ups" found out too, and they logged everything down . . . "Mr. Manicone could handle a class, any class."

My newfound "rep" turned out to have many ramifications. The most obvious one was my presence in the hall. Let me explain. In any New York City junior high school, the attending students "rate" all their teachers. The student's definition of an effective teacher is "how powerful," "how weak," "how good," "how bad," meaning does he control the class, can he intimidate, does he know his material, and is he a poor grader? Well, one way to know if a teacher is "powerful" is to measure the distance between the student body and himself in any hall he walks! I can modestly tell you that the empty space between the students and me as I walked in the halls of J.H.S. 22M was about twenty feet! Believe me, that was powerful stuff.

Well—maybe 15 feet, but no matter. The other end of my rep was that I could handle any class, especially those that were labeled as "difficult." Once a teacher gets a reputation among the class of supervisors and administrators that he or she is "weak," that teacher is held in contempt for the duration, in the school building. I did not want to be judged as "weak" or "not able to handle the load," so I took what was assigned me, and I got "my reward" the following year. It was a class of undisciplined, unruly and as completely unteachable a group of young men as I had ever seen. Most were nearly sixteen, two years behind in grade—and all were on a 2.5 testing score in both reading and math. It was an eighth-grade class!

9

As usual, I had my confrontation in the first week of class that September, and I established my "rep" once more. But this "put-down" was only a small potato, while the "cruisers" were still biding their time for the "true" test to come. I knew it and, more importantly, *they* knew it. They tried everything, from "staging" fights in class to see my reaction, to throwing all sorts of weighted spit balls around the room. I would no sooner turn around the write on the blackboard, when a missile of various determined weight would splash on the board or on my back.

Attempting to fix blame was useless.

After weeks of this behavior, and remember, in junior high school, it was the usual practice to assign a homeroom class with the same subject teacher, so I had these "gentlemen" assigned to my care for almost 25 percent of any given day, I was now approaching a panic situation. I had recently married; I just passed my regular teaching J.H.S. exam, and I wanted to impress the powers that be. I wasn't going to let this get me down. I had to reach into my gut and find "something," and that "something" turned out to be a beaten-up edition of the *N.Y. Daily News* I happened to locate in the top desk drawer in that classroom. I was saved!

"*The Golden Gloves!*" The answer to my problem was staring me right in the face! Instead of letting them direct their fury at me, I let these "gentlemen" direct their fury at each other. I would challenge their manhood by having them "earn" these applications to fight in the Golden Gloves. They were almost sixteen years old and by the time I "processed" their applications, I knew I could whip this class into shape.

I went on a Golden Gloves application hunt! When I had acquired about a dozen or so, I made my move. On a bright Monday morning, I announced to my class of social incorrigibles that from this day forward, I would only "honor" those individuals in class with applications to the Golden Gloves if they proved to be "worthy" of that recognition. It worked like a charm!

As soon as I made my announcement, the demeanor of the class changed dramatically. The major "toughs" emerged and wanted the recognition they felt they were entitled to. The minor "toughs" (they were the skinny, wiry type who always had to prove something) gave way and became subservient. I warned everybody who wanted to be seriously considered for the Golden Gloves that they had to really "earn" their application to it. The moveable chairs were neatly lined up, the scraps of paper were gone from the floor and the spit-ball display ended abruptly. If any infraction occurred, I had one of the major "toughs" take care of it. Believe it or not, three of my charges got into the Gloves, and one actually made it through the first round. They got their asses truly whipped and by the end of November, I was in control again. The administration was duly impressed.

The following September I became a grade advisor. I was relieved of the Home Room class and two teaching classes. I was rewarded after three years. More was to come.

My "reward" was a mixed blessing. Grade advising allows an individual entry into a world of social dynamics that requires a tremendous capacity to understand human nature. At J.H.S. 22M, this included broken homes, child abuse, alcohol and drug dependencies of parents and students alike; divorces, separations, live-in boyfriends and girlfriends, incest and problems like, "the dog ate my homework." There are tragic days and very funny moments. Most of the problems cannot be solved.

The runaways usually made it into this category. One of my earliest cases involved a young eighth-grader whose parents were undertakers. The girl lived with her family in an apartment above the mortuary; she was acutely ashamed of anything associated with the livelihood of her mother and father. So, she began to run away from home. One day, I interviewed her. She appeared pleasant, but as soon as we got near the "problem," she tensed up, became fidgety and spoke in short, monosyllabic phrases. Then I noticed the black fingernail polish, and her make-up had no traces of red. It appeared whitish. Yet, when she replied to my questions, she was visibly assertive on the subject of death. She said she didn't want to touch her mother or father because they handled dead things. "How would *I* like it if *I* had to be driven around in a hearse?" she asked me. I was at a loss. A hearse? Really? I guess I would run away too!

I tried to bring in things like, "This is what your mother and father were trained to do," and "Somebody has to do it," and further, "Look, it's almost like being a doctor." Nothing worked. The girl kept running away and we had to refer this case to the Bureau of Child Guidance in Brooklyn.

Then there was the case of the young Jewish boy who had difficulty with English and history. His mother came in during Open School Night and when we discussed his lack of progress, she said she had the solution. She had been saving $300 for a vacation, but instead, she was going to buy the *Encyclopedia Britannica* for her son. I advised her to save her money, as we had an up-to-date edition in our library, and I advised her to use the money on tutoring, or on an "educational" vacation like visiting museums or historic sites. She agreed that my solution was "very wise."

In the Guidance Office where I had my quarters, we shared our meager space with the truant officer. His name was Jerry and he was not only effective at what he did, but he worked very closely with us in cases that we shared. Truancy, poor grades and poor self-image were basically the problems we handled day in and day out.

I remember a particular instance in which Jerry was very instrumental in tracking down one of our worst truants off the street. After many weeks of attempting to find this young man, Jerry was successful in getting the boy's mother and a translator into the office for interrogation. The questioning was creepingly slow because the mother had to wait for the question to be interpreted and then translated into Spanish. She had difficulty in hearing and might also have been retarded, which didn't help the situation at all. After some fifteen or twenty minutes into this prolonged process, it appeared that the mother had known the whereabouts of her son all along. When Jerry asked, in desperation, where the young man might be currently, the mother casually answered that her son was living with a grown woman in her thirties! Jerry went berserk. A fifteen-year-old male with an adult female? Incredible!

In a flash, Jerry jumped out of his seat and started searching for certain official forms on top of his desk and inside the desk drawers, muttering to himself. "Where's that form?" "Contributing to a minor?" and that one on "Aiding and abetting?" He went on like this for several minutes, all of this while the mother and the interpreter were watching with greater and greater concern. "¿Que pasa?" the mother kept repeating. "¿Que pasa?" over and over again. When the interpreter attempted to answer her, the mother started to yell, "No, no."

"Don't you want to help your son?" Jerry called back. "I'm trying to help your son, and we don't want him to get sick with venereal disease and other things!" But the mother kept shaking her head. "No, no."

"What do you want?" Jerry replied. "Don't you want to get your son back in school?" You could hear the urgency in his voice.

The mother told the interpreter, who later translated that, "No, the mother understands the needs of a man. She doesn't want any trouble with the police—she just doesn't want anyone arrested."

"What? Are you kidding?" Jerry screamed. "What does she think we've been trying to do all this time here?"

Now the translator tried one more time, and when she asked the mother Jerry's question, she went into a fit of laughter. The more Jerry and I pressed, the more the translator screamed with laughter. "What the hell did the mother say to you?" we repeated and repeated. It was only after some time, and with a great deal of persuasion that we finally got our answer. The translator said, "The mother wasn't concerned with the truancy, or even the possibility of venereal contact. No, she wanted Jerry to speak to this woman and tell her to stop smoking, because that was serious. Her boy has asthma! And, smoking is very bad for asthma!"

Some people are always a pound short or a day late. This mother wasn't even in the train station.

In today's world, the truant officer is now called the Attendance Officer.

Two

Violence—Who Needs It?

Many people find violence, any type of violence, unimaginable, intolerable, or even inexcusable. Maybe so. But in my experience as a junior high school teacher, I found something rather interesting about my school. It had a lot in common with prisons. People in both places bring hostility with them, and attempting to teach, train, or instruct that kind of clientele is almost impossible. In most work places, the atmosphere is pleasant, and we never read about any of them until we learn of a tragedy in a post office or a Burger King. Then it's too late. The shooter brought the violence with him that day.

Teachers are not saints. We can be provoked and, that said, let me attempt to explain the nature of violence in the New York City Junior High Schools. Students are always "testing the waters." In many cases, territorial claims are either "understood" or established by the proponent. Sometimes these claims can be challenged or disputed, but the result is always the same. "Who won?"

In my first year at 22M, during the Fall of 1960, I was one day walking back to my classroom to prepare for the next class. As I got to the end of the corridor, I had to make a right to continue down the next corridor. At the elbow of this point was the typing class run by Mr. D., who had just swung open the door to his room and was ushering out a male student in a very brusque manner.

15

The kid had a red slap mark on his left cheek and when he threw the young boy up against the wall, the kid said something to which Mr. D. summarily punched him in the side, dropping the boy to the floor.

As I witnessed this incident, neither Mr. D. nor I were aware that the Assistant Principal was watching, too. He had emerged from one of the rooms when the trouble broke out. The A.P. asked Mr. D. what had happened in the typing class in the first place, and Mr. D. told the Assistant Principal that the young man had made a vile comment about Mr. D.'s mother. When he brought the student out in the hall, the young man repeated the comment.

"Fine," said the A.P., and with that he reached down and grabbed the young boy's left heel and started to drag the helpless kid down the hall to his office.

The boy was still doubled up in pain as the A.P. pushed open the swinging door in the middle of the hall. As they both passed through, I distinctly saw that the A.P. got his body through the door, but, unfortunately, the young man's head took a good shot as he went through. Mr. D. and I looked both up and down each of the passageways. We saw absolutely no one. Violence made a deafening sound to everyone concerned, especially me. If the tool is appropriate, use it!

This type of violence, keeping the students in check to maintain "peaceful control," was manifest on many levels. I distinctly remember an incident which involved one of our best para-security guards and a very insolent eighth grader. I happened to be at the head of the landing in a side exit staircase when I noticed that this nameless student deliberately shoved herself past the female security guard in her haste to exit the building. The security guard tried to restrain the child to learn her identity, but the girl refused to cooperate.

At this point, the guard attempted to grab the girl's notebook to ascertain her name, and the confrontation became physical. The student was no match for the guard in this brief struggle, because she outweighed the girl by at least 200 pounds and years of know-how.

As the guard wrestled the notebook away from the student, the girl screamed, "You got a big black ass!"

With that, the security guard dropped everything and, walking over to the kid, said, "Honey, my ass is as black as yours!" and slugged her right in the mouth.

I rushed down the steps and told the guard to write up the incident as I escorted the dazed student to the nurse's office. We called her mother, reported what happened and the issue was closed, but our security was better for it and I believe the young girl also learned from her very "painful lesson."

Thinking back, after all these years, one would like to sanitize the events. I could have rushed down the steps and grabbed the security guard's arm and defended the health and welfare of this child. But I didn't, simply because the teachers maintained their end and the security personnel held theirs, no pun intended. We supported each other, but the support was always to keep order so that everyone at J.H.S. 22M could do their job—teach the children. You can't teach anyone in an atmosphere of anarchy or disrespect for institutional values. Most of the parents of our students wanted it that way, because we constantly got the feedback that 22M was tough but fair. Other junior high schools in our district told us the same thing, and our principal directed this policy. He didn't want any variations; he rewarded his disciples and got rid of the "trouble-makers."

Again, there was nothing novel about this approach

or philosophy in the junior high schools of New York City. In the fall of 1959, when I was attending New York University to get my Master's in Education, a six-credit course (ETA) involved getting hands-on practice teaching with an experienced teacher. As I sat in the back of the class, I distinctly remember that these classes were frequently interrupted by fire gongs. Our NYC Board of Education takes great pride in the fact that we have never lost a student in a school fire in nearly 100 years!

Fire drills are conducted with a great deal of soberness and dispatch. Everyone must exit the building; that's the law. Well, after several weeks of observing the teaching method, I became puzzled over the frequency of these alarms. Remember, I was only attending this activity once a week. It must have been sometime in late October or early November when we experienced another legitimate alarm. As I arose from my seat in the back of the classroom, I overheard one student say to another, "Are you on the list?"

What list? And why are they discussing it at this particular time?

"I don't think so," replied the other student, "but I know Reggie is." As we got into the hall and headed for the staircase, I noticed for the first time that members of the Phys Ed department were at the top of the stairwell. They were still in their gym clothes, whistles and all.

"There he is! Reggie and that other kid!" someone yelled, and like a shot the two took off down the stairs, pushing their way down through the mob of kids. But it was no use. The gym teachers below grabbed the two young people and banged both up against the wall. They were slapped and punched senseless.

"What the hell is going on here?" I asked as we continued down the stairs.

"There's Billy!" someone else yelled out, and the same thing happened to him. He was grabbed and punched against the wall. It then dawned on me what the "list" was. The gym teachers had written names on a piece of paper and they were the "executioners." I later found out that this was the policy of this particular junior high school and it was very simple and very legal.

Everyone knows that a teacher is not permitted to strike a student without running the risk of losing his or her job and getting arrested if the parent presses charges. However, there is one exception to this rule; and that exception is during a fire drill, regardless of whether it is a practice drill or the real thing. According to the law, a New York City teacher may use whatever force is deemed necessary, including striking a student, to maintain and expedite the purpose of the fire drill: namely, get the kids out of the building safely and quickly.

Someone in this particular junior high school believed in "creative fire drilling." Using the pretext of conducting regular fire drills at the height of perfection, lists of disorderly students were gathered by the Dean's Office from various sources and the gym teachers carried out their mission—pick up the listed students as they exited the building and "discipline" them for "behavior unbecoming during a fire drill which puts the rest of the student body at risk." It worked; it was legal. The school ran like a well-oiled machine. So much for "excessive" violence.

The nature of junior high school violence has and continues to have many "fathers." Administrators (who condoned it), teachers (who practiced it to keep control in their classes), students (who pursued it in their pecking scheme of things), and parents (who knew what was going on), all used and needed violence for their own purposes. However, we all dreaded the day when one of these "fathers" would decide to cross the line and go into the other guy's bailiwick. And as luck would have it, that dreaded day came in the Spring of 1964. A parent came to school with a bolo knife!

That morning, Mrs. O., our regular Spanish teacher, who was born and educated in Spain, was attempting to explain a particular word and its meaning to her class. As things turned out, when she asked this one designated student to say this word in Spanish, he did so in his own vernacular patois. She tried to correct him and he insisted that he had said the correct word in Spanish. After several attempts, she said to him, "That is not correct. You said it in Puerto Rican."

The boy continued to insist and said, "That's the way we say it at home and we speak Spanish! My mother says it the same way!"

Mrs. O., in desperation, said, "I'm sorry, but that is not Spanish and if your mother says it that way, she doesn't know Spanish either!"

With that, the young man, obviously humiliated, bolted out of the room and ran out of the building. He came back with his mother and she brought with her the bolo knife, screaming at the top of her lungs as she walked up our ramp into the building, "I'm going to cut her heart out!"

Lucky for the Spanish teacher, someone in her class had warned her that the boy was on the way home to get his mother, otherwise, we would have had a tragedy at 22 that morning. Mrs. O. prudently left her class and ran into the principal's office which was down the hall. One of the secretaries suggested that Mrs. O. hide somewhere in the building while someone else called the police. For one reason or another, I was instrumental in opening the auditorium door which was locked and we ushered the frightened Spanish teacher down the darkened aisle. Someone suggested hiding her in the folds of the auditorium curtain, and that's where we left her as I relocked the doors. Then we waited.

When I saw the mother and the kid rushing up the rampway, my heart literally sank. I had never seen such a huge knife before. It was the type used in Central America to cut down bananas. The woman was screaming and ranting even as she pulled back the doors leading into the building. No one attempted to stop her.

"Where is she? That bitch! I'll cut out her heart! You heard me, where is that Spanish bitch!" she screamed as she went from the principal's office down the hall, opening and closing closet doors and marching herself and the boy toward the Spanish language classroom. We followed her—at a very safe distance, you can be sure. More and more classroom doors were being held open for a second, and then very discreetly closed again.

When the mother reached Mrs. O.'s classroom and found it to be Mrs. "O." less, she turned and marched back down the hall toward the principal's office. We all beat a very hasty retreat. The mother kept screaming and brandishing that knife throughout this sequence, which had to be an unbelievably long ten minutes or so, but the police finally arrived, disarmed the woman and arrested her. The aggrieved mother never caught up with Mrs. O. that day, needless to say, Mrs. O. was shaking like a leaf when we retrieved her. She had to be coaxed away from the auditorium curtain.

Everything ended as quickly as it started. And, by the way, Mrs. O. never returned to J.H.S. 22M after that term. Who could blame her? She wasn't qualified to teach Puerto Rican.

I kept telling myself that things couldn't get worse, but given enough time, they actually could. A case in point involved some of the members of the class of those incorrigibles who "promoted" me to grade advising. Some of them actually made it to the 9th grade and in my first year as a Grade Advisor, a couple of these "boys" were in my care.

Picture a warm May night down on New York City's Lower East Side, somewhere near Rivington Street, close by to Pitt Street Park. A police car with its windows down is quietly "cruising" the neighborhood when one of the officers smells the odor of gasoline. But there were no gasoline stations on Rivington Street. It was after midnight during the wee hours of Saturday morning. I got the phone call that Monday.

I went down to the 7th Precinct on Grand Street and spoke to the investigating detective and he told me the most incredible story I'd ever heard. After he finished, he said, "You talk with Joachim, and I'll bet you'll ask him the same question I did when he's all through. Okay?"

Sure enough, there was Joachim, sitting dejectedly in the police interrogation room. We exchanged the usual pleasantries and he told me how and why he was picked up. At 16, he was facing felony charges of mayhem, attempted arson, conspiracy to riot and a few other things which I can't recall now. I also learned that he was the War Lord of the Pagans.

I had always known that gang activity was rampant on the Lower East Side, but Joachim was the first gang member I had actually met in person. The actual names of these gangs like the Dragons, the Bishops, the Pagans, were in reality associations of ethnic groups like the blacks, Puerto Ricans and/or Dominicans. Believe it or not, a girl gang associated with the Pagans was called the Bopping Ballerinas! But, I digress . . . Joachim, being the War Lord of his gang, was to procure the necessary "armaments" for the scheduled fight. His choice was Molotov Cocktails! He went around the neighborhood siphoning gasoline from the gas tanks of various cars parked near the school. He then continued scrounging the neighborhood for any and all types of bottles.

On that Saturday night, he got help from one of his brothers and brought a couple of cartons along with the bottles, the gasoline and several towels he had stolen from his home. He shooed his brother away, "made" the cocktails on the corner and waited. He said he "made" about 40 or 50 cocktails, all primed and ready. Then he waited for his gang to show up. Fortunately for the Lower East Side, he got the days mixed up. The rumble was to take place next Saturday!

"How long were you waiting there?" I asked him.

"Oh, a couple of hours and then the cops came and grabbed me and took all my stuff," he said without too much remorse. I was still thinking about "that question" I was to ask Joachim, and then it hit me. With all those bottles, the reeking aroma of gasoline in the night air, and patiently waiting all that time, had Joachim ever been tempted to test one of his concoctions? So, I asked him. "Why didn't you try out one of the bottles?"

"I didn't have a match!" he replied. I later learned that the detective asked him the same question. We both just shook our heads in disbelief.

As I left the station house and returned to school, I couldn't help wondering about what had just transpired. "How stupid can one person be?" I asked myself. "It's bad enough that that dopey kid is in trouble with the law, but we averted a catastrophe by an eyelash! What the hell am I doing with my life? I just want to teach! This is not teaching. This is being a warden, being a referee, being a witness to madness. I've got to get out of this junior high school and go to a high school where I can maybe do some good," I said to myself.

A couple of months later, a new twist to the theme of violence came by way of a frightened seventh grader. That September term, I picked up the 7th grade, which meant that as an advisor I would stay with these students until they graduated. The seventh grader was very shy and she was a potential runaway.

The girl was referred to me by her homeroom teacher who had overheard someone say that Matilda was planning to run away from home. "She couldn't take it anymore because of all the fighting in her house," the referral said. When I questioned the student, she admitted that there was a lot of yelling and fighting between the young girls in the house and the mother. And, she proceeded to tell me that her uncle and the girl's grandmother also got involved in the fighting and that the uncle usually ended up hitting the mother.

"What?" I said. "Your uncle hits Matilda's mother? Why?"

"I don't know, he just slaps her around after he waits for my mother to come home," she said. The more I questioned her on this point, the more frustrated I became. The student wasn't making any sense. Then I noticed that the seventh grader had a sister in the 9th grade in our school, so I sent for her to see if she could shed some more light on this puzzling situation.

Believe it or not, the ninth grader said the same thing. She further told me that she had run away from home herself on two or three occasions, and that she was planning to leave again with Matilda this time. I realized that I had to send for the mother. The girls were very distressed at this, but I persisted and I gave them a note to take to their mother for an appointment with me. Boy, did I get a jolt!

Several days later, as I was returning to my office, I casually entered the room and was instantly greeted by a pair of legs. And, what legs! I was immediately reminded of that expression, "Legs that never quit." Remember, this was the mid-sixties, and the mini-skirt was in fashion, but as Benny Hill would put it, "This girl abused the privilege!"

She was simply the most voluptuous woman I'd ever seen. She didn't belong in a Guidance office, but rather in a modeling studio. So, with as much poise as I could muster, I asked her if I could help her.

"Are you Mr. Manicone?" she asked.

"Yes," I stammered. "What can I do for you?"

"You sent for me," she replied.

I hadn't sent for any 30-ish young woman that I could recall, as I took the piece of paper from her. And then I realized this was from the interview of the two sisters a few days previous.

"I sent for the mother," I said, "not a sister of Matilda's."

"I am the mother," she said. I was startled beyond belief. How could this gorgeous creature produce such plain girls? With that incredible news, I ushered the woman into my cubicle and proceeded to relate what had transpired.

The interview was going reasonably well until I got to the part where I questioned the mother about the violence in the home—in particular the slapping alleged by the girls. "Is it true that your brother hits you?" I asked the mother.

"Yes," she said.

"Does he live in the apartment with the girls and your mother?" I asked.

"Yes," she repeated. "He's like our father."

"Whose father?" I asked, somewhat puzzled.

"My father," she said. "My real father is dead."

This conversation was going nowhere; nothing made sense. Why would a thirtyish-year-old woman allow herself to be reprimanded by her brother in front of her kids? Why did the grandmother permit this? Why was this woman going out frequently during the school week? When I asked these questions, this mother could provide me with no satisfactory answers. I then did something quite extraordinary, I asked if I could see *her* mother. She agreed!

When the grandmother showed up alone, I knew I was going to get some real answers. She was a "real" grandmother type, if you know what I mean. She wore dark clothes, her hair in a bun, and she carried a handbag that could double as a weapon. She was pleasant and very cordial and appeared eager to help her grandchildren. She informed me that her daughter was a mother at 15, and was 31 at the present. She also told me that the two granddaughters, though not as beautiful as their mother, had frequent fights over boyfriends.

"What?" I asked. "What boyfriends?"

"That's where the problem always begins. It's the boyfriends," she insisted. "When Matilda, or her sister, invites a boyfriend over, the boy takes one look at them and then they stare at my daughter. The boys always pick the girls' mother!"

I couldn't believe my ears. Young boys of 16 or 17 going out with a 31-year-old woman! Incredible! And, she went on to tell me, she likes the "slow ones" even better.

"You've got to be kidding," I said. "This is crazy!"

"That's what my son keeps saying. Don't you understand? It's all jealousy. My granddaughters are jealous of their mother because she's prettier and she's always taking their boyfriends away. My son has to hit my daughter when she gets in very late sometimes, like two or three o'clock in the morning."

I said, "Mrs. Sanchez, we must stop this. Your daughter is not fit or able to understand or control herself. Your granddaughters' education and health come first. I'm going to call in my supervisor and see if he can help us." The grandmother, already in tears, thanked me for understanding and consented.

Once my superior, Mr. G., heard the whole story, he recommended that we bring this to the Bureau of Child Guidance and have them take the mother to court. He warned the grandmother that she would be called in to testify against her own daughter and that the net result could possibly be the removal of the three grandchildren—the two girls and a boy—to foster care. The grandmother had indicated that she had a serious heart condition and that she could not raise the children. All she could do was to keep house for her son and daughter.

Several weeks later, the case was heard. I was not present, but Mr. G. was and he told me that when the hearing began, the mother of the two girls was jovial, smiling and appeared to have no understanding of what was going on at all. It wasn't until the ruling came down from the judge that the weight of undertaking finally took root. She screamed and carried on at the defense table that Mr. G. described as "The most heartwrenching thing he ever witnessed."

In retrospect, one could say that these very unusual situations are the exceptions and let it go at that. My point is, that far too often, these exceptional cases become quite routine during the lifetime of any given teacher. We are just not ready when they occur, and the educational systems and universities which are supposed to prepare the potential newcomers to the field of education do a rather poor job. I was reminded of such an instance when I was getting my degree at NYU.

Our instructor told the story, when he was attending Columbia for his degree, that a student asked the venerable professor of her most difficult or threatening situation when she taught in the school system in the 20s.

"Now, let me see," she said, as she tapped her finger on her cheek. "Oh, yes. Once a boy" (said with a prominent Harvard accent) "got up out of his seat when I asked him for his homework, and stormed out of my class!"

Every teacher takes into the classroom all the tools of his or her trade; that being the training (for what it is worth), life experiences that are appropriate for the classroom, and the talent to influence and instruct youngsters. I tried to do that each and every time I stepped into my room, regardless of whether it was to teach the developmental lesson, go over practice Regents questions, teaching in the summer school program, or giving a guidance lesson as a Grade Advisor.

It appeared to me that one's life experience should be imparted to young teenagers along with the materials printed up by the Bureau of Child Guidance. But I found that they were lacking in those strengths that had sustained me and my generation. For example, where could I find material about moral values, or doing chores around the house, or being thrifty and having a savings bankbook? How could I allocate materials about citizenship and accepting responsibilities to parents and other figures of authority? When I wrote to the Bureau to send me material about these qualities that my middle class upbringing stressed, I received an unexpected reply.

"How dare you to ever attempt to impose your middle class values on your students!" it went. The letter further reminded me to use only the required and approved materials which we were instructed to employ. I was so angry, I tore the letter to shreds.

Three

It Gets Better!

One day, in the middle of the fall term of my fifth year at 22M, I was called into the Dean's office because one of my male charges and his friend were accused of molesting a young girl—I think a first grader—in Pitt Street Park.

Gathered in Mr. R.'s office were the two accused students and their mothers; the Dean, the other Grade Advisor and myself. The Dean proceeded to relate how information about the alleged molestation had been obtained, and then he read the statements each boy gave him.

He proceeded to question the two boys, in front of their parents. The boys readily admitted that they had lured the little girl over to the park bench where they were seated, and began to grope her privates. Then they went behind some bushes near the bench; the boys exposed themselves and they "played" with the little girl.

As one of the boys related the incident in detail to all of us in the room, I noticed that one of the mothers appeared thoroughly bored and even somewhat impatient during the proceedings. She kept swinging her crossed leg back and forth as the two boys continued their confession. The Dean also noticed this bizarre behavior on the part of the parent. Finally, he interrupted the hearing and directly asked this mother, "Is there a problem here, Mrs. P.?"

"You bet there is!" she replied. "What's all the fuss about? The girl should know something about boys, shouldn't she? And, after all, she's almost 7 years old!"

I was just too dumbfounded to speak. I got up and left the room. Sometimes the problem is not with the children as much as it is with parents. Here, we obviously have another case where intelligence is not a requisite for parenting.

Cases like this one were not as rare as one might suspect. The pressures, whether they were student-created or parent-made, exacted a toll on everyone. Parents were constantly imputing on both our level and on the superintendent's. During the early 60s, every imaginable program was kicked around in the New York City junior high schools, ranging from adopting the middle school mode to abolishing junior high schools altogether. We had the two year SPE Program, a three year SPE Program, bi-lingual classes, Two Bridges Program and my favorite, Higher Horizons.

The Higher Horizons Program was an outgrowth of a very poorly conceived idea that was strongly supported by the Hispanic Community in our district. Basically, the concept was why were there so few Hispanics in the SPE Program? In the junior high schools of New York City, it was the pride and joy of all principals to have as many functioning SPE classes as one could program. Unfortunately, at our school, where we could have as many as 21 or 22 classes in grade, the best was only 1 or 2 SPE classes at any one time. The potential SPE student had to meet certain basic standards. But the parents in our district didn't want to hear it.

To them, all conditions or pedagogical standards

were merely euphemistic terms which served to exclude Hispanics from these SPE classes. For example, one prerequisite for taking a foreign language, even Spanish, was that the applicant had to read on grade level, meaning 7.0 or better. Very few Hispanic students at 22M could attain that score in English.

"It doesn't matter," the parents said. "We speak Spanish at home and if our child takes Spanish in school, he will have a leg up on those who don't."

It didn't matter to them that most Hispanics on the Lower East Side spoke a dialect, or that a student has a better chance of success in learning a foreign tongue if he or she has mastered at least the English language. All our arguments fell on truly deaf ears, and the concept of permitting a Spanish-speaking child, regardless of his or her reading grade, some as low as 2.6, was called High Horizons. Politics or education? Politics wins hands down.

Without too much fanfare, I was called into Mr. Z's office in the Spring of 1964 to get the new eighth grade ready for the September term and to pay particular attention to the development of our new Spanish SPE classes. I was to follow the strict guidelines as set down by the district. I was to program three classes of in-coming eighth graders who were exclusively Hispanics, disregarding their reading and writing scores, which they took in the 7th grade, and pick "the most qualified" (meaning no discipline problem).

I selected about 85 or 86 students out of a pool of hundreds who had a strong math scores, no record with the Dean and who were given recommendations by their home and subject teachers. Some of the "qualified" had reading scores as low as 2.3 and 2.4! All their classes were to be conducted in Spanish; even their gym and shop classes! This was the "new" SPE class; but would it fly?

Within two weeks of the new fall term, difficulties began to develop. "The work is too hard," "the gym teacher speaks Spanish funny," "I don't understand my shop teacher when she talks." On it went, and we kept encouraging the students to persevere. "Not enough time to make these judgments," we said. "Give it more time," we insisted. Then the parents began to arrive, asking for transfers. They didn't realize how difficult the SPE classes were going to be, and they didn't want all this stress and pressure. Kids were literally crying to get out of the program.

Mr. Z. told me to "hold fast" and try to persuade as many parents as I could not to transfer out. But, when Open School Night came, in late October, it became obvious to the principal and to me that the Program was not working. Good kids, who never had a Dean referral before, were being sent down for infractions like, "disrupting the class," "fighting with other students," and "talking back to the instructor." These were commonplace. Something had to be done.

Both the principal and I knew that if we allowed one transfer to take place, many others would follow. How much "damage" could be acceptable and still maintain a viable program? Soon after that Parent-Teacher conference, Mr. Z. permitted the first transfers to be effected, "for the good of the program." We removed one or two "disruptive influences" and two or three very sensitive girls who had become emotional "wrecks" at home and in school.

In the weeks that followed, other transfer requests came in fast and furiously. "Hold the line, Mr. Manicone," Mr. Z. advised me; but the best I could do was to hold the enrollment at 75 students by January. We still had three functioning SPE classes with 25 students each. We "lost" about 15 students, and then we had to wait out the Spring term.

It didn't get any better. More wanted out. More and more excuses, problems and disruptions kept mounting. Minor arguments and spats blew up into major confrontations. "You transferred Margarita out, why can't you take me out too?" Or, "I have the same problem with Mr. J. that Juan had, why do I have to stay in that class?" Or "My son can't understand Mrs. F. and you transferred his cousin for the same reason. I want my son out too!" In addition, the referrals to the Dean's office didn't help either. By May, Mr. Z. told me to reduce the Spanish SPE Program to two classes. "Keep the best 60 you have!"

When we started in September, due to moving out of the district or parochial transferring, we really had about 54 or 55 students still left in the Program. During the fall and spring terms, the rate of attrition remained constant. The upshot was this: when it was all over, by June of 1966, we graduated about 40 students! Of which, only a dozen or so received a first rate, SPE-quality education. The remainder, in my professional estimation, lost two valuable years of education. (The District Superintendent and the New York City Board of Education called it "a success!") It goes without saying that this "experiment" was never repeated. We at 22M echoed an oft-repeated axiom about programs and mandates sanctioned by the Board, and that was: the Program was "doomed to succeed!" End of story.

After five years of living on the junior high school level, I decided that I had to get out. I had made some wonderful friends at 22M, and I was treated very well by the administration; but, in my mind, all I was doing was spinning my wheels, and I decided to take the High School (Reg) exam in Social Studies. I won't make any excuses, I failed. No matter, I'll try again when it's posted by the Board. I still have a job here.

When I was working at 22M, I always put my name down for all kinds of paying positions, like the after-school tutorial program, summer playground positions, and teacher-in-the-summer-school-on-the-junior-high-level. After three years of trying, I finally got my first after-school position: working in a playground position on the Lower East Side during the summer.

The summer school playground program was eight weeks long. It didn't pay very much, but it was the opening to other, better paying summer programs in the future. This particular program involved "enriching" the Lower East Side elementary school kids, both male and female, in a world very similar to a day camp in the suburbs. We had the traditional swimming lessons at the Pitt Street pool, an Arts and Crafts program, Health Ed, and occasional trips in and around the community. As a senior counselor, I had a class of some 25 students assigned to me and we did each of the activities, weather permitting, of course.

Approximately half way through the playground program, I ran into my most serious situation. Whenever an adult takes a group of children around the neighborhood, whether it would be to escort them to the pool or take a little nature hike near the park, the usual group of misfits, malcontents and/or para-criminal element hounds your very steps. You just have to put up with the catcalls, the mimickers, and badgering as part of the job. However, what I ran into was quite different and far more serious.

We were sitting in a classroom, doing our usual arts

and crafts work. My class of students were all first graders, and because they were young, we were situated on the first floor alongside the main lobby. In this way, if a parent wanted to escort her child home early or would want to bring rain gear if the weather was bad, we were easy to locate. In this setting I was seated at my desk, helping a student with his project. We began to hear a ball bounce off the common wall between our room and the lobby. At first I didn't pay too much attention to it, because little distractions like that are somewhat common in any grade school. However, the noise persisted and in fact grew louder. I excused myself to the class and went out to the lobby area to check the cause of my problem. There I found a gang of 8th or 9th graders playing handball against the lobby wall. I asked them to continue their game outside. I also reminded them that the lobby was not a handball court and that they were marking up the wall. They seemed to understand; they nodded their heads, appeared to leave, and I went back into my classroom.

Ten seconds later, the ball bouncing began again. I went back to the lobby and ordered them to stop or I would call security. (We had no security!) They again appeared to leave and I went back to my room. I no sooner sat down when the ball bouncing began again. This time, I was angry.

I returned to the lobby area and watched the gang play. When the ball hit the lobby wall, I caught it on the fly, and went to the room and closed the door. I went back to my desk and tried to help my student with his project. The door burst open and a surly-looking 13- or 14-year-old said, "I wan' my ball!"

I told him, "I'll give it to your mother when she come to school for it."

With that the kid went over to the first desk on his left, threw the first-grader out of her seat, picked up her chair and approached me. "I wan' my ball!"

Rage filled my entire body. I had a helpless child on the floor crying, a child who was totally innocent of the on-going events here; I had a terrorized child at my desk quivering with fear; I had an entire class being menaced by this piece of garbage. Behind him was his gang of quasi-criminals hooting and abetting his actions with yells of encouragement. Slowly I got up from my chair and said to him, "I hope you have a soft chair in your hands, because if it isn't, I'm going to use it on you!"

I must have surprised him with my quickness, because I rushed him in a second, and grabbed the chair with my left hand, throwing it to the floor. Then I seized him by his neck, twisted him around, and grabbed the back of his pants so that he now appeared to be a human battering ram. I moved toward the door and using my "ram" I sliced through his gang and walked out into the lobby, with his gang right behind me. I then kicked open the front door with my left foot and threw the little bastard out onto the sidewalk. He went sprawling in a heap. I then turned to his gang and asked, "Do you want to go out the same way?" With that, they all exited pronto, running out the other set of doors. The name of this gang leader was Hannibal C.

As luck would have it, when I went back to 22M that September, guess who was on my homeroom roster for that term? You got it! It was Hannibal. I couldn't wait to see his face!

When I greeted my new charges as they got to my door, Hannibal spotted me. He stopped at the doorway, looked up to see the room number, gave his program a quick peek, turned, and walked down the hall. I never saw him again.

From time to time, my thoughts return to these kids. What are they doing right now? Did the brief moment we had, significantly change anything? Many of the hundreds of children who pass by and through the life of a teacher can be intimidating, but that one actually did a constructive thing, whether it was positive or negative, can only be as relative as the circumstances make it out to be. Sometimes, one can do absolutely nothing.

I remember one such instance when I was leaving school on a fall afternoon. It was raining.

As I was attempting to pop open my umbrella, I noticed one of my students, a girl, standing under one of the main columns that supported the school structure. I walked over to her and asked her if she would have a problem getting home because of the drizzle. She was facing Columbia Street and the Baruch Projects, where she lived.

"No, Mr. Manicone. I'm just waiting," she said matter-of-factly.

I noticed that it was almost 4 o'clock and already getting dark. "Is there a problem?" I asked. "Do you have a key?"

"Oh, I have a key, I'm just waiting for my mother."

"What time will she be here?" I persisted.

I could see that I was making her uncomfortable, but she answered my question with a little reluctance. "Oh, about five o'clock or so."

"Five o'clock!" I repeated. "That's an hour from now!"

"I know," she said. "I don't mind. I do this every day."

"For heaven's sake, why?" I asked.

"Mr. Manicone, my mother's boyfriend lives with us in our apartment. He's there right now," she said.

"So, what's the problem? Won't he let you in?" I asked.

"Oh, he's let me in all right, but he's naked," she added.

"Does your mother know this?" I asked.

"Sure, she knows. I told her and she beat me for telling her lies!" she said. "So, not to make any more problems for me or her, I've decided to wait here under the building. Then we walk into the apartment together, and everything is fine."

I stood there stunned and transfixed. Here a 14-year-old had solved her major problem, one which had the potential for disaster. And, how did she resolve her dilemma? She used her *common sense*. You can't beat common sense.

However, "common sense" is a relative term. It depends on the circumstances and on how it is applied. I found that some teachers and some administrators never had common sense in the first place. I recall that when I was a student observer in the ETA Program, a rather convincing tale was circulated around the Lower East Side about a principal who used used to lock himself in his office and play his cello when problems began to mount up. As I heard the story, this particular principal had the school safe against his hall door and a school secretary who acted as a guard at the other. No one was allowed to knock on either door, and the secretary would ring him up for emergency proposes only. I was also told that he played the cello rather well.

In my personal experience, I remember an assistant principal of English and foreign languages, a Miss W., doing a similar thing. On a particular working day, a new

English teacher sent me a note for help via a student. It appears that the Dean's office was closed and I was "available" in the Grade Advisor's Office, so I rushed out with the messenger to see what the fuss was all about. The security guard was standing in front of the room and the teacher was in the hall sobbing. A male student had been deliberately taunting her and passing lewd remarks about her in class.

"I can't take it anymore!" she said. "I've sent down referrals, but it's no use! He says that he's saying it to someone else!"

"Let's go see Miss W." I said. "I'll get her to transfer him out of your class. Let's go right now, and I'll tell the guard to mind your class for a couple of minutes. Okay?"

I could see that she was tremendously relieved that "something" was going to be done about her situation. As we climbed to the second floor, she actually stopped crying. I was hoping that she wouldn't because it would help her case with Miss W.

I knocked on the door. I noticed that the window shade was pulled down to its limit in the window frame. I knocked again; Miss W. opened the door and I could see that she was visibly annoyed. "Yes?" she asked.

"Miss W., I'm sorry to disturb you," I began, "but Anne here is having quite a bit of difficulty with a young man in her class right now, and the Dean's office is closed. We were hoping that you could help her out."

"What can I do?" she asked. The situation was becoming awkward as we all stood there by her door. Miss W had no intention of inviting us into her office and here I was pleading a case for a teacher in her department. I had the boy's guidance folder in my hand, attempting to give it to her to support my contentions.

I said, "We were hoping to have you transfer the kid out of her class."

"Absolutely not!" Miss W. replied. She then turned her attention to Anne, who was standing on my right, and asked her, "To what extent have you provoked the child?"

Young Anne just stammered, then remained absolutely quiet and puzzled. Miss W slowly closed the door, leaving the two of us in the hall like complete idiots.

That particular lesson served me very well. I always believed in taking care of my own problems "my way." A few weeks after that incident, I was asked to cover the dismissal period of someone's class for a week or two. It was a personal favor because the teacher had requested an early dismissal for herself due to an illness in her family. I really didn't mind because I also used the same room for my Social Studies lessons.

As usual, the class of boys and girls was eager to get home, laughing and recounting the events of the day, as they struggled with the book bags and articles of clothing to pull from the room closets. On one particular day, as a girl was attempting to remove all her belongings from her desk, she gave out a subdued yelp. "Someone's been spitting in my desk!" she screamed. I went over to investigate. It wasn't spit . . . it was semen.

"Oh, my God!" I said to myself, "what little bastard did this?"

Trying to dismiss the situation without embarrassing the young girl or her friends, I did not contradict her but said that I would get the custodian to clean it up. I got a chalk rag out of my desk and cleaned off the book and we got ready to leave the room as a class. It was Friday, and I made a mental note to get to this when we got back from the weekend. As luck would have it, I forgot. That next Monday afternoon it happened again! "He did it again!" I heard from the back of the room.

"Damn it to hell!" I said to myself. "Why didn't I remember?" But aloud I said, "Okay, okay, let's not make a federal case, okay?"

I escorted the class out and then returned to the room. I was hoping to find some incriminating paper or quiz with a name on it to identify the culprit, but I found nothing. Since I shared this room with Mr. F., also a Social Studies teacher, I would attempt to get some names of boys in his classes who might sit there. Meanwhile, I went over the cards in my Delaney book to see if I could come up with a name from my class. No luck.

The next day, I quizzed Mr. F. about it and he supplied me with some "prospects." Sure enough, "it" happened again on Wednesday afternoon. This time, the "spit" was inside two desks! I knew it wasn't in my class because I had deliberately left those seats vacant. It had to have occurred in Mr. F.'s class exclusively. On Thursday morning Mr. F. supplied me with the names of the only two boys who had been seated in those seats. Later that day, I paid a solo visit to Mr. F.'s class and called to two boys to step out into the hall for a minute. Mr. F escorted them and I proceeded to ask, "Who was playing with himself?"

At first, stony silence, then the embarrassed grin, then the naughty chuckle. "He made me do it!" one of the boys excused himself, as he pointed to his friend. The other, feigning surprise, countered this accusation and both began to giggle hysterically. At this point I really got angry. Maybe because I was a new father and I wouldn't have wanted my daughter to experience this truly crude exhibition of teenage debauchery, I grabbed both boys' throats with each hand, shook each kid violently and said, "Do it again, and I'll make you guys clean it up with your tongues!" Well, it never happened again. And I didn't provoke anybody.

The last two years at 22M seemed to go on forever. I really was just "spinning my wheels." I wanted to teach, but it wasn't going to happen on the junior high school level for me. Others were taking Assistant Principal exams, and for a year or two that recourse looked tempting. In the fall of 1966 I took the regular High School exam and passed. Perhaps that last year went even slower; the situation at 22M never got any better. A new principal came in, but it appeared he was just overwhelmed by the growing chaos and breakdown of classroom discipline we were all experiencing. In the seven years I was at 22M, our Junior High School led Manhattan in student suspension five times! Even though our building was relatively new then, built in 1958, it looked "tired" by 1967.

During that last year in particular, vandals did their worst to destroy the building by throwing rocks at it from Pitt Street Park and, believe it or not, from the inside open courtyard as well. Tiles from a mosaic, which had won a special city award, dropped off like petals from a flower each day into the middle courtyard of the school. When I first had come up the ramp of that courtyard seven years before, everything was still spanking new and fresh. Now, it was just another example of urban decay.

That last spring in 1967, as I went to my car which was parked by the courtyard, I encountered one of my students. She was in tears.

"What's the problem, Mandy?" I asked her.

"I have to fight some girl because she called our

school a shit school," she replied between sobs.

"You don't want to fight her, is that it?" I continued.

"Na, na," she answered. "I can beat her!"

"Then what are you crying for?"

"Don't you understand?" she said, as she got up in desperation. "I don't have any panties!" Then she turned away and crossed through the school's courtyard. She was still crying.

To me, this was a very poignant moment. I'm not kidding. In a sense, it encompassed all the truly human emotions that revolve around a public school. The "honor" of Gustave Straubenmueller Junior High School depended on a female fight which never took place for want of a pair of underpants. A movie could be made around stuff like this.

Four

Just Say "Good-bye"

It's very difficult to say farewell to something that was part of your life for so long a time. I had spent nearly one quarter of my life at 22M. I know I affected the lives of many students there, but more importantly, they affected my life even more. I went to instruct, to teach, to aid, to advise, and to comfort. But in reality, it worked out the other way around.

Besides the students and parents, there was the faculty at 22M. We had such support for one another! The camaraderie was infectious and genuine. It had been tested. We had some old-timers who started their careers at P.S. 188 across the street, on Houston; continued and finished them at 22. They came from as far as Long Beach, Long Island, or were as close as a couple who rented an apartment just blocks away. We had a naval hero who flew a dive bomber during the Battle of Midway and had a steel plate in his head to prove it. We also had those who were avoiding the draft during the Vietnam War. What a collection!

Talent abounded in the shop classes, whether it was home economics, or boys' and girls' wood shop; in the music and art classes—whatever. Everyone did their jobs professionally because of the tight supervision generated from the top. We once had a newly transferred science Assistant Principal who made a point to tell everyone, even the Principal, how hard he worked, regardless of the fact that he was given a cleaning closet as his temporary office. One day, a teacher friend of mine went to visit him in his "office." While waiting for him to end a telephone conversation, my friend noticed a graduated cylinder in the corner with yellow liquid in it.

"I'm so busy," the A.P. said to him, "that I can't even get to the men's room!"

When it came to minor or major quirks, the administration did not hold a monopoly, by any means. The year after I left, I found that a dressmaking shop teacher used to give baby showers for her pregnant students in the school. It became the stylish thing to do, and because she didn't realize what she was promulgating, someone on the staff actually had to tell this twit that she was encouraging teenage pregnancies. Then the partying stopped!

As a Grade Advisor, it was always necessary to have a staff of monitors. They helped locate and escort students to the advisors' offices. These monitors would earn "service credits" toward the requirements needed for graduation as part of their citizenship development. It was good training. But it was always a case of feast or famine. Sometimes I would have three or four in one period, or, no one in the next. Time was wasted if a counselor or advisor went searching. We could have been completing some important paper work rather than spending half a period finding Jimmy.

It was on this type of mission, walking the halls, that I had two impossible-to-believe things happen to me. The first was the time, middle of May or thereabouts, when I walked into an English room and spotted a raging fire going on in the back of the classroom inside a student's desk. The teacher was in the front of the room, chalk in hand, pointing at something on the blackboard, when I interrupted her.

"Mrs. F., do you know that there's a fire in the back desk?" I screamed.

"Where? Where?" she stammered.

"Where?" I asked. "Right there!" I pointed.

"Oh, my God!" she said, as if I had interrupted some deep thought she was holding.

I ran to the back, and with the assistance of a fire extinguisher, the blaze was out in a second.

I got the names of the two arsonists who had been "building" the fire and took them to the Dean's office. But, as I walked down the hall with the two culprits, I couldn't help judge Mrs. F and the incident that took place in her room. She apparently was so preoccupied with teaching the first two rows of students before her, that she physically excluded the rest from sight and mind.

I clearly remember that when I passed by the opened back door of her room, I smelled smoke; that's what brought me into the room. Perhaps the draft sent the fire smell into the corridor, but how could she not see the column of smoke coming from the desk? As soon as I entered the room, I noticed the two culprits feeding the fire with paper to "keep it going." Prejudgment or not, how could a teacher be so dense, or so preoccupied with her lesson as to permit that?

The second unforgettable incident involved a substitute teacher whom we managed to acquire in the late days of June. By the time June rolls around, junior high school teachers are either delirious with expectation or completely "burned out," and the call for substitutes becomes a high priority need. We have to scrape the bottom, literally. I believe that we did this on that fateful day in June.

I was returning from a Guidance Meeting, and I was late for an appointment with a parent. As I passed the front, opened door of this classroom, I noticed a gentleman in a three-piece striped suit. It was a hot day, and here was this guy in a three-piece suit! His hair was combed back, a la George Raft, Irish-looking, short in stature, instructing the class.

"I'm your substitute teacher for today," he said, "and I want you to behave yourselves so that I can hand in a good report to the office."

I stopped a pace or two away from the front door in order to see the class in summer wear, and yet, discreetly enough so that I didn't let on that I was watching what was going on.

He continued. "And, if you are really good, but I mean really, *really* good, at the end of this period, I will show you my wooden leg!" I couldn't believe my ears! His *wooden leg?* I didn't think a New York City teacher could be that handicapped and pass the physical. I had to pursue this.

Sure enough, I complete my conference with the parent and made sure I was standing (again, very discreetly) against the wall opposite the front door of the class. Several minutes before the bell rang for change of period, I noticed that the substitute arose from his desk and took the same position he'd had before. He was gesturing with his right hand, index finger pointed upward and standing very erect.

You never saw such a well-behaved class at 22M before! The students all had their hands folded in front of them and you could literally hear that proverbial pin drop. He pulled the desk chair next to him and said,

48

"You all have been good, really, really good. Now I will show you my wooden leg." I still could not believe what I was witnessing.

With that, he turned toward the chair. He noticed me at the same time, standing by the wall, and he placed his left foot on the chair and hiked up the trouser leg of his three-piece suit. To my total disbelief, he revealed his wooden leg—right up to the knee joint! The children and I gazed at it with our mouths wide open. He had scored a pedagogical triumph, but—unfortunately—he could perform this feat only once with the same class. I told this story for years, and it always topped anything someone else had ever experienced.

In the same vein, parents of our students did some odd things too. Once, I had a student referred to me because the teacher complained about "the odor" of this student's hair. When I questioned the child, he told me that he washed daily, using a face cloth, but that washing his hair was difficult.

"Why?" I asked.

"Because we don't have a bath or a shower in our apartment," he replied.

"What do you mean, 'no shower'?" I asked.

"They forgot to put one in. Our bathroom doesn't have a shower or a bathtub," he said.

"Who do you live with?" I asked.

"My grandmother. We live alone in the apartment."

" . . . with no shower," I said. "Did your grandmother ever complain?"

"She can't speak English too good, and doesn't want to bother anybody," he replied.

"Well, I speak English very well, and I'm going to see that you and your grandmother get a shower. You live in the Baruch Projects, right?"

"Yeah, but, please, no trouble. My grandmother is going to be very angry with me if she gets into any trouble."

"There won't be any trouble. Please, don't worry. I'll get in touch with the super and make sure we correct this problem. Okay?"

"Okay," he said. He didn't look that confident about my abilities as he left my office. I called the super of the Baruch Projects that afternoon.

I set up an appointment with the grandmother through the kid, and we all marched across Columbia Street several days later to see for ourselves. I believe we were four—the boy, the school nurse, the super and myself—who found ourselves ringing the doorbell. The grandmother let us in and we were very impressed with the obvious neatness and cleanliness of her apartment. Then, we asked to see the bathroom. The grandmother very obediently showed us the way and we all tried to squeeze in. A couple of us had to content ourselves with looking from the corridor. The woman confidently waved her arm around the room to express, "So, where's my tub and shower?"

I couldn't believe my eyes. The woman was standing right next to the tub! Instead of a shower curtain ringing the top of the tub, she had hung all her clothes on the curtain rod that encircled the tub. And, in the tub, she had placed a series of shoes and sneakers that lined the device right up to the rim! Trying not to embarrass the woman or her grandchild, we all said something like, *"Uno momento, senora,"* and we ushered her from the bathroom.

Trying very hard not to laugh, but we did smirk quite a bit, we started, using the "bucket brigade" technique, removing all the articles of clothing and shoewear from the tub. I was just amazed at how much clothing the woman had managed to put on the shower ring! It was my task to keep finding new places in the living room to deposit the clothing and shoes. The grandmother was completely transfixed. She didn't say a word. When we finally finished the task, one of us—I think it was the super—invited her into the bathroom and turned on the water. You should have seen her face! She was actually startled as she grabbed her breast and shouted something in Spanish. She was so embarrassed! But, I think we handled it all very professionally and, through her grandson, we attempted to tell her that it was all very understandable.

Since it was getting late in the afternoon, I told the boy to say out of school and help his grandmother put all those things in the closets of the apartment. The three of us left, and we talked a bit in the lobby of the building. It was very sad. I honestly can say that we did not laugh at the grandmother's expense. We attempted to understand how something like that could happen. The woman even had hosiery hanging from the spigot and shower handles! Didn't she ever have company or relatives over to tell her what those "things" in the bathroom were supposed to be used for? We just left the building shaking our heads. Sometimes reality is more unbelievable than fiction.

In telling this story, it always impressed me to relate how we, at 22M, tried very hard and very professionally, to bring others, with their strengths, to help us with dilemmas that begged for answers.

I clearly recalled one such episode when I had the unenviable task called "lunchroom patrol." It appears that if you are a male teacher in a JHS this lot falls on your shoulder. Well, in any case, I was confronted with the "missing mustard" syndrome. Someone was "stealing" our mustard!

At times, we could feed 400 to 450 students at one seating. At 22M, we had three lunch periods, and many of our students could go home to eat, but most chose not to. We always had two male supervising teachers in the lunchroom, with three or four paras to assist us. It was very difficult to maintain order and at the same time feed all those students within the 50 minutes scheduled. Aside from all that, we had to solve the immediate and not so immediate problems as they sprang up daily. Of course, we are not even discussing the fights among the students that could erupt at any time. Just let me say, that it was a rare day if the lunch period went by uneventfully. Now, the mustard case.

It was a typical hectic lunch period, and they were serving hot dogs that day. As customary, we always put out the mustard. We took our supply from the 10 gallon jars that were stored under the counter. I had faithfully filled the large dish with an ample supply of mustard, and then began to patrol my sector. The other teacher was by the large set of doors, counting in the students, ten-at-a-time. Everything looked normal until a student came up and said. "Mr. Manicone, we're out of mustard."

"Out of mustard?" I said to myself. "How can that be? I just filled that dish!"

Sure enough, the student was telling the truth. The mustard plate was wiped clean! So, I took out the 10-gallon supply jar and filled the plate " . . . That should hold them till the end of the period," I said to myself, and I returned to supervising my area. Not 10 or 12 minutes went by when another student complained about the same "shortage."

"What the hell is going on?" I asked myself again. "Why are the children using up so much mustard today?" I filled the mustard dish for the third time in less than 25 minutes and thought no more about it. Right at the bell, I happened to walk by the dish—and it was empty! Something was very screwy here. I had put out over a quart of mustard, and there were two or three dishes scattered around the lunchroom. This one was empty, the others were about half full. In keeping with dietary regulations, we weren't scheduled to have hot dogs until the following week.

We did, and I was missing mustard again! This time, I didn't move from the table and just watched. I pretended to do some paperwork, and within a minute or two, a slight girl meandered over to the mustard table, set down her metal lunch tray, and filled up on mustard. I mean, she *filled the separate compartments with mustard,* and then returned to her seat. I had caught my mustard thief!

I sat down next to her and asked her a few questions as she gobbled down mustard.

"Hi," I said. "I'm Mr. Manicone. What's your name?"

"Nancy," she said.

"Boy, you really like your mustard. Shouldn't you try eating it along with something else?" I inquired.

"No, I like it plain," she replied.

"How long has this been going on?" I pressed.

"Oh, a couple of weeks or so," she replied.

I was very disturbed watching her eat the mustard with her spoon as if it were ice cream. I got her name and official class and immediately referred her to the guidance people, who in turn referred her to the nurse. It turned out that she had a severe depletion of several minerals that had dropped to a serious level in her body as she reached puberty. Without any conscious effort on her part, she had seized upon mustard to satisfy this shortage that was chemically lacking in her body. With proper medical attention, I was told, she could return to normal in no time. True to this evaluation, Nancy did, and the case of the missing mustard was solved.

However interesting as this mustard case might be, nothing prepared me for a situation that was to take place several weeks after this incident. Mr. O, the other teacher with me, was an old veteran of the "wars in the lunchroom." So, he gave me the opportunity of counting in the students. From painful experience, those in charge had found that it was not a wise thing to let the kids rush the lunch counter to get their food. Fights would break out and people could get hurt. Counting them in, ten-at-a-time, was the best method. It was orderly and we could regulate the flow to the counter as the children picked up their trays of food and milk. We always served a hot meal.

The students formed this long line outdoors, parallel to the lunchroom. Only in severe weather did we permit the students indoors where they waited in the auditorium and had a line form as far back as the stairwell. Whether it was outside or inside, we had to maintain discipline. Any rowdy behavior meant instant demotion to the rear of the line. This also included those who wanted "to hustle" the line, meaning to creep up or break into the line. "Hustlers" were invariable upperclassmen. So, there I was, counting off the students, ten-at-a-time, very professionally, watching for infractions, seeing where Mr. O. was, checking the lunch counter and keeping the line straight. We didn't want the kids to bunch up so that they could sneak a friend or two inside the line. It was a nice late autumn, early winter day, and then I spotted this rather large ninth grader coming from my left. I was standing on the stoop counting the kids in. I became momentarily distracted, and when I resumed my post, the kid was already inside the line. There was no way that he had taken his rightful spot at the rear, but because I didn't actually see him hustle the line, I said nothing. I would wait for another opportunity.

My opportunity came a day or two later. Again, he was walking parallel to the building, going from my left to the rear of the line. He kept turning as he walked, to see what I was doing, and again I was distracted, and again he hustled the line. His arrogance and my stupidity was getting me real steamed, but I knew that one day, I would catch him.

Off and on it went. Sometimes he would show up, but most of the time he didn't. All I knew was whenever he was anywhere near the line, he invariably hustled himself in. I just had to catch the right moment. He knew of my preoccupation and he took full advantage of the situation, but time was on my side. I would get him.

And I did. Using the same technique, he moved along the line, pretending to go to the back. Always turning his head, he waited for his opportunity. This time, I pretended to be distracted, but I jumped back to my position on the stoop, and there he made his mistake. He hustled the line and I saw him!

Then, still not able to see me, but I could see his every action, he started to move up the line, just as one would if he were doing the Virginia Reel. He would grab a shoulder of someone in front of him and pull them to his rear. He was moving at a rather good clip until he came to a little Hispanic boy in front of him. The kid grabbed his shoulder, pulled the small boy to the side, but then, the most unexpected thing happened. The smaller boy literally climbed up the kid's back and locked his legs around his neck.

Securely perched on the hustler's body, the little Spanish kid went to work, punching the hustler around and on top of his head with some very effective blows. The Big Kid was flapping his two arms about, trying to hit the boy, but with no success. The rain of effective shots were getting in and the Big Kid was getting badly bloodied.

What sweet justice! Little David at work again. As I took my time getting over to the fracas, the Large One started to fall to his knees. The small boy continued to hammer away until they reached the ground. I got to the fray just as the little boy hopped off and returned to the line.

"What's going on here?" I asked as sternly as I could. But the bloodied kid on the ground could only shake his head, as if to asked, "Did you get the name of that truck?"

"All right, then," I continued. "I don't want any more fooling around here! Get me, buster?" I was addressing the fallen hustler to his feet and then I pointed him to the rear of the line. "You know the penalty for hustling. Back of the line!"

There was much drama here, and I took full advantage of it. I never once admonished the Hispanic kid, but in a sense, I was praising him for his courage and tenacity. No one was going to pull that stuff on him, no sir! Meanwhile, the Large One was banished to the back for all to see. What incredible justice!

I ran that lunch line for the remainder of that year and something very good came from that David-and-Goliath struggle, and it was this: Every time I spotted the

Big Kid on the line, the small one was always in front of him. Maybe I wasn't successful in stopping *all* the hustling, but, at least, we made a small dent in it.

I took the high school exam again in the fall and winter of 1966, and passed. In the spring of 1967 I was appointed to the High School of Fashion Industries, which was located on the west side of Manhattan. At the same time, my wife and I decided that now was a very good time to move, and I persuaded her to investigate areas in New Jersey. I just didn't like the congestion of Long Island. We settled on New Jersey for several reasons, one being that I could commute to the Port Authority Building and walk to school which would free up the car for her needs.

In September of 1967, I was in a new house and I would be teaching in a new school. The "new" house was 12 years old and my "new" school had been built in 1940.

The High School of Fashion Industries is one of the Special High Schools in New York City, meaning that in order to attend our school, a student must take a qualifying entrance examination. Originally, our school was the brainchild of Mr. Mortimer Ritter, who began his enterprise along with two others, calling it the High School of Central Needle Trades. It was located on the third floor of the Greeley Arcade Building in downtown Manhattan. By 1938, the school had become so successful, that ground was broken to build the ten-story building at its present location on 24th Street.

An interesting sidelight to this brief history of "my" high school, is that my mother-in-law, as a young teenager, went to Central Needles when she first arrived here from Italy and attended evening classes in school garment construction.

Mr. Ritter's concept of building a high school to "feed" the garment industry was bold and imaginative back in the 20s. Other high schools followed like Printing, Art & Design, Performing Arts, Aviation, to help build up the many industries for which New York City is famous. Our school was considered "vocational" in the Directory, but it was more than just a vocational high school. It really was special.

For starters, a successful graduate of Fashion has to satisfy two basic requirements. She or he had to not only complete both a vocational course, but had to satisfy the requirements for an academic diploma. We had a strict dress code, so that anyone could immediately identify an undergraduate's class by the color of the smock he or she was wearing. And, a student had to accumulate the necessary number of service points in order to graduate.

However, the biggest obstacle in all of this was the entrance examination which had three parts. Normally, some four to five thousand eighth graders took our test; only 900 to 1100 passed it. The test included the English and Math part; plus an example of their special skill, like an Art Portfolio and an Interview Evaluation. We were very selective; that's why we were so special.

This type of high school was just what I was looking for. In many ways, it was quite similar to a parochial school with very highly motivated students who wanted an education. At times the overall school population could be about 2300, but the number of male students never exceeded 125 or 150. So, for all intents and purposes, Fashion High School was male segregated. This factor alone made discipline in the classroom "a breeze!" I loved it.

In June of 1967, I was invited by the Chairman of the Academic Department at Fashion to introduce myself and become officially welcomed by the Principal. As I approached the Academic Office on the 8th floor, I bumped into a young man coming out, who asked if I was just appointed to Fashion, too. When I replied in the affirmative, he pointed to the door and said, "He's crazy!" and left. That young man was to become my godson some fifteen years later.

Five

Some Cracks Appear

"Ed, come in here! I got that 'something' I want you to do today. Remember? We talked about it yesterday?"

"Yeah, Jake, I remember."

We were in the last days of June, 1968, in the process of reorganizing for the upcoming September. Ed was told to come in jeans. It was highly unusual, believe it or not, in the mid-sixties to wear jeans during school time. Our chairman, Jake, ran a tight ship, and if he told someone to come in in jeans, there had to be a reason. The reasons was to count books! Ed, with pencil in hand, was told to go to the various book storage rooms of the Academic Department. He was to make an inventory of all our Social Studies textbooks. In this way, the chairman could get a handle on which texts were to be re-ordered and which could go for a year or two. Given the limited amount that a chairman could spend on re-supplying textbooks, an accurate number was essential.

Ed took his job very seriously. From time to time, as I would check on his progress, I would see him on all fours, making his tally, including books that had fallen behind radiators and shelves. He was covered with dust.

Ed took the better part of a week to complete his assignment for the chairman. As it turned out, I was in the chairman's office going over some paperwork when Ed practically crawled in. Jake popped out of his seat as

Ed handed him his final tally. Ed was thoroughly exhausted and glad that he was finished. He stood waiting in front of Jake's desk for a "Well done!", a "Great job, Ed!", or something similar. What he got wasn't a compliment!

"Ed, these figures are all wrong!"

"No way, Jake, I personally counted each and every book! Those are the numbers!" contradicted Ed.

"I'm sorry, Ed, but these can't be the numbers," Jake reported. "I'll have to show you how to do it." And with that, he took Ed's tally with one hand, seized Ed's hand with the other, and shot out of the room. I raced right behind the bewildered, confused tally-taker and my chairman. This showdown was one not to miss! I knew that Ed, with all his Teutonic efficiency could not be wrong, but a chairman is always THE CHAIRMAN. As I scurried down the hall after the pair, I was followed by other colleagues. They had smiles on their respective faces. Then I knew that Ed was in for a shock.

The bookroom door was wide open. Jake, still holding on to Ed's hand, entered the room. I was right behind them. And, just a pace or two behind me were the others from the department. Jake stopped at the first book stack, loaded to the ceiling with books and, dropping Ed's hand, started to count with his right hand. Moving his right index finger from left to right in a straight line, Jake continued, "twenty, forty, sixty, eighty, one hundred!" He continued like that right down to the last shelf and then, writing down a figure like "580," he proceeded to the next stack, doing exactly the same thing. Within 45 seconds, Jake had "his" figure of 9790. Ed and I stood there transfixed. Behind me I heard a muffled giggle.

"Ed, that's how you do it! Do you understand? Your

numbers were way off!" With that, Jake finished the count for that room in the next several minutes and rushed out with the "correct" tally. I moved to let him exit. Ed never moved. He just stood there without even blinking. He never knew what hit him.

That day we had a liquid lunch to ease the pain.

Back in the 60s, the High School of Fashion Industries enjoyed a wonderful dualism—that is to say, that the vocational section of the school was separate and distinct from the academic. In the Academic Department, chaired by Jake, teachers of English, typing, social studies, foreign languages and the library fell under his control. Apart from our department, there was the Science Department, which supervised the instruction of all the Sciences, Math, Relative Tech, and Health Education. We also had a terrific Art Department.

In the vocational area, there were two chairwomen who divided the responsibilities in supervising, and for all intents and purposes, the curriculum of Vocational Studies for our students. Each department, whether vocational or non-vocational, had its own set of book rooms, labs, and even their own set of classrooms, which they used exclusive of the others. These "fiefdoms" were jealously guarded and maintained by the respective chairpeople. I was always rebuked by the Program Committee at the beginning of each term whenever I requested all my classes on the same floor, or next to a book room, or whatever, with this injunction, "You can't teach in that room, it belongs to the Science Department, or the Vocational Department." It didn't matter, that as the low man in the Department, I had to lug books or wall maps up or down three floors because I was the interloper of the "system."

Recalling my first days at Fashion, I was very

impressed with the array of courses the Vocational Department offered. There were classes in upholstery, millinery, draping, interior design, foundations (women's undergarments), pattern making, men's clothing, women's clothing and textile design—just to mention the ones that come to mind. In addition, each freshman who was not an Art major took an Exploratory Vocational Class, three periods long, for an entire year to determine in which area of the vocational track he/she did best. With the recommendations of the chairperson and the Guidance Counselor, the student was placed in the vocational major that provided the greatest option for success. Most students remained with that particular major for the next three years. When the pupil completed the required academic work along with the vocational subjects, he/she graduated. Many went on to attend the Fashion Institute of Technology, or Parsons, or even to the prestigious Rhode Island School of Design.

My first year at Fashion was great. I was finally teaching, for the first time in years. I had a couple of American History classes, along with three Economics classes. My students were practically all seniors with a few juniors thrown in. I had no more than 6 or 7 male students in the entire five class set; students answered by questions in complete and cogent sentences; they all did their homework, and most were attractive to boot.

But my idyllic bubble burst in the first week of June, 1968.

On the evening of June 5th, Robert Kennedy was assassinated in California. All the newspapers, all the TV and radio reports on the morning of the 6th were filled with the events that had taken place in Los Angeles the night before. I went to bed completely transfixed with all the information I could gather before class that

Thursday morning. I wrote out a brief outline of a lesson plan on the bus to the Port of Authority, and when I got into my classroom I pored over the *New York Times* to get down as much information in my lesson plan as I could. (I certainly was not going to teach the scheduled lesson on the Containment Policies manifested in the Eisenhower foreign policy of the 1950s!) Unfortunately, because of the time factor, I did not tell Jake that I was deviating from lesson plans that we submitted to him a week in advance. My lesson plan for June 6th was on a single sheet of composition paper, hastily drawn up with many side notes in the margin. I thought that in keeping with the breaking story and because of its spontaneity, I would be allowed this "transgression." It turned out that I wasn't.

That first period was incredible. I never saw such student involvement in a subject before. For the first time, my students realized that history was truly relevant. They were seeing "history in the making!" And what a bag of mixed emotions I was confronted with that day; students were angry, they were visibly upset, many were crying—and they all wanted to know the "why's," the "what's," and the "how's." "When are these killings going to stop?" "Who's behind it?" On and on it went; my lesson plan was absolutely no good. I wasn't following it and it was pointless to try. My next class, a period or two later, was exactly the same. I felt like a referee. There was too much social and student interaction. I wasn't following the script. A student asked to be excused, and when he returned, he was pointing with his thumb toward the hall.

"What?" I asked. All he did was point to the hall and then he whispered the Chairman's name, "Mr. M."

I went out into the hall, and there was Jake, with his

back to my side of the room, taking in the lesson. I invited him in with, "Mr. M. what are you doing there? Come in. I'm sure the class won't mind." He came in, quite upset and did not sit down but remained for the rest of the period standing by the class bulletin board, jotting notes on a piece of paper. When the bell rang, he came to my desk and demanded to see my lesson plan. I showed him my improvised sheet.

"This was not your assigned lesson for this class today," he said, and walked out. I couldn't believe my ears.

When one joins the system, known as the Board of Education, probation is a good and necessary thing. Usually this probation period is for three years, which I completed when I was in JHS 22M. Now that I had gone up to the High School Division, I needed only to complete one more year of probationary time if I received a "S" rating (which I did). As I headed up to Room 806, I really believed that my "Satisfactory" rating was in jeopardy, all because of a monumental and historic event like the assassination of a future President of the United States!

I was steaming! I wasn't some new kid on the block. I was a mature, 34-year-old teacher with eight years of teaching experience under my belt. And I was reprimanded for the first time by a supervisor.

"Jake, I'm really angry with you!" I started. "What's the big idea?"

"You weren't prepared and that was not the lesson for today!" he countered.

"How was I supposed to know that Robert Kennedy was going to be murdered yesterday?" I shot back. "I had to improvise because of the extemporaneous nature of events. I *had* to, because I knew the kids wanted a lesson on the assassination and not on the Eisenhower Doctrine." I knew I was in trouble as soon as I uttered that last line.

"The students don't dictate what is taught in this department. I do!"

"Jake, be reasonable! You mean to tell me that some significant historical event like an assassination, or a declaration of war today doesn't supersede some past event of equal importance, just simply by the mere fact that an event of today or yesterday is relevant and the policies of Eisenhower are not?" I said.

"Okay, okay," he said ". . . but you should have cleared it with me first. That's all. Okay?"

"Okay," I said. I got my "S" rating, but things were never the same. I even went to the Principal and told him what had transpired, and I invited him to drop by my class anytime. But he never did. I just didn't like these tactics and I never wanted to "play the game." I liked my independence. Obviously, Mr. M did not.

My second year went pretty well, but I made it a point to avoid 806 as much as I could. However, there were times when that was just impossible, like our monthly departmental conference, or during the end of a term when he had to grade papers or enter grades. Another would be when we had to write up the finals. Mr. M would select a candidate during a meeting and advised him or her that he wanted an outline or a mock-up of a final in World History I by such-and-such a date. During the Spring term of 1969, it was my task to write up the American History II (Vocational). We had many back copies to use as models, and I did the test, which included 50 multiple choices, a political cartoon, a reading passage and the essays. I submitted the test in late April or early May. Jake crossed out everything except 5 or 6 multiple choice questions and the reading paragraph. "It needs more work," he said as he dismissed me to revise the test again.

Not to belabor this incident, I went back three or four more times and each time, Jake would accept the same 5 or 6 multiple choice questions, cross out the other 44 or 45, accept the cartoon, but reject the essays. Jake obviously did not want to see factual questions like, "When did George Washington cross the Delaware?", or "How was Benedict Arnold caught?" He wanted essay questions like, "Comparing the English form of democracy with the American, how is the Executive Branch better controlled under our present constitutional form?" It didn't matter if the test was given to non-Regents students or not. I attempted to differentiate when I wrote out a test if I believed that the students could not handle 50 thought-provoking questions.

However, by mid-May, I thought I handed in my last revision. I was wrong!

Since Jake had accepted all the parts of the test except the first part, the "Multiple Choice" section, I walked into 806 confident that my task was done. This time Jake ran a red pencil through all the pages I submitted, including the 5 or 6 questions he thought were "superior" from the beginning! I couldn't believe my eyes. Fortunately for me, the Social Studies Coordinator, Herm, was standing next to the desk, waiting to run off the exam.

"Jake, Jake! What are you doing?" I snapped. "How can you cross out all 50 questions like that? Don't you remember you always accepted those first 5 or 6 questions in each revision?"

"He got you there, Jake," muttered Herm, and with that, Jake said, "Okay, okay," and accepted the test as was. I was getting too old for this crap! If it wasn't for the fact that I'm just a poor excuse for a social drinker, liquid lunches would have become my steady diet at Fashion.

The fall of 1968 and the following spring were also memorable for what took place outside the building as well as inside. We were hit with student protests and boycotts stemming from the Vietnam War. Starting with draft card burnings up at Columbia University, the student movement quickly escalated down to the high schools within weeks. Especially around Election Day, the students began these disruptive marches through the streets of Manhattan, originating at one high school, emptying it, and then moving on to the next target. It was incredible to see an area like 24th Street filled with students, from 8th Avenue to 7th, screaming and yelling, trying to force their way into the building.

These protests went on for days. Thankfully, the Board of Education had established a hot line, warning the principals about which schools might be targeted. Since Fashion was located in the Chelsea area, it seemed we were always "the next to get hit." Schools like Printing, Haaren, Washington Irving and Brandeis were successfully "cleaned out," so, the students always appeared to march down to clean out Fashion. I honestly believed that the males from those schools were really not politically motivated, but were in fact looking for girls! No matter; our Principal and his small security staff were determined not to let those kids in to disrupt our school. Being ten stories high, we had an excellent vantage point to see the trouble coming and grouping at each end of the street.

In addition, the Principal complemented his security by "arming" the staff, both male and female teachers, with golf clubs—believe it or not!

As it turned out, the Gym teacher had found a couple of golf bags in storage. The golf clubs were distributed as our "weapons" when we were assigned to the lobby area during these student protests. Since Fashion was shaped like a large H, we had a south side and a north side with four doors at each wing. Guarding sixteen doors, plus running ten floors of students plus three periods of lunch, with about 700 students at each seating, was a monumental effort. But, in all those days of protest, as frightening as they actually were, our school was never "cleaned out." We had only one close "scare," and one "almost."

In the first case, two or three intruders actually penetrated the building and were apprehended by security in the lobby. Some believed that our girls had abetted their entrance by letting them in through the back door during their lunch period. No matter, the interlopers were caught, and the police officer assigned to the building actually drew his weapon when they attempted to run back out. It was quite dramatic to see high-school-aged students with their hands up against the marble wall, assuming "the position," with a New York police officer holding a weapon on them, waiting for his partner to handcuff them. Remember, this was 1968 in a very safe high school lobby—not in the 90s on a South Bronx street corner. It was very frightening.

The second incident was not dramatic, but in fact, quite comical. A petite, but quite determined trade teacher was walking her rounds when she heard a noise emanating from the recessed door at the end of the hall. As in all public buildings, the exit doors are always encased by another set of doors to keep heat in and prevent drafty hallways. In any event, when she went to investigate the inner chamber, armed with her golf club, she found that the male students from the outside had broken the transom windows above the outer door and they were lowering an intruder, head first, down the side of the door.

He almost made it! She rushed at the dangling subject, screaming at the top of her lungs all the while, and clubbing the unfortunate victim as hard as she could! I wasn't present for this one, but I was told that the teachers who got there to support her efforts, were crying with laughter. The kid was begging for his comrade to let him up. They couldn't see the commotion from their vantage point, and kept asking if they should let go.

He kept screaming, "No, no! Let me up! She's killing me!" They finally pulled him out, and our emergency was over. For weeks, this brave little shop teacher was the cock, or should I say, the *hen,* of the walk! We talked about this one for weeks.

During that second year at Fashion, Ed and I both were assigned the lunchroom. It was policy then to allocate only males for this duty because, quite frankly, it could turn hazardous at any given moment. As I said, we used to feed about 700 students at any one time, and there was always the potential for an "incident." These incidents could consist of anything from hustling the line to a major brawl. It was bad enough if boys duked it out, but the worst free-for-alls always involved girls. Ask anyone who has broken up school fights, and you will find that girls' fights are the hardest to disrupt. Boys want to punish or teach someone a lesson; girls want to incapacitate or "kill" their opponents.

I particularly remember a brawl between two rather well-endowed upper-class female students, that started at one end of the lunchroom and ended up outside in the hallway, right in front of the Principal's office door. When we first noticed the altercation, the teachers and the lunchroom attendants attempted to intervene. But it was useless to try because the girls were so intent on destroying each other, they didn't care who they hit.

We backed off, waiting for a secondary lull. It never came. Tables and chairs went in all directions; even their friends became concerned over the viciousness of the fight. Each girl had clumps of torn-out hair; each of the girls was bleeding quite badly from her scalp. The altercation finally proceeded into the hall, and when one girl attempted to run into the girls' bathroom next to the Principal's office, one girl fell. As they wrestled on the floor, tearing off their garments, two of the heftier teachers and I pulled away the one on top. The girl on the floor was naked from the waist up. Her bra landed on the door jamb of the Principal's office just as he ventured out to witness what he hoped would be the end of the brawl. I took off my jacket and covered the hapless bloody student as I helped her up.

As the lunch aides were picking up jewelry, articles of clothing, books and pens from the floor, I vividly remembered the Principal, with his arms folded in front of him, without a word, pointing with his right foot at a bra left on the floor. He certainly wasn't going to pick that up.

The fight had started over a simple thing: one girl forgot to get the other a bag of chips!

The other thing that always comes to mind during that lunchroom assignment was the "activities" of the few male students who came "to eat lunch." Most didn't; many of them were constantly socializing, either by a table or in the boys' bathroom. An attempt had been made in the past to minimize the activity in the toilet by removing the front door. There was some smoking, not heavy drug use—yet—some shakedowns, and a lot of cutting. Since the dress code had been voted out by the students during my second year there, it was very difficult to catch the cutters, unless they produced a program card, and some of them had several.

Back in my first year at Fashion, each grade had to wear a smock, which they made in their first year in the Exploratory Trade classes. Seniors wore gold, juniors wore green, and so forth. With the dress code eliminated, the students had won a major victory in the war against cutting. I always believed that the smock also neutralized apparel differences which separated rich from poor, and the students looked more professional.

The use of the smock served another purpose. It immediately singled out the intruder, because no one was permitted to attend class without his or her smock. If a student forgot the smock, he or she was given a demerit and assigned a replacement garment only for that day. I thought it was wonderful. But, somewhere or somehow, a vote was taken by the student body and the dress code was history.

Which takes me to the point I want to make. During my assignment in the lunchroom that year, I had a particular problem with a heavy-set male student whom I challenged during the first weeks of the new term. I really thought he was quite "old-looking" to be one of ours, so that when I asked him for his program card in front of his male friends, I had made an instant problem for myself.

This faux pas was further aggravated when he established his credentials by baiting me with his little games. He would "pretend" to have a fight with friends so that when I got there, he would laugh up the joke at my expense. Another thing he would do, because it was so outlandish, was that he would deliberately count huge wads of money in front of me, hoping to see my astounded reaction. When I "pretended" not to see it, he would count all the louder, saying things like, "How much do teachers make now?" I couldn't completely avoid this tactic because we did have a small problem then with marijuana and when I reported him to the Dean's office, he really got on my case. "Why did you report me?" he wanted to know.

I told him straight out. "Keep it up and see how many times your parents can come up to the school this year! Just eat your lunch and we'll have no more problems. Okay?"

"Okay," he said, and the "little tempest" never hassled me again.

For my labors, for my independence, for my two positive years, I was rewarded with a small "plum"; Jake told me that I would only be teaching four classes in the Fall of 1969, with one period a day in the Guidance Office. Shades of JHS 22!

Four teaching classes, no Homeroom, and a desk in the Guidance Office, after only two years. Perhaps it had to do with my "guidance," or my junior homeroom twit who went ahead and filled out his college application form even though he wasn't supposed to. He said he did it because he had been left back and wanted to graduate with his friends. I told him it was impossible and not to waste money for college fees and the like. He not only disregarded what I said, but was accepted by a junior college, even though he "owed" almost a year in high school credits with us.

You had to see his face when he presented me his program at CUNY for the Fall. I wonder what my face looked like! Waving the yellow card under my nose, as a gesture of defiance, because he "knew," and I didn't, was his Program. "Remedial Reading, Remedial Math, and something that looked like "Opth Lab." I said, "What's this Opth Lab thing?"

He pointed to his eyes, "You know, opthmallany!"

I said, "Ophthalmology?"

"Yeah, yeah. The eyes!"

I made it my life's work to stay clear of any optometrist who opened an office in the Bronx after the 1970s.

Six

"When the Going Gets Tough . . . "

"Mr. Manicone, how would you like to work in the Dean's Office? Hmm?"

"The Dean's Office?" I repeated, trying to stall for time to answer. Here it is, just three years on the high school level, and the principal is offering me a very prestigious and very important position in the table of organization. In most high schools, the Dean answers only to the Principal and works hand-in-glove with the Administrative Assistant in the day-to-day operation of the school. At Fashion, at the time, we had two aging Deans, one for the boys and the other for the girls, who shared a rather comfortable suite on the second floor.

The Principal continued, without bothering to hear my answer, "As you know, both Mr. T. and Mrs. F are close to retiring, and we would like to give you the position because you are young, you have an outstanding record here as a teacher and grade adviser, and frankly because I think you have earned the position, which by the way, is for a 6-year-term. What do you say?"

"Mr. K., what can I say? I'm flattered that you even considered me for the job and if you're offering it to me, my answer is 'yes.' Absolutely. Thank you!"

"Don't be so quick to thank me, young man, because there were some people on my staff who opposed your nomination. You'll have to win their support. The other thing I must tell you," he added, "is that within a year or two I want to combine the two Dean positions into one, I don't want a boys' and girls' Dean, just one dean for everybody. Do you understand?"

"Well, won't Mr. T. or Mrs. F. get upset over hearing that piece of news?" I asked.

"That's not your problem, that's theirs—and we'll just keep that news between us for the time being," he replied. "Right now, just concentrate on what I have offered you. Start slow and then pick up speed as you go along; try to learn as much of the job as you can from the people you will ultimately replace. Good luck!"

My "tête-to-tête" with Mr. K. that June morning in 1970 had nothing to do with my teaching or advising. It had much more to do with my attempt to become the Union Chapter Chairman at Fashion the month before. In early spring, the position of Chapter Chairman was open because the gentleman who had the position for several years was stepping down. So, I decided to run, and with my friend, Ed, we waged a vigorous campaign for the job. The outgoing Chairman was a vocational teacher; I came from the academic side, and before long, it soon escalated to a "war" between the Vocational People (those who came from the sweat shops, earned their degree at night, spoke the New York dialect and were a little gruff in the trade classes) and the Academic People (those who went straight into Fashion from college, were spoiled because their parents paid for their education and were polite and permissive in their classrooms)!

As it turned out, the outgoing Chapter Chairman wasn't supposed to run in this election; he was stepping aside only to permit another Vocational person to run. That person backed out, and I found myself in a hotly contested race of personalities that divided the school into two camps as never before.

In my campaign literature, I stated quite emphatically that the current Chapter Chairman was a personal friend of the Administrative Assistant and that it would be impossible for him to argue any case for a teacher against the Administration. That particular piece really tore it, because the counter-literature to my attack was that I personally was not a "friend" of the ethnic Vocational people. I lost by one vote!

A week after that bitter contest, I was offered the Dean's job. Somebody had told the Principal I "was hungry for something, and should be offered a plum before I stirred up more controversy within the school." I neither wanted or sought anything but to be the Chapter Chairman, but since that Administration saw it differently, I took their offer. I began an eleven-year ride that topped anything I had done before.

Before I stepped into that second floor Dean's Office in September of 1970, I unconsciously brought with me ten years of teaching and related experience from the Junior High, the J.H.S. Camp Program, the J.H. Summer Schools, and my three years at Fashion. It was mainly the Junior High School experiences, especially those situations which involved all those physical confrontations I needed to learn from and avoid. I had to become aware of my own naïveté and try to use the "reasonable man" approach in attempting to reach an equitable solution between student and teacher, between student and student, and between me and the student.

I had to remind myself that tolerance, compassion and understanding had to be my goal. Boy, did I get tested early!

Mr. K., or "Iron Mike" as we affectionately referred to him, ran a tight ship. He wanted professional record-keeping and he wanted substantiation when a student was charged with a violation, especially if the Dean called for a parental visit and especially for a pre-suspension hearing. He got neither with the aging Deans. Mr. T. was a gentle giant. Everybody was a giant to me, who believed in writing 'something' on a scrap of paper and then 'gently reminding' the male perpetrator not to do it again.

As for Mrs. F., who really ran the day-to-day operation of the office—she would write down her personal comments on the referrals which were kept on file. The files were something else again, with slips of paper of unsubstantiated accusations, meaningless items like a patch of cloth or a teacher's memo of some long-forgotten incident. And worst or all, the files were all out of date. We retained files on students who had graduated or left the school years before. Double and triple files of the same student were very common because they were not properly filed, or because Mrs. F. had her own file on her desk. She had many of them along with all of her vocational materials which were strewn all over her desk. She also had another bad habit, she loved to bully her female charges over the dopiest things.

I particularly remember very vividly one incident whereby a girl was sent down to the office with a monitor and a very strong piece of incriminating "evidence."

The "evidence" was a scrap of paper, delivered in an envelope via the monitor, which said, "She is a shitty bitch." Without attempting to ask the girl who the term referred to, Mrs. F. immediately assumed that the comment was directed at the teacher. The girl said nothing, only nodded that she had written it, but sat there petrified as the Dean of Girls laced into her as if she committed the crime of the century.

"I'll have you suspended right now! This instant! You could go to jail for this, do you know that?" On and on went Mrs. F., and the more the girl heaved and sobbed in her chair, the more abusive became the threats.

"I know what I can do," Mrs. F. added. "I'll call the police right now and have you jailed instead of being suspended. How do you like that?"

By now, the offender was so physically hysterical, she almost appeared emotionally disturbed.

"All right, young lady, we've had enough of that! Stop your whimpering and sit up straight. Here's what I will do. Are you listening to me?" she demanded.

Between sobs, the young girl nodded, and Mrs. F. continued, "Now, I want you to sit over there" (pointing to a desk in the corner of the huge suite), "and write a sincere letter of apology to the teacher, Mrs. C. Do you understand?"

The girl attempted to interrupt, but Mrs. F. would hear none of it. "I said, do you understand? Now go over there and start writing! Otherwise, I call the police!"

I just believed that all this was unnecessary, disturbing and certainly very painful to witness. I later went up to Mr. T., the Dean for Boys, and said to him, "Wayne, can't we do something about this?"

"What the hell do you want me to do?" he snapped. "She's the Dean of Girls, and that's practically the whole school. I'm responsible for the boys, the lunchroom and all major fights between anybody. And that's our jobs. Sometimes, I'll sit in on a suspension hearing. I teach too, you know!"

Wayne's greatest help came in separating combatants during a fight. He was the best! He knew where all the major pressure points were on the shoulders, arms and hands. He tried to teach me these points, but I didn't possess his arm strength.

I also became aware of other subtleties that I came to appreciate with time, and that was the deployment of student desks strategically placed inside the Dean's office. We had some outside in the waiting area as well. These desks, at times, were completely occupied by students, all writing their letters of apologies to the various offended teachers, a group which, on the whole, was made up close friends of Mrs. F. What a sham!

Once, Mrs. F. tried to humiliate and bully another student in my presence, but this time, the girl reacted quite differently. She got up and started to strike the Dean. I shot out of my chair and separated the girl from Mrs. F. Needless to say, the attacker was promptly suspended.

I had to bide my time. Iron Mike told me that both Mrs. F. and Mr. T. would be retiring soon. Then, we would do things somewhat differently. The first thing proposed to start on were the records. In my own fashion, I could begin to weed out the dated folders; up-scale the referral forms with areas marked on them to stress what actually happened while keeping personal comments to a bare zero, and delete all those scraps of papers with annotations such as "she's a shitty bitch." If a student did in fact, actually call a teacher a "shitty bitch," I wanted it on the proper referral form, devoid of any comments about what the teacher thought of the student's parentage, and then signed by the offended teacher. I wanted the document to look professional, and I stapled the forms in triplicate so that one was mailed home, one went to the counselor and I kept the third. If there is anyone thing I do proficiently, it is record-keep, and if Iron Mike wanted a record-keeper, I was his man!

But, I digress. I want to relate my first serious case as a dean. Remembering all my objectives and goals of professionalism, and my desire to avoid confrontations at all costs, I relate the following incident.

Since Fashion High had so few male students within the school population, it was not unusual to have only one or two in a class of 34 (the contractual limit in a day high school academic class). Class disturbances common in the junior high school were rare. Believe it or not, most of the referrals involving male students usually originated because of hall activity, smoking in the bathroom, or because of infractions like attempting to cut school, or not being prepared in a gym class. When we did have a fight between two male students, Wayne would take care of it. I handled the more complex problem in this regard—that is, if a fight was between two gay boys, Wayne just wouldn't touch it; Period. He thought it was more of a guidance problem than a conundrum for the Dean. Maybe he was right—but that was the problem I was forced to confront. What to do? It wasn't just a matter of writing a referral, as much as I wanted to tackle the issue and attempt to solve it.

Fights between a gay and a straight were one thing, but what did you do if it involved two or three gays? My priority was always to promote a safe environment for everybody; and safety was a Dean problem, not a Guidance one.

To complicate matters further, the gays would attempt to 'win over' straights by 'offers' like an "A" grade design or pattern for homework in exchange for their companionship in school, or where ever. In addition, these gays would dress to the nines with exotic clothing like net shirts that revealed their nipples to any viewer who was so inclined. Many times, gay men would have serious altercations with female students in class because they were so well dressed and so attractive.

The dilemma I faced that fall was a major problem bearing all the earmarks of a Shakespearean tragedy. This real-life drama involved two gay boys who had been dating for some time. The more aggressive of the two, Mario (and perhaps the more unstable), became jealous when his partner had a surreptitious date with another gay in school. To get even, the first boy went "recruiting" quite openly for a "straight" so as to register more points, because any gay could get another gay, but to get a "straight" was something else and something of a "prize." When the second boy found his partner strolling arm-in-arm with the "straight" in one of the school hallways, all hell broke loose. After a near brawl, the second one declared he would kill them both if he ever saw them again.

Fortunately, Mr. T. was in the vicinity and brought all three down to me because he had a class next period. As usual, he handed me a scrap of paper scribbled with last names and official class data, and left.

I called in the first gay for a brief interview and left the other gay to cool his heels in the waiting area outside my office. I then instructed a monitor to escort the straight kid to the A.A.'s with a note from me to wait for my call. I interviewed each boy separately, jotted down some comments to myself, and never gave either fellow an opportunity to talk or argue with the other. This procedure took almost the entire period of 40 minutes. In fact, I was just concluding the last interview when Wayne stepped in.

"How ya doin', kid?" he asked quite jovially. "Solve the case, kid?"

"Not quite," I replied. "I just got some preliminary

things down first, and then I thought I could dig deeper and try to resolve this thing."

He pointed to one end of the office and I followed him over to the windows. "Don't dig too deep," he said, "you might not like what you'll find. Let them hash it out among themselves. You can't waste your time on something like this. It's not our concern. Turn the whole thing over to the Guidance Department, and let them call for a parental conference," he continued. It sounded more like a warning than anything else.

"It's O.K., Wayne. I think I got a handle on this one," I lied, and he left the office much like the old-timer who had just wasted a fine glass of port on a teetotaler.

I needed time, and so I dismissed the first gay and the straight, and I called in the second gay, the one who had made the original threat. After some persuasion, I got him to promise that he would do nothing about activating his threat until I had had time to find a solution amicable to all parties. He agreed, somewhat reluctantly, but he promised. I further added that if he saw the two together after my warnings to both, he was to let me know immediately. Again, he promised. I wanted to show the "old-timers" a new way of thinking, and apply a little effort and guidance where ever possible.

The truce lasted just one day! I had all three of them in the office twenty-four hours later. Mr. T. could hardly contain his chuckle. But I was determined!

I tried again. This time, I interviewed the two gays simultaneously and left the straight boy in the waiting room. I got nowhere. The two gays just accused each of past sins and how "he said this" and "you said that." To make the situation almost comical, the first gay was wearing his provocative 'net shirt' which infuriated his partner.

"Why are you wearing the shirt I gave you?" the second asked. "Just to get me mad, or are you dicking for someone else?" he screamed. "I can't stand you!"

"Oh yeah?" countered the other. "What did you do with the scarf I gave you? Sell your ass for it?"

There was no end to this litany of abuse, so I had both boys wait outside while I tried to reason with the straight. "Are you really interested in Mario?" I asked, "or can we come to some kind of agreement here?"

"I don't give a rat's ass for Mario," the straight said. "I'm doing this for some bucks! That's all!"

"What!" I said. "All this crap over some *money*? Please explain, right now!"

"Mario just wanted to see how far he could go to get his boyfriend jealous, that's all!" he replied. I told the straight to leave my office and never darken my doorway again. He saw that I was furious and meekly made his departure. Then I called in the two gays, who could see I was fit to be tied.

"Get in here, you two. I've had about enough from both of you and we're going to resolve this thing right now in this office, today! Get it?"

They both nodded in agreement.

"Do either of you think that this has been some kind of joke for your amusement? Well, think again! And, Mario, where do you get off teasing and paying off people to play your little games? I want some answers, and now!"

Mario proceeded to relate his soap opera. The only thing he left out were the commercials.

"So—where do we go from here?" I asked. Looking over to the second gay, I asked, "Are you going to control this undisciplined rage of yours?" And, without bothering to get a reply, I further asked, "When are you both going to grow up? I've spent the better part of two days with this idiocy, and what do I get for my troubles? A typical love spat, with 'you said,' and 'I said.' And then I get this moron," (pointing to Mario) "to go pay someone to rile things up even more. Real bright, you know. Real bright! And, to top everything off, somebody could have gotten hurt here if we continued to play out this farce. Well, it ends here, right now. Right?"

The truth of the matter was that I was nowhere with this. Once I excused these two twits from the Dean's Office, I would be back to square one with the situation and no resolution in sight. What I needed was another "Golden Gloves" piece of inspiration. I was fishing and I needed help!

Then I saw it.

My Constitutional Law textbook from my one year at Brooklyn Law! I brought the text in to show the students how Marbury v. Madison was written up by the Supreme Court, including the arguments for both sides of the issue. This was my godsend. I told both students to stand up and face the desk. I told them I was empowered to act as a justice of the peace because I had attended law school and with this solemn text, I could officiate their "marriage." Both boys stood up, and, looking very solemn themselves, agreed to the ceremony. Then and there, in the dean's office at Fashion High, I, John A. Manicone "married" two gays. Problem solved!

After I read some passages from the text, I closed the tome very deliberately, the two gays kissed and left my office quite content and happy.

This was the second time in my career, I believe, that a decision of mine was truly inspired. From nothing, I achieved something and I'll be condemned or commended later. I knew from the beginning that I was just "reaching." I was inadequately prepared for this job, but with time, I could make it. Mario had deceived me and what did I do but play right into his hands. This entire episode reminded me of that situation at Junior High School 22 when a female teacher complained to me that she was having problems with her all-boys class. They were taking advantage of her, she claimed. I really got steamed and began an investigation worthy of a Congressional hearing. As it turned out, she was lying and they were telling the truth.

I just hate it when I'm being used, but because it's my nature to accept something at face value, I fell for that "helpless female" line. As it turned out, this particular math teacher complained that the boys were deliberately stroking her backside whenever they were called upon to work out problems on the blackboard. She didn't want to take this to the Dean because she was ashamed. I told her I would take care of it and requested names. I interviewed each boy separately and I soon came away with a very disturbing picture: the teacher would deliberately put herself in harm's way as they were going to the blackboard.

She readily admitted to me that there were occasions when she was "leaning over the desk" when the student was called up. When I suggested that she stand by the window when the fellows worked the blackboard, she gave me the excuse that she had to stand in front in order to give them a grade.

It's one thing to be molested, and quite another to abet the abuse. With time, I would get it. I had many, many opportunities to sharpen my skills. Meanwhile, I never told anybody, especially not Mr. T., about once being a temporary, acting, substitute Justice of the Peace. Wayne didn't want to be bothered with small details.

I suppose that Mr. K. was duly impressed with events, not withstanding the "marriage," and with my performance in the Dean's Office after my first year on the second floor. He was very supportive in my request to have an aide assigned. I had a small army of monitors, who did nothing but staple the three referral sheets, sandwiched by two carbons, so as to have a steady supply of dean referral forms. In addition, I instituted a policy of establishing a hierarchy, or chain of hearings, for any one particular student who was a repeat offender, culminating with a Principal Suspense hearing. Each step triggered its own act of goals and purposes. Iron Mike had found the right man. I was born for the job!

Meanwhile, Mrs. F. and Mr. B. liked my spirit and wished me well. They were both calling it a day. In September, 1971, the Dean's office was unified, just like the Heavyweight Division in boxing; there was no separate Dean. It was an awesome responsibility. I had no classes to teach and the entire business was my call from now on.

I had the pick of teachers assigned to the office, but there was one drawback; the suite of offices was divided. One half went to the chairlady of the Art Department. I could live with that because one of the first things I did that September morning was to get rid of all those writing desks!

That fall, I scored two successive coups which enhanced my position and silenced the critics. The first situation involved a student whose family was close to Iron Mike. The girl, for whatever reason, had decided to wear a fur jacket to school—I believe it was around Yom Kippur. Well, anyway, the jacket was stolen and the girl came running down to my office hysterically, to report the crime. She gave me all the particulars, including what, when and where, and she personally tried to solve the theft before the culprit could leave the school with it. No one can leave our building, not even for lunch, without a pass. That was a strict rule enforced by our very capable security staff. I had only one good thing working for me: the jacket size was a petite.

I immediately ran down to the lobby floor and alerted the security not to let anyone out, and check all bags and parcels. We are looking for a fur coat! If anyone has a pass, look for anything unusual. We didn't have radios then, so everything had to work by word of mouth. I advised our female guards to check bathrooms and look around. Top priority on this one!

Sure enough, within one hour, we had our fur coat and the thief. The student attempted to sell it to our petite security guard, believe it or not! We laughed about that one for years.

The second case came a few weeks later, when a student reported that she was constantly having her handbag rifled of money. The Spanish girl maintained that all the thefts took place in the trade class. When I asked her who she suspected, she immediately claimed, "Those colored girls across my table."

I told her to give me all the facts—names, dates, amount taken and where she had left her handbag. She complied. Then, I had a brainstorm, I took out a dollar bill from my wallet and marked it by circling several numbers and placing a star on the corner of the bill. I gave her the bill and I told her to fold that with her own money when she came to the same class tomorrow. I gave the girl a pass from me to the trade teacher instructing the teacher to send a monitor down to me immediately if another theft took place. And it did.

I went to the class, which was as busy as a hive, with students working, cutting, sewing, standing, ironing and the like. I announced my presence to the class and asked everyone to sit down, which they did. Then I told them my purpose for coming to their class. I told the class that I was looking for a blue cocktail ring that one of the students had reported stolen yesterday and I wanted to search the class and their handbags for it. I said I would start from one end of the room and I needed their cooperation. "All handbags and bags on the table—NOW!" I demanded. Of course, I started with the table with my planted dollar first!

I took great pains to look for a small item as I began my search. I could glance from time to time and see all the faces at the tables watching my every move. Good, that's exactly what I wanted the thief to believe, that I was looking for something she did not have. I pretended to give the wallets and paper currency a perfunctory look. Then I got to a Spanish girl who was seated next to the plant. And, bingo! I found the marked dollar bill.

"You!" the victim screamed. "You stole my money!" She got up angrily and before she could deliver a blow, I was between them. I told the victim and the suspected thief to come down to my office right that minute. You could have heard the proverbial pin drop.

When I got the two ladies down to the office, I had them both sit on opposite sides of my desk. The victim was seething; the thief just held her head down and glanced from side to side.

"I give you money every day, you bitch!" she started, "and yet you steal from me!"

I told the victim that everything was under control now, and to stop remonstrating. I then informed the thief what the dollar amount was that she had stolen and that I wanted it repaid by the end of the week. She agreed and I forwarded a copy of the referral to her counselor for a parental conference. I dismissed them both, but I first called the victim to the side and told her to apologize to her black classmates. She promised she would.

Seven

There's More

Nowhere in the script does it say that I could win them all—no way. Many times it would be downright frustrating in that I knew a kid was stealing, but a source I was counting on had given me the wrong name, or identified the wrong item. Or, if I had the right kid, he decided to cut out of school that day and the evidence was gone. However, two situations come to mind, neither of which was a case of wrong identity or improper pursuit, but students at Fashion were involved and my office, although witness to the events, could not dictate the outcome. The first took place in the fall of 1972; the other, about a year or so later. Neither kid was an American citizen.

Heidi was a very pretty German girl, who came to the United States with her rather elderly parents in their mid-sixties. She wanted to be "American" in the worst way, and after she was accepted by Fashion as an Art major, she started to hang out with her classmates and eventually began cutting school.

Sometime, around October or November, this small, intimate group of friends was introduced to someone named Pacho. Unknown to these class cutters was the fact that Pacho was a pimp constantly recruiting new girls to his stable. I never met Pacho, but in several interviews with various girls who were apprehended later, it became very obvious that Pacho was some charmer.

"He could really turn it on when he had to," said one girl. Another said, that despite his greasy looks and "pimply face" he really attracted the girls. Perhaps it was the money he flashed, or that he was about six or seven years older than most of the guys who hung around in front of the building across the street by the stoop—but he interested Heidi.

Heidi became his girl. Girl friends of Heidi's who were a little bit more street-slick began to hear rumors about Pacho and tried to discourage the romance. Heidi wouldn't hear of it, accusing the girls of being jealous because she had an "older" boyfriend with money. Heidi broke away from this group and her classmates saw her less and less. Her grades and her attendance dropped off, and late in November, I had a visit by Heidi's elderly mother and father, who were quite upset because they were having to report Heidi missing.

Right off the bat, we had some rather serious problems. They spoke very little English, I spoke no German; the elderly father was hard of hearing, and when we did attempt to communicate, the mother spoke rather quickly between fits of sobbing. These people had no business trying to raise a fifteen-year-old in such an alien nation. They were just overwhelmed with feelings of guilt, helplessness and an inability to understand that the American authorities were not as sympathetic and as understanding as the Germans were. Our initial contact lasted almost two hours, which included instructions on my part on how the American system did in fact work, and what various rules and procedure meant. Little by little, we made headway.

After they gave me a brief but thorough history of their lives up to the present moment, they showed me Heidi's report card. It was terrible. They also showed me the report cards of her primary grades in Brooklyn, which were outstanding; it was as if we were talking about two different individuals.

"It's all because of this man, Pacho," said the mother. "Now she's gone and we don't know where she is. He would always call at night and they would talk for hours and hours! When I told her to go to bed or do her homework, she would go like this" (and the mother would wave her right arm to the father in deep contempt). "Heidi's changed when she came here. She was never like this to us before!"

The parents were very cooperative. They answered all the questions I posed; that by 5 o'clock yesterday, when Heidi had not come home, they began to worry. By 6, they called all her known friends—except for Pacho, whose phone number they didn't have. At nine that night, they called her friends again, some who had not answered the first time. No, they didn't know where Heidi was. Yes, they would call back if they heard any word.

It went like this until midnight. This was the first time Heidi had ever stayed away from home without telling Momma or Poppa, the parents claimed. A relative told them to go to the police or go to her school the next morning without delay. They chose to visit the school first.

I asked them to describe Heidi; they did better than that, they showed me her graduation picture from elementary school. She was very pretty. Then I told them what to do next. They had to go to the police station in their precinct in Brooklyn, even if they thought she had run away from school or from another part of the city. They could not file a "missing persons" report until a full 24 hours had elapsed, which would make it between 5 and 9 o'clock on this day when they believed their daughter to be missing. On hearing the words "Missing Persons Report," the mother gave a shudder and began to sob, at times, uncontrollably. It was hard to witness.

The father was full of questions: why wait until 5 or 6 tonight to make out the report? Friends had said she was in school yesterday, but she didn't get home; so shouldn't we use the precinct closest to the school? Can't we interview any of her friends in your presence, or better yet, in the police station? When I said no to all their questions, I also gave them full explanations about New York City and Board of Education Law. You can't force a student to be taken from school to be questioned at a police station if a law or regulation is broken outside of a school. In fact, I told them, a police officer can't come into a public school building, uninvited, to question any student about a police matter that occurred outside a school building. That's the law.

I helped them look up the phone number of the precinct next to their home, and called the station. I spoke to a detective who handled missing persons and explained the situation. The parents were quite relieved that some wheels were being greased and help would be forthcoming. I tried to encourage them, but I also tried to paint a realistic picture at the same time. I promised that I would begin to question as many of Heidi's friends as possible today and that I would keep in touch. I made them promise that if they heard anything, they would inform me immediately. They left, and I began to dig.

I did not like what I had unearthed after several interviews with Heidi's close friends. They were very frank about their observations and what they believed about Pacho.

"But, who is this Pacho guy?" I asked, like a typical

father with a personal stake here.

"Oh, you know, that skinny Spanish guy with all those pimples on his face. He's always hanging around outside across the street in the afternoon. You must've seen him a hundred times!"

When I told them that I had not had the "pleasure," they all appeared unbelieving. Once I finished with the interrogations of my students, I then called the 10th Precinct and spoke to a sergeant there whom I knew quite well. In fact, I knew quite a few police officers there because of all the "business" we did with arrests and having police officers assigned to our building. They knew of Pacho; knew that he was a suspected pimp and had a police record, but didn't know his current address or where his new "stable" might be. I told the police sergeant what I knew of the Heidi situation, and he was interested. I was to keep him informed.

The next morning, Heidi's parents called and told me that the police Missing Persons form had been made out and completed, and that Heidi had not yet come home. They were very upset; I told them what I had done, but did not inform them about Pacho's occupation—yet. I tried to be optimistic, but I don't think I was successful.

I then called the precinct in Brooklyn and spoke to the same detective I had spoken to yesterday, telling him all I knew so far. He was very concerned and I gave him the name and number of the 10th Precinct. He advised me that if Heidi, being a minor, was apprehended and Pacho had forced her into prostitution, we definitely had "just cause" for an arrest and the Attorney's Office might be necessary. "If—and only *if*," the detective said, "Heidi cooperates. And, that's a big if!"

A few days passed. Nothing. I re-questioned Heidi's

friends. They swore they knew nothing. Then, I got a phone call several mornings later from Heidi's mother, who was hysterical. This time, I couldn't understand a word.

After several long minutes, I finally heard something about "Heidi."

"What about Heidi?" I asked.

More unintelligible gibberish, a mile a second, and again the name "Heidi, Heidi."

Finally, in desperation, I yelled at the mother to please put her husband on the phone, as I couldn't understand her at all. Poppa got on the phone. He was more collected and he spoke very deliberately, saying that Heidi had phoned just a minute or two ago and had given them the address where she was being held, and asked them to come and get her. (I believe he said, "save her.") All the while, I could hear the mother screaming hysterically in the background.

I asked the father if he was sure he was accurate about the address, and he said that his wife had written it down on a scrap of paper. The address was five blocks from the school!

I told them to get to Fashion as quickly as they could, and I would make sure that my buddy there sent two officers to my office, to escort the parents to the address. I waited.

The officers arrived first. I asked if they needed a search warrant, and they claimed that if a crime is in commission (namely, prostitution involving a minor), a warrant is not necessary, especially if the parents can identify the child. About an hour later, the elderly pair showed up, quite breathless. They held a scrap of paper with an address and an apartment number.

"Let's go!" said one of the officers. I wasn't needed.

I was told afterward what happened.

When they got to the address and the police banged on the door, literally all hell broke loose. Screaming and shouting emanated from the room, with the squealing and scraping of furniture thrown against the door of the apartment. As the police officers attempted to batter down the door, Heidi's mother—from down the hall, where they had left her—started running through the hall screaming, "Heidi! Heidi!" at the top of her lungs.

With a great effort and much shoving against a weighty set of beds, mattresses, box springs, bureau drawers, and other impedimenta, the officers were finally able to squeeze into the room. A great deal of time was wasted attempting to effect entry, but, the end result was that neither Pacho nor any of his ladies were there. The room was empty. Pacho was very smart. He rented two apartments, just in case of this eventuality, the policeman said. Now they did need a search warrant. Pacho and the girls were long gone!

Late the next morning, I receive another phone call from Heidi's father, who said that Heidi had been located; she was at St. Vincent's Hospital. I got there as soon as I could, and the two parents were absolutely distraught. Their beautiful Heidi was badly beaten up, especially around the face. She looked awful. Her nose was broken, teeth were missing and she had sustained fractures to her cheek bones and collar bone. She also suffered a concussion and an eye socket hemorrhage. She was in such pain that I had to walk away. What could I do there? I felt helpless.

I told the parents that I was available when—and if—Heidi came back to school. Absence from school was not an issue here. Full and complete recovery was far more important. They said they understood and thanked me for my efforts.

Two or three weeks later, I received a very cordial, but brief, phone call from the father. In his very deliberate Germanic manner, he regretted to inform me that he and his wife had made a very big mistake in attempting to fabricate a new life for Heidi in the United States, and that they were departing that very evening for Germany to raise her properly. He thanked me again for all my efforts, and hung up.

I never heard from them again, but I still can hear that woman screaming her daughter's name.

Then there was the episode of the thieving student, the anguished father and the duplistic math teacher. If I sound a bit Perry Mason-esque, it's because we had here all the elements of a TV sit-com, with a rather startling and dramatic ending.

In early spring of 1972, I was visited by a college-age student who accompanied her father. They were Italians who had arrived in America about eight or ten years previously. The father was escorted by his daughter because he spoke no English and required an interpreter to discuss a rather serious situation which involved a younger daughter, who was one of ours. We got along very well because this time language was not a barrier. I speak and understand Italian quite well.

The problem, in a nutshell, was the father's and mother's suspicion that the girl, Maria, was seeing a teacher on the sneak. They had found incriminating letters and notes which were translated by the older daughter, and they suspected that the person was Maria's math teacher; he was black.

I asked the parents how they had arrived at their conclusion. The older girl, Carla, said that her sister's behavior and actions had changed quite remarkably right after Christmas. Maria, who worked in a supermarket after school and on weekends, started to return home later and later. She had never stayed out really late, but Maria, being sixteen and pretty, the parents became concerned. Once the letters and notes were found, the family staked out the supermarket, and that's when they realized what was going on. On several occasions, both late in the afternoon and on Saturday, the teacher would walk into the superette, in the Bronx, and spend time at the cash register as Maria worked. Sometimes, he would wait for her in his parked car. The parents saw the couple kissing as well.

"What can the school do?" the father asked, in Italian.

Of course, there was a problem. A teacher seeing and dating a student from the same school was certainly an ethical problem—but could a school legally be held accountable? No laws had been broken, as I could see it, but still, there was something immoral going on. Should the school administration speak to the man? What about the Guidance Department?

The father was a baker by trade. He was short and round, and I don't believe he had a mean bone in his body. Never once did he make a threat or mention doing anything physical. All he wanted was that I, or someone of authority, speak to the man and stop what was going on before the situation became more complicated or somehow directly influenced his daughter adversely. He and his wife were at a loss. I could see that the man was in pain. I asked his permission to call his daughter into the office to see if all this was true. I sent a monitor to get her.

Maria was not like her sister at all; she had blonde hair and looked German, or Swiss. Her sister, on the other hand, had dark hair.

As Maria took her seat, I could see a transformation take place. She brought her head down, slumped in her chair and looked very surly. She knew what was coming. I began to question her about some of the things that had been discussed before her entrance. She either didn't answer my questions, or she was so evasive, that little information was forthcoming to help us resolve the situation amicably.

Finally, the father, in frustration, asked his daughter very forcefully (and in Italian) whether she was going to cooperate, *si* or *no?* The girl remained silent and hostile. Much of her anger appeared directed at her sister for abandoning her in her hour of need. The side-show between the sisters was quite revealing and informative because Maria, up to that point, still did not know that I understood Italian very well. Seeing that for the most part, I was carrying on a one-sided conversation with Maria, I sent her back to class. The father, not to be out-done, advised Maria to get home without delay after school.

Not much later, after exchanging phone numbers, the conference was over. I really had a dilemma on my hands. What to do? I decided that I would feel my way around this one by picking the brains of some people I respected and trusted, I then would speak about it to the A.A. and the principal in an off-the-record meeting and see where it would lead. I needed time to crack this nut. But it never happened.

Two or three days later, I got a phone call from a police precinct in the Bronx about an alleged series of thefts which took place at the supermarket where Maria worked. The detective told me that he spoke to the parents, through a daughter, Carla, and the girl gave them my name, phone number and a brief synopsis of our conference earlier in the week. They wanted to speak to the student, Maria, and since the supermarket was pressing charges, an arrest was possible.

I said, "No way."

I reminded the police officer that he could not arrest any student inside a school building for an alleged crime that took place outside the school environment. He said he knew that, but could we simply hold her there until they got to Fashion. Again I said, "No way."

At first he couldn't understand why I was protecting a possible criminal. I simply would not budge. Then he tried the gambit of "inter-city" and "inter-agency" cooperation. Again, I stood my ground.

Then, he asked if he and his partner could come up to see me in my office. I said O.K., but with the strict understanding that I would not permit any attempt on his part to roam the halls to look for the girl and that our conference would start and end without seeing or interviewing her. He reluctantly agreed to my conditions.

I checked with the Attendance Room to see if Maria had come to school. She was marked present. Then, I went down to the lobby and gave Security their instructions. After the detectives signed in, they were to be personally escorted to my office and one was to wait in my foyer until our meeting was concluded. I then went to the A.A.'s office and told him that two cops were coming to question me about a possible theft of funds in the Bronx that might involve one of our students. I told him nothing else. He reminded me of what I was allowed to do and not to do, and I assured him that I would take care of this matter. No problem.

The cops knew everything. Boy, was Carla a blabbermouth! The policemen told me quite a bit to get me to soften my stance about them seeing Maria. It appeared that Maria had been short-changing the store for several days and attempting to pass it off as "I must have given someone too much change," or "I must have been distracted." However, yesterday Maria's count was off by hundreds of dollars and she also fudged and erased figures on the tape. The store wanted Maria arrested.

I told the officers that I would in no way help them and that the best I could offer was that they could stand discreetly across the street in an attempt to arrest her outside, or at her home. The police officers said that they understood and left my office. I understand that Maria was arrested at home in the Bronx later that day.

The older sister, Carla, called me the next day and told me what had happened. Her father made restitution and that for the sake of the honor of his name, he would spare his daughter the shame of jail. Maria, according to Carla, remorseful for what she had done, confessed to her parents that the teacher "needed" the money and had her steal for him.

I asked Carla, what was Poppa going to do now? She said, that "my father will come up with something." And he sure did!

A couple of days later, I was very surprised to see Carla and her father strolling into my office, all smiles.

"You solved the problem?" I asked, rather stunned.

"My father did!" Carla announced very proudly.

"Well, well, don't keep me in suspense. What did he do?" I asked.

"I'll let Poppa tell you," she said and he proceeded to tell me a tale and a solution worthy of King Solomon.

After the restitution, and after Maria's confession, the father asked his daughter what were her feelings about the math teacher. Despite what he had led her to do, she said, she still maintained an affection for him. She said she loved him because even though she stole for him, he hadn't taken advantage of her at all during this whole time.

"Fine!" said the father. Then he promised the following: "Spend some time in Italy until all this blows over (the scandal and the rumors in the neighborhood). Then, after six months, if you still love him, you come back—you'll be almost seventeen—you can marry him. Is that all right with you?" Maria immediately agreed to the proposal, and started to pack as the father went to buy the plane tickets.

He continued on to say that Maria was giddy with happiness and that she had her parents "all wrong" and that they were "wonderful" and "so understanding."

When they arrived at the Rome Airport, her father had a small surprise waiting for Maria. She was met by her father's sister, a very stern and very strict woman, who took no nonsense.

Then, turning toward Maria, the father—holding Maria's passport in his beefy hands—ripped it to shreds, and said, "*Qui tu sei nata, e qui tu rimani!* (Here you were born, and here you stay!)" And bought Maria a one-way ticket to Italy.

There is absolutely nothing I can add to either of these stories because I did not affect the outcome nor in any way play a major role. I was merely a spectator. Yes, I might have facilitated a situation here or there, I was concerned for the people who were hurting; but no person or organization is equipped to handle such complexities as now have invaded the public schools of today. I took courses at NYU and Columbia's Teacher's College, and nowhere in their curriculum of study are these situations addressed.

Unfortunately, too many educators go into their careers ill-trained for the job ahead. I am reminded of that story again of Teachers College professor's reaction when asked about her worst day in teaching youngsters back when she graduated in the twenties. "Let me see," she said as she tapped her right cheek. "Oh, yes; once a boy got up in class and walked out of the room without permission! Yes, that was the most singular case of bad manners that I can remember." There is a woman who has no business teaching teachers-to-be.

Although neither of these two cases involved classroom disruptions, they were disrupting in other ways, because education was lost, lives were altered, and remedies were not forthcoming from the areas that were addressed. Are schools capable of these solutions? Can a grade advisor or counselor, who normally has a caseload of 100 or 150 students, ready to spend the time that is quasi-legal at best? Can the police handle everything, no matter how marginal to the law it might be? Who's responsible?

I wish I could tell you, but I can't.

Eight

Drugs & Alcohol in Fashion

"What you hear, is what you get!" That, dear reader, was how I once had a parent answer his phone when I called and asked, "Hello, Mr. Brown?"

The man had absolutely no idea who was on the other end of the line. I had called early in the morning from my office to catch parents at home before they went to work. It was my custom to reach parents any way I could to acquaint them with the fact that a problem had developed, and suggesting that we talk about it. If the phone calls didn't work, then we sent out form letters to announce an appointment for a Dean-Parent conference.

Mr. Brown's kid liked to wear new Banlon shirts everyday, which I knew retailed for $25 apiece. I was getting suspicious; wearing a new Banlon shirt, per se, isn't a crime, but, this kid's activity in the lunchroom and in the boys' bathroom had brought his case to my attention. When he was discovered cutting classes several times, and was caught in the bathroom several times by security without a pass, the young man, Clinton, began to interest me. Then I remembered the shirts. He always had a brand new shirt on every time I saw him, sometimes two or three days in a row. I questioned him about it, "Hey, Clinton, how come you get to wear one of those shirts new each day?"

He told me that his mother did not have the time to wash the dirty ones, so he always took out a new one! Mr. Brown the father, really interested me now. I kept my eye on Clinton, and through my well-established network of informers that I had recruited over the years, we got lucky. We caught Clinton in possession of some marijuana joints in a bathroom "sweep." That's when I called his home and got that most curious reply.

Mr. Brown came into my office wearing his postman's uniform; we had arranged it so that everyone would be in my office at the same time. We got down to brass tacks right away because Mr. Brown did not want to be late for his shift, so I produced his son's statement, the security guard's statement and the five or six sticks of marijuana. The boy said that he was not selling them in the bathroom, but, that he planned to consume them himself, one at a time, during the day.

When I asked him, "Where did you buy them?" he said "From someone outside."

"How much did you pay for them?"

He replied that he paid a dollar each.

"A dollar each?" the father screamed at his son. "A dollar *each?*" he repeated. "What do you think that money grows on trees?"

I interrupted that line of questioning with something that I thought needed answering, by asking him about those new Banlon shirts. To me, Clinton had to be dealing and to support my claim, I wanted to establish the fact that the only way Clinton could have afforded those shirts was through dealing and not by consuming marijuana. So, I asked the young man, "Where do you get the shirts?" pointing to the one he had on.

His father immediately jumped in by saying that he

bought them. He didn't have time to wash the soiled ones!

"You see," the father continued, "I'm divorced, and I have to do everything—the cleaning, the cooking, the shopping."

"But, isn't it very expensive to buy him all these shirts?" I countered.

"I get them wholesale," he replied.

The kid didn't say a word.

"Look, Mr. Manicone, I have to get to work, and I want to wrap this up to your satisfaction and mine too! Clinton promised me last night that you will never find him cutting class or carrying grass again. It was his first trip. Let's take those joints down into the toilet, and I want to be with him as you destroy that stuff. What do you say?"

Since I had a weak case, only possession of five or six joints (in New York State, one must have one ounce of marijuana for a felony arrest, which by the way, is equal in size to a jar of oregano or parsley flakes), I went along with the deal. The three of us went to a men's room, and as I flushed each joint down, Mr. Brown poked his kid and said, "There goes another one of my dollars." Later, I found out the real story, but by then, the kid had transferred out of Fashion. Clinton not only was dealing in our school, his father split the take! How about that one?

Usually, my spy network operated very well. Once I had a kid indebted to me for a minor infraction: their information always proved to be invaluable. So much so that in eleven years as the Dean, I only had to pay for two locks I broke to get into a locker. It was my standing rule, that if I had to open your locker with the cutting bolts, and I found something incriminating, I owed the student nothing. I must have popped open dozens and dozens of locks, but I was wrong only twice!

I remember in one case I had the name of a supplier of needles in the school. I called him down and he said that he would cooperate. We went to his locker, he opened it, and we found nothing. I was slightly chagrined and allowed him back into his class. I phoned my snitch and he said, "Didn't you look and search the top of his locker? It's in there!"

I said that it better be, and I had Security bring the kid back to my office again. Again, I questioned the kid, and again, he said that his locker was clean.

"Prove it to me again," I ordered him. We went back to the same locker; again he opened it, but this time, I ran my hand along the top shelf, where some gym things were stored, and sure enough, it rained needles. All different colors, pastel yellows, greens, light reds and blues. I couldn't believe my eyes. Dozens of syringes and needles fell to the floor. My security chief had a tight grip on the kid's arm, and after I picked everyone up, we all went to my office for a "chat."

In his confession, the supplier said that he worked at St. Vincent's Hospital in some capacity or another, and when no one was looking, he would sneak into the supply room (this was before AIDS), and help himself to the syringes. He commanded top dollar because his customers loved the tint of his wares. I duly had him arrested, informed his parents where to bail him out because he was only 17, and informed them that a suspension hearing was imminent. A dangerous supplier was terminated because of "my system." I never made any apologies for it—ever.

Unfortunately, drugs, and their availability were a very serious problem for us in the early and mid-seventies. We heard stories of roasting banana skins, snorting and sniffing aeroplane glue and, believe it or not, inhaling the smoke from burning photo negatives. In the boys' bathroom, we always found a steady supply of bent spoons, to free-base, and McDonald's stirrers (the old model) so that the user could sniff cocaine. Some of you old-timers don't realize that McDonald's was asked to change the spatula end of the stirrer as a public gesture to combat drug users from raiding McDonald's for the coffee implement.

Another valuable tool that drug users employed were nail files which they bent up to a 90-degree angle, so that the drug user could prevent the valuable material from blowing off the grid of the nail file as he or she sniffed! Based on how many of these things would litter a bathroom floor, we could get a basic idea of how we were doing in our war on drugs.

We weren't doing too well.

Which brings me back to the photo negatives and the twit who tried it.

One afternoon, as I patrolled the fourth floor and to take a quick look-see in the boys' bathroom, I smelled smoke coming from that direction. I immediately raced into the bathroom and found a student lying unconscious on the tiled floor. Next to him was a burning, smoldering one-pound bag filled with photo negatives. The kid was as cold as the floor, I really thought he was dead until I felt a very weak pulse. There was no one around, and so I started shouting (this was still before hand-held telephones) and a teacher emerged from her room and immediately sent one of her kids down to the A.A.'s office to get help and call for an ambulance.

I stayed with the kid—who never came out of his coma. I was certain we would soon have a D.O.A. here and I tried everything to waken him. Not even cold water helped. Finally the EMS people arrived and he was rushed to Bellevue Hospital on the East Side. While I was waiting, I looked through his things, and got his name, address and phone number, which I gave to the ambulance people. Because of the lateness of the afternoon, it was already past three o'clock, and practically all our aides and security were gone for the day, so I went with the student to Bellevue as the school's representative.

While the emergency crew worked on the boy, I called his home and spoke to his mother. I told her what had transpired and that her son was now in Bellevue being treated. She said she understood and that she would get to the hospital from Brooklyn as soon as possible. I waited. The doctor emerged from the ER and told me that it was essential to give the boy certain drugs which he needed.

"Give them to him!" I said.

"I can't do that unless I get parental permission."

It was almost 4 o'clock now, and I tried his home again. The mother answered the phone again.

"Mrs. Harvey," I said, "your son is in great need of additional drugs to keep him stable. You have to get here right away! Why are you still home?"

"I need to wait for a ride," she answered.

"Why can't you take the train?" I asked. "You could be here inside a half an hour!"

After I kept insisting that she wait no longer, she promised that she would get to the hospital.

"Where is it?" she inquired.

"Bellevue! Bellevue!" I shouted. "Just tell the transit guy that you want to get to 23rd Street on the East Side. Hurry!"

It was almost 5 o'clock now, and still no mother. The doctors were on hold. There was nothing more for me to do except wait. I tried another phone call. Mrs. Harvey answered, "Hello?"

"Hello?" I yelled. "This is Mr. Manicone! Why are you still in Brooklyn?" I yelled again.

"I have to wait for my daughter to take me," she said.

I was livid. "Mrs. Harvey," I said as calmly and as controlled as I could be, "your son is still in the Emergency Room, and they cannot give him the medicine he needs until a parent gives them a written O.K. Do you understand?"

"Where is he again?"

"Bellevue! Bellevue!" I screamed.

"How do you spell it?" she asked.

"Spell it? My God! *Everyone* knows Bellevue!" I yelled.

I tried to gain my composure, and attempted to help this woman. She had to be stupid! "B-E-L-L-E-V-U-E," I said, slowly. "On 23rd Street, in Manhattan. Did you get that?"

"Yes," she said. I could see her spelling out the words on a scrap of paper, using a thick pointed pencil.

"Please," I said, "get here as soon as you can! I will wait for you, just a bit longer, but I have to get home myself." I waited till 5:30, then left. I called the hospital the next day, and they told me that the mother of our student didn't arrive until nearly nine. I would have shot her.

To get the whole picture at Fashion, you have to understand that our drug problem was not helped by the fact that on the East end of our block, 7th Avenue, we had the VA Building. Guess what the VA Building had on the first floor? A methadone clinic! Our discharged veterans from the Vietnam War, who were hooked on heroin, were treated at the clinic in that building. We couldn't understand the dimensions of the problem at first when we saw the veterans overdosed and on occasion, dead on car hoods around 24th Street. Wasn't methadone supposed to make the former drug user a functioning and viable member of his community? What was happening?

Through our drug coordinator, we discovered the truth. The veterans, instead of taking their methadone with their orange juice at the clinic, were in fact ingesting double and triple amounts of the methadone, in pill form. Pretending to take the substitute, they then would go outside and sell the methadone for cash to our students, and then would buy the illegal heroin to maintain their habit! The Federal Government was, in fact, subsidizing the veterans' illegal drug habit! We just couldn't believe our eyes.

To prove it for yourselves, the drug coordinator and I went into the cafeteria in the VA Building, and we saw the transaction taking place. We saw the veterans, very discreetly, handing over the methadone to the buyer for cash. Then both parties left the area. We followed them out, and saw the veteran make his buy on the corner of 24th Street and 7th Avenue.

We then returned to the building and demanded to see the Director. He was very cordial about seeing us on such short notice, and yes, he knew about the "problem."

"What are you going to do about it?" we asked.

"We're planning to shut down the clinic. We can't deal with the problem anymore. We know it's an outrage, but, that's the best we can do at present," he said.

End of story.

The drug problem was pervasive throughout that

area of Chelsea. In fact, I remembered that once when I stopped in a rather large coffee shop on the corner of 23rd and 7th, which once was a Bickford's, to get some coffee and a roll, the place had tables and booths, recently installed, in the center of the shop and also, along the huge plate glass windows. The counter was in the rear, and the recessed lighting gave the place a very warm and comfortable feeling. As I left the counter, to find an unoccupied table or booth, I noticed a booth was occupied with several men and a scruffy, dirty-looking woman, referred to as "Grandma."

Again, I couldn't believe my eyes, because, right before this group, on their table, was a huge pile of marijuana, which Grandma was dividing into smaller shares. And as she handed the grass to one of her cohorts in a plastic bag, she ordered, "And this goes to Johnny, right?" or, "This goes to Benny, right?" With every "Right?" the answer was "Right, Grandma."

All the while, people came and went past this drug transaction with their little paper sack of coffee or juice. Not to be believed!

I immediately went outside to the bank of telephones on the corner, and dropped my dime to the 10th Precinct, whose number I knew by heart. I got the desk sergeant; I revealed who I was and I told him what I had just seen in the coffee shop. (In New York City, location of a crime is very important, because if their jurisdiction does not cover the area, the precinct will tell you, "We don't handle that shop." I once reported a fight between two druggies that was taking place on the East side of 7th Avenue, and the desk sergeant told me, "The 10th doesn't cover that side!"

But, back to my story of Grandma and her little band of runners.

"How do you know that it's marijuana?" the sergeant asked.

"Because, I'm the Dean of Fashion and I confiscate grass at least once or twice a week, that's how!" I replied. "Also, you can smell it!"

"Are you sure?" he asked.

"Look," I said, "I'll be here for another ten minutes or so, but then I have to get back to the office. If you want to send a car, I'll be right here on the corner to point them out. If not, you can reach me at my office in the school. O.K.?"

I waited fifteen minutes. The police car never came, and they never called. Grandma and her "boys" didn't even have coffee cups on the table. I hate it when someone doesn't believe you.

A case in point was when Security caught a kid drinking wine in the boys' bathroom. The bottle was empty and they had him discard it. He was brought down to my office to make a statement, after which I set up a parental conference.

His mother came to school, on time, and I had her and her son escorted into my office. After I finished my presentation, she looked right at me and asked, "Did you *see* my son take a drink? Did your Security take any pictures?"

"Take pictures?" I said, quite puzzled. "No, we didn't take any pictures, but I have your son's statement and the eye witness account of my Security people. What more do you want?"

"Without pictures, you have nothing!" she said triumphantly and marched herself out of the room, leaving me with her son. I was so angry, I could have spit. But, every dog has his day, and mine came several months later.

It was my practice to always patrol the staircases that led to the basement locker areas around 7:30 or 8 A.M. Since my office had been down to the first floor for better access with the Security, it wasn't much of a hardship for me at all. One morning, during my sweep, I ran across an interesting scene. A young man and his date were sharing a Schaefer beer from a quart-size glass bottle in a stairwell between the first floor and the basement level. The were sucking its contents from two straws, one for him and one for the girl. It looked romantic, and yet cheap at the same time, if you get my meaning.

Recalling my sad experience with the other kid and his mother, I took no chances. I seized the bottle and the straws first, then demanded to see identification. They showed me their train passes and now I had them! I took both the students and their sipping breakfast to my office and had them complete their statements. Then, I stored the bottle in my closet and I sent for their parents. The father of the young man came in first.

No problem. He took one look at his son's statement and another at the bottle of beer, and appeared terribly ashamed for his son's action and how could his son could do such a thing? This parent couldn't hide his embarrassment. He promised me that his son would never repeat this offense again, I had his word on it. But the second parent wasn't like that at all.

She came, after one or two postponements, with her daughter to see me about the infraction. She looked at me very coldly and aloof. I read the statement I had prepared, her daughter's statement and the young man's statement. When I finished by asking, "Why is your daughter drinking beer at 8:00 in the morning?" the mother responded with, "Do you have any pictures?" Another parent demanding to see pictures! Well, lady, I got you now!

"I'll do better than that," I replied. With that, I went over to my locker, which by now was reeking from the smell of the brew, and brought forth the bottle with the two straws intact.

"If you will observe carefully, ma'am," I pointed out with glee, "your daughter's straw has the same color purple from her lipstick still on it!" Her daughter happened to be wearing the exact same shade that morning. The mother never flinched. She gave the straw a distant look, collected her handbag, and promptly walked out of my office without a word. (She *could* have said "Have a nice day . . .")

Marijuana, especially bad marijuana, always had the potential for something screwy to happen when kids ventured into the dangerous game of drug pushing. Fights that on the surface appeared to resemble the fights of a generation ago, were usually disguised as "area-tampering" or "hustling" someone else's customers; and when everyone involved suddenly clammed up, I usually suspected the "unobvious." Then, a new wrinkle appeared one bright morning as I put my key into the lock of my door.

"Mr. Manicone, Mr. Manicone!" I heard from behind a marble pillar some twenty feet from my door.

I turned just as a young man emerged from behind the pillar, looking dreadful, with his shirttail hanging out, as he lunged for the partial opened door. No one was around.

"Quick!" he said. "Let me in, and shut and lock the door!" he commanded. "Please!"

"What the hell is going on here?" I demanded.

"Please, inside. I'll tell you everything inside."

"O.K., you're inside," I replied. "Now, tell me what you're doing here, in the building, so early?"

"They just let me go," he said nervously.

"And, just who is 'they'?"

With that, the young man slumped down in a chair and told me this horrific story about being kidnapped from the school yesterday as he was walking up 24th Street toward 7th Avenue. He said that about 2:45, as he was walking along the curb next to the first set of houses east of the school, a car with two men, stopped, and the driver asked for directions. As the boy leaned over the driver's side of the window to give him the information, the other guy got out from the rear door, and "kidnapped me!" The second man was very large and strong, and he lifted the student up and threw him in the back seat, slamming the door.

Unfortunately, there was no one on the street at the time of the abduction.

The boy related that he was told to lie down on the floor in the back seat of the sedan, with the large man holding a gun at his head. He also was told to put a bandanna over his eyes and they began to "drive around the city."

"They just let me go this morning in front of the school! Just now! I haven't even been home yet! We drove around all night!"

When the "kidnap victim" said that he hadn't been home all night, it rang a bell in my head. Perhaps, it was the way he said the phrase, perhaps, it was the inflection; I don't know, the story just didn't make sense to me. I've heard hundreds of stories from students all my professional life, and a story either rings true—or it doesn't. I've had a very good track record when I rate stories, and I was willing to bet the farm that this one was a fish story, so I started to see if I could trip the kid up.

"So, they had you all night long on the floor of the car? All night? No stops? All night long?" I began.

"That's right, Mr. Manicone, all night long!"

"All night long?" I repeated. "No ransom demands, or a phone call to Mom, that you were aware of?"

"No, no demands or phone calls that I was aware of," he said matter-of-factly.

"Do you think they had the right kid?" I asked.

"Oh, yeah. They called me by my first name. Yeah, they knew me, all right."

"But, if they didn't demand anything, why take the risk of kidnapping you in the first place?" I asked.

"I don't know. They just did!"

Now, I decided to break his story with, "So they had you all night long? Where do you think you went all night long—just around Manhattan?"

"Well, I think we went to Queens and Brooklyn, too," he added.

"And you didn't even stop once?" I asked.

"No, we didn't even stop once," he said.

Now I had him.

"What about the toll booth? Didn't you stop to pay the toll?"

"Yeah, right; we stopped once to pay the toll."

"But you came back into Manhattan again? Didn't you have to pay the toll again?"

"Right. That's twice. That's all, twice."

"When you stopped to pay the toll, couldn't you yell out, or scream, or something?" I pressed.

"Mr. Manicone, the man held a gun to my head! I couldn't do *nothing!*"

"Besides the toll gate, didn't the car stop at all? Not even for you to go to the bathroom?"

118

"Oh yeah, we did stop to go to the bathroom, once!" he replied.

"Now, son, according to my count, you stopped at least three times. When you first told me your story, you didn't even stop once, remember?"

"Well, I forgot. Now I remember. It was three times!"

"Didn't you stop at any time to eat?" I kept pressing.

"Oh shoot, that's right. We stopped once to eat!"

"That's four stops," I said. "And the man held the gun to your head the whole time? Didn't he get tired?"

"I think he switched hands . . ."

"And, you saw him switch hands?"

"Sure, well, no. . . ."

"Please," I said, "you're not telling me the truth. Who would kidnap you? You aren't wealthy. There wasn't any ransom note. The kidnappers held you for over 12 hours. For *what*? To risk getting caught with a kid in the back seat of the car? Why would they drive all night with you and then let you off, so conveniently, right in front of the school? Give me a break!" I finished.

"O.K., O.K.," he said. "I wasn't kidnapped, but I did tell you the truth about not being home last night. I'd like you to call my mom and tell her I'm alright!"

"I promise to call your parents, immediately after you tell me the whole story, and this time, I want the truth!" I demanded.

"Some guys were after me and I knew they would be watching my house, so I stayed out all night, and I pretended I got kidnapped so that my mom wouldn't know what I did."

"What did you do?" I asked.

"I sold some guys some bad marijuana, and they wanted their money back!" he replied.

"Bad marijuana? What's bad marijuana?"

119

"You know, all seeds! Now they want to beat my ass if I don't give them back their money," he said.

"Well, the fellow you have to worry about is not some guy outside, but *me*. You concoct an incredible story about a kidnapping that never took place, and if I was more gullible, a cop would be here, taking down your statement, and then when they discovered the lie, you really would be up a creek, making out a false police report . . . Right now, I'm going to call your mom and *you* tell her the whole truth. Then I want the phone back to set up a Dean's hearing, if not a Principal's suspense hearing for selling drugs. You made a big mistake this morning reporting your 'kidnapping'!"

Nine

"It's Always New Year's Eve"

Iron Mike retired in the early 70's and our new Principal was Mr. B., the former Administrative Assistant. Mr. B., as it turned out, was one of the Assistant Principals who had vetoed my selection to become the Dean. Years later, as Principal, he told me, that in his opinion (and to his eternal chagrin), I was the best Dean in the City!

Perhaps, it was due to the way I handled the daily flow of traffic that passed through my office and/or the way my staff and I preserved the traditions of the old-fashioned Fashion.

One of the first things that Mr. B. did in the Fall of 1973, was to move the Dean's office to the first floor. Here I was in a better position to monitor the lobby area, supervise the Security staff, and—better yet—I was in easy access to the elevators which could take me to any floor in a fraction of the time it took me when I was located on the second floor. I can't tell you how many times I was frustrated when the elevator would skip the second floor as I banged the outside doors to the elevators trying to answer a desperate call on some upper floor.

Within weeks of the new term, the student demonstrations began again. These student protests were reminiscent of the late 60's, because they were attacking the current administration's domestic policies, but were also

121

aimed at City Hall and the Board of Education. The high school teenagers and their college counterparts wanted liberalization of the curriculum, input in selecting material to study and they wanted more student rights—Not civil rights, per se, but more freedom to express their particular life styles, like wearing jeans and doing their "thing," whatever that was.

It was during the first week of these demonstrations and I was stationed behind the first set of doors watching the commotion. Outside our building were literally thousands of students, mainly high school age, ranting and screaming to the upper floors and urging our students to join them so they could march to another targeted high school. Our building has two sets of 4 doors on the 24th Street side, and a corresponding set of doors on the 25th Street side. However, there is one major difference. On the 24th Street side, we have six 15´x 12´ picture windows that display tools and fabrics, the lovely work done by current students, and mannequins dressed in beautiful student-made garments. As I looked on in horror, I saw one of our own pick up a garbage can from across the street, carry it to our side, and to the screaming delight of her fellow demonstrators, heave it right into the picture window.

The roar that followed that willful act of vandalism reminded me of a scene in the movie, *A Tale of Two Cities,* when the guillotine fell! The young lady was the darling of the crowd until I rushed out and, while her back was to the building as she was taking a bow I grabbed her (with the help of a security guard) and escorted her into the building. The mob yelled for her release, but our doors were locked. I escorted the young lady right to the Principal's office.

When I related the incident which just had occurred,

Mr. B. immediately suspended her, and she was already scheduled to be suspended by the Superintendent to boot. A double whammy!

Approximately two weeks later, we all gathered in the Superintendent's office in Brooklyn for the hearing. This hearing was attended by the Hearing Officer, his secretary, the young lady, her mother, a friend of the family and myself. Mr. B. said that I could speak for him, if necessary. Suspended students may not have legal counsel. If they come with an attorney, that person must sit outside the hearing room. That has been Board of Ed policy from Day One. During the hearing, the student may consult with his or her attorney, but, it must be done outside in the hall—not in the hearing chamber.

The Hearing Officer went over my disposition and asked me if I wanted to add or subtract anything already written down. I said no. When he questioned the young lady, she stunned me when she said that she *didn't* throw the garbage can into the plate glass window, someone else did; and that I couldn't have seen the exchange from my vantage point. How do you like that?

"What?" I said. "It wasn't you?"

The Hearing Officer held up his hand to give me a moment to collect my thoughts and regain my demeanor. Then he gave me the floor to challenge her denial.

"Miss Ortega," I said, "your statement is absolutely ridiculous because I saw you carry the can to our side of the building. Now, don't tell me you didn't carry the can?"

"Yes, I carried the can, but someone else threw it," she insisted.

"And, when I grabbed your arm," I asked, "where were you?"

"Standing on the sidewalk," she countered.

And I helped her finish her statement by adding "bowing to the audience. Right! Why were you bowing, if you didn't throw the trash can in the window? Answer me that!"

"Were you bowing to the crowd when Mr. Manicone grabbed you, Miss Ortega?" the Hearing Officer asked quite sternly. The silence was deafening. She didn't say a word. She just looked down at her hands on the table.

She and her parent were presented with the bill for the damage, which came to over $2,000 for materials and labor along with a Superintendent's transfer to another high school. Everyone was stunned. As the parent and student got up, the mother slapped the kid hard on the arm and said something very quickly as they left the room. The secretary translated for us that the mother had said something like, "See! I told you to admit it! They caught you in a lie and now we have to pay the whole thing. You'll never learn!"

Several months later Mr. B. informed me that I had to return to the classroom because of the budget crisis. However, I would have an assistant, Mr. G. Rocky, as he was affectionately known, used to love to say "this is like New Year's Eve," whenever things got hot in the Dean's office. We had it scheduled that he was in the office during my two periods away from the trenches. At first, Rocky taught four classes, then we got it down to three, then just two when he went to run the lunchroom. He simply couldn't believe that I had been alone for two and a half years in the Dean's office. "How did you do it?" he would always ask as we handled one crisis after another. I don't think I ever gave him a straight answer. Ever.

I was very fortunate to always get good help simply because I had first pickings within the faculty. Every teacher was assigned an administrative period once every two years, according to our contract. Based on their previous performance in the Office, I could request or reject any possible candidate. But, when it came to the uniformed Security Staff, that was something else again. We had some outstanding people during my tenure, and then, we had some real winners. Frank Corchado was just outstanding. He could read my mind. Many times we would chase after someone, and without telling him a thing, Frank would instinctively cut the kid off on one floor, and drive the culprit in my direction; or, he would scout the bathrooms, or run up to the 9th or 10th floor and shoot down the staircase, with walkie in hand until we "got our man."

Very early in my career as the Dean, he literally saved me from getting smashed with the business end of a heavy floor lamp when we cornered this particular girl drug dealer in the Assistant Principal's office. As it turned out, I had suspected this girl for some time and had used a ruse to have her report to the A.A.'s Office, where she reacted by trying to smash my head in. It was only because Frank was behind her and grabbed the lamp as I attempted to duck, that I don't have a permanent headache to this day. I was very fortunate.

Then we had those security people who would put on their uniforms and then later take off their uniforms. They did very little else between changes. We had those who loved the uniform and attempted to put every known piece of metal on to display their authority, but did little more than use metal polish. We had the steady and reliable types who would always come when called, but then, would die on the job. Without direction, they were very rigid and autocratic. I remember once telling a female security guard to mind a class as I escorted a distraught teacher from the room because of a nasty fight in her class, with "stay with this class until I get back." As luck would have it, I couldn't get back, so I sent another security guard to tell her to dismiss the class when the bell rang. "That's not what Mr. Manicone said. He said I was to stay until he came back." Well, you can just imagine the confusion. The class could not go on to their next period; students were milling around in the hall and two bickering, uniformed females greeted me when I eventually got back almost an hour later!

We also had the "operators." Those are the ones with a hidden agenda who will, with some street smarts, take advantage of their situation. I particularly remember this one Security Guard, whom I'll call "Greg" who really fit this bill. He was very handsome, young and charming, and he looked very good in a uniform. But, he was like a fox in a chicken coop, because in a high school which was 98 percent female, he had his pick. Not only that; we later found out that he had rented out an apartment just minutes from the school and when he made his move, he would hustle the young thing to his "pad." The problem was that Greg was *married*. That was his undoing—thank God.

To Greg's credit, he was always respectful and attempted to volunteer instead of being ordered to do something. But, I later discovered that all those signs of respect and apple-polishing were really to give him the opportunity to "operate." Thinking that he was "checking the 10th floor," for example, I would later discover him somewhere else like outside a trade class on the 7th floor, looking inside an opened door. When questioned, someone always furnished a ready alibi for him like, "I think he ducked into one of these rooms," or "his friend said he might be with this class." It wasn't until much later when we started to put the pieces together—all these alibis, all these excuses, all these acts of volunteerism led to the obvious conclusion that Greg was always on the lookout for a pretty face. When the rumors of this behavior surfaced, I began to make discreet inquiries. That's when I found out that he had two addresses: one legitimate and the other for hanky-panky.

Within hours of obtaining this information, a senior female had just "unloaded" a tale of woe to the principal, Mr. B., about Greg and an apartment near the school. Mr. B called me up to his office and wanted to know what I knew. I filled him in as the young lady cooled her heels in the outer office. Mr. B, smelling a huge problem here, told me that the girl outside had noticed her girlfriend exiting this notorious apartment yesterday afternoon. "Greg had told her that he was her steady, and now, being cheated on, she's willing to testify against him."

Mr. B. immediately got in touch with the director of School Security in Brooklyn and gave him a brief, blow-by-blow description of the facts against Greg. A meeting was scheduled in Mr. B.'s office for the next morning and I was to get Greg to report to Mr. B. right away to his office. The girl complete her statement and was dismissed with the warning not to say anything to anyone. Greg reported to Mr. B. and was told to be in his office the following morning to "discuss a security problem in the boys' locker area." I couldn't wait for the A.M.!

With the scorned young lady waiting in the A.P.'s office, all the participants to this meeting were present in Mr. B.'s conference room. Greg was surprised that his boss from Brooklyn was at the table along with our new A.A., the Principal, and myself included. As Mr. B. began to read my report, the girl's statement and finally the

A.P.'s Evaluation Report, Greg knew he was in deep trouble. When Mr. B. asked Greg to explain his actions, Greg the charmer re-surfaced, as he stated, "I didn't break any laws!"

"What?" Mr. B. exclaimed. "You slept with at least two of our girls that we know of, and you're married! What about the charges of statutory rape, I might add?"

"There's no rape, statutory, or any other kind. I only dated girls who were 18! I *checked.* You think I'm stupid, or something?" Greg shot back.

"Mr. Manicone, is that right? I want you to personally check this out! We'll wait until you get back!" Mr. B. thundered.

I left the conference room and scrambled down eight floors in seconds and raced into the Guidance Office. Sure enough, both girls were eighteen! I went into the A.P.'s Office to retrieve the complainant, and escorted her to the Principal's Office. I then entered the Conference Room. It was quiet as a morgue. When I handed the piece of paper with the birth dates on it to Mr. B. the room got very small. I knew Mr. B. had just lost his argument, but he tried to put his best spin to a terrible situation.

Turning to the Director, Mr. B. exploded with "I don't want this young man in this building one more minute! Take him with you and I don't care what you do with him! He's not fit to wear the uniform of a Security Guard or be with young people, especially girls, ever again! Meeting closed!" he shouted.

I cannot end this terrible story without a postscript of some sort. It turned out that the young lady who had complained to Mr. B. withdrew her statement the following day, either by pressure from her girl friend or from Greg. Not only that, Greg, with no serious charges now pending, was permitted to transfer to another high school. And, yes—and he kept his apartment, believe it or not, because his wife, who appeared to have a lot more character than either of our two students, threw him out. End of story.

Security Guards became far more effective when we were authorized to have walkie-talkies. Now, with a push of a button, security guards could be sent to any part of the building within a minute or two. The problem in our building was the elevators. It's one thing to get hold of someone to respond to a problem, but it's another to get him or her actually there to be truly effective. Our building has six elevators, but in my eleven years in the Dean's office, the most we ever could really count on was three! Maybe four if the wind was right! It got so bad, that the Principal permitted people in the Administration to be issued elevator keys! I ran elevators many a time, taking passengers to various floors for expediency's sake.

The problems with the elevators were really two-fold. First, only union personnel were permitted to operate the elevators. If an operator called in sick, we had to get a union replacement. The custodial staff was forbidden to run the elevators with passengers in them, according to their contract. Secondly, the six elevators were vintage originals, installed during the building's original construction, circa 1939–40. When an elevator broke down we were in big trouble, because the original parts either had to be cannibalized from another building or they had to be hand-made. Things got so bad that the mechanics began to cannibalize parts from one or two of our own elevators, so that in reality, we only had 4 working lifts at any time. This problem was not solved until the late 1980's when I was ready to retire. Meanwhile, we did the best we could, city budget notwithstanding.

With all this overuse of the elevators, it became routine for an elevator to break down with students and/or teacher in it during a change of periods. Since I was on the first floor, students and security people alike would race into my office to make a call for help.

"Mr. Manicone, they're screaming in the elevators!" as they would point in that direction. I would either get 911 or the Emergency Fire Department (because they had the ladders and levers to do the job), and then shut down my office (New Year's Eve, remember?) and stand by with my talkie to coordinate things with the A.P., Security and the Principal's Office. Once, it was so bad, I'm surprised we didn't get hit with a ton of lawsuits.

It must have been around 1974 or 1975 when one of our diminutive and easily bullied elevator operators allowed her car to go way over the legal limit of passengers permitted to ride at one time. I believe the capacity then for each car was about 28 or 30. With that number in the car, it was comfortable to move about to permit passengers on or off without shoving or pushing people out of one's way. But this young woman, as we found out later, permitted almost 70 to get in on the first floor! When she finally closed the doors to this vertical "suitcase," she put the elevator in motion on automatic to stop and let everyone off on the seventh floor.

It never got there.

The elevator stalled between the sixth and seventh floors. When she couldn't compel the car to go either up *or* down, she rang the emergency bell and then the screaming started. It was a late fall morning, and the kids still had on coats, scarves and gloves. The temperature started to soar and panic set in. It was almost an hour later when the first passengers were assisted out by the firemen who came through the ceiling trap door and forced the elevator doors open.

The firemen, using a portable winch and operating all their equipment via the elevator shafts on either side of the stricken car, got the car to stop about 4 feet above the eighth floor landing, some 20 feet from the Principal's Conference Room. Out the kids came, one by one, crying, wailing hysterically; others came out in stony silence and in shock, as if they had just come away from a street brawl. Little by little, the room took on the appearance of a MASH Field Hospital, with teenagers strewn all over the floor of the room and our Security people and Drug Coordinator administrating to the individual calls for assistance.

I couldn't believe my eyes! Out they came! Twenty-five, thirty-five, *forty-five*. How may kids are still in that car? The fireman brought out the operator and she was absolutely hysterical, screaming, "No more! I quit! No more! Do you understand? *No more!*" And still more came out. I believe the final count was 67 or 68! I personally carried a female student, her eyes half-closed and her skin clammy to the touch, into the room. As I carried her to a spot near a leather couch, she shot her hands out to the base of a heavy floor lamp and wouldn't let go. She started yelling, "We're going to fall! We're going to die!" The Drug Coordinator, who knew the student, had to talk the kid down for over fifteen minutes before she released her grip on the lamp. Many students were taken to the hospital for observation, but I know that the trauma of that day still lingers in somebody. I know it still does for me.

That particular elevator operator retired that afternoon. Now we were down to three working cars.

After I would return to my office following an episode like the one just described, everything became anti-climatic. I was physically drained, but the nature of my office was such that within minutes of a life-and-death situation like the one on the eighth floor, the "nonsense" would resume. Now a trade teacher just sent a kid down because the student failed to close her work box properly and store it under her seat as previously instructed. Or, I would get a phone call from a parent because she wanted to see me about her daughter's treatment at the lunch counter. Or whatever. However, when I got a referral from the Drug Coordinator, or from a Grade Advisor, I knew it was worth looking into, like the referral I held in my hand from the 9th year advisor. The student was doing poorly in school, but when the advisor questioned her about it, the student said she didn't care and wanted to leave anyway, and warned the counselor not to telephone the parent or her father would kill her. Maybe I could be of some help? So, I called in the girl.

As soon as the frightened student sat down next to my desk, she began to tremble. Was it me? She was obviously very nervous. When I told her that she hadn't done anything, that I just wanted to go over the matter of running away, she began to fidget and shake some more. I quickly changed the subject and little by little I gathered her confidence. It took over a half hour, but she finally told me that she couldn't stand living with her father anymore. "He beats me every Friday. He beats my brothers and sisters too, and I can't stand it!"

"What?" I said. "He beats you? On Fridays? Why Fridays?"

"I don't know. He just does. He lines us up and he hits us and then he goes to bed!"

"Where's your mother? Does she let your father beat you for nothing, just like that, and not say or do something?" I asked, almost out of my seat.

"Oh, she ran away, or something. Nah, we just live with my father." Then she stopped and pleaded, "You're not going to call him or anything?"

"I can't let your father beat you and just not say or do something!" I replied.

"Oh, please! You *can't* call him. He'll kill me! He'll *kill* me!"

"First of all, no one is going to kill anybody. You know that, because, you just told me something incriminating about him. If we find you dead, we'll know he did it! So, stop worrying, and let me do my job. Give me a phone number where I can reach him. Please, don't worry."

She reluctantly complied and I called him at work, which was right down the street from the school in a scrap yard, and he sounded affable and eager to assist. When he asked about the nature of my request for his visit to my office, I was very general with something like, "It's about your daughter's class work." He agreed to come in early the next morning, and then he said something quite odd.

"I hope you don't mind the dirt!"

Sure enough, bright and early, about 8 o'clock the next morning, in walked this dirty, soot-covered, curly-headed man wearing a greasy T-shirt Holy Hannah! This guy looked just like William Bendix did in the movie, *The Hairy Ape!*

"Please sit down," I requested; his smile sincere.

"I want to talk to you about your daughter, Clarice, O.K.?"

"Sure, that's why I'm here!" he said.

133

"She's planning to run away," I started.

". . . just like her sister done last year," he interrupted angrily.

"How are you going to stop her?" I continued.

"I'm not! She can't get far!" he replied.

"Are you going to beat her when she gets caught, or comes back?" I asked. I knew I was walking on thin ice here, but, the father wasn't one bit troubled by what I asked.

"Maybe she'll go live with her mother, my ex-wife. It'll be one less headache for me."

"You call your daughter a *headache?*" I asked. "A headache? She looks like a very nice person. Very mature."

"Look, Mr. Manicone," as he searched for my name plate on the desk, "I work long hours. From a quarter to six to six, maybe six-thirty every day, five days a week. It's dirty work. I load scrap iron on a conveyer belt all day long. *You* wouldn't do it! I'm tired when I get home. I'm responsible for five kids—used to be six. My wife left me, she called me a dirty animal, but I bring home good money and I always come home sober. She left me, but, she didn't take the kids. That was five or six years ago. So, I'm stuck, and I can't do everything. I come home, the older girl does the cooking, I shop on Saturday. I don't expect much, but I do want respect."

"So, you beat them to get it?" I asked.

"Nah. Nah. I'm tired when I get home, I can't handle that petty crap, too. All I want is my meal and I go to bed. But, I know those kids have been doing their poking, and fooling around, and their teasing and screaming when I'm not there, so, I take care of it on Fridays. That's my system."

"System? What system?" I asked.

134

"I know they did something during the week, so they get theirs on Friday!" he replied with an air of satisfaction.

"That's no system, to punish the guilty along with the non-guilty. Maybe the younger kids did something, but not the older ones," I reasoned.

"Nah, nah. They're all guilty," he countered.

"And, what did it get you? I don't know the circumstances of why your wife left you, but one daughter did, and now, another one is planning to. This system of yours is not working," I said with some built-up conviction. I was attempting to help this kid, and all this man was, was a parental bully.

"So, what do *you* think I should do?" he shot back.

I was caught off my guard for a second because I didn't think I could get him to this point of the solution so quickly, but I recovered as best as I could with, "Let's call in your daughter."

"Clarice, please sit down and let me hear what you think of this suggestion," I began. "What if I get your father to promise me that he won't hit you or your other sister if you two share in running the house for your dad? In other words, you would be like the mother, and your sister would be your helper, but, you must reprimand the younger ones if they do something naughty. You must report to your father every night when he comes home. What do you think of that idea?"

". . . and he won't hit me and embarrass me again, ever?" she asked.

"Yes," I said, peeking over to where the father was seated, and he appeared to be receptive to this proposal (to my delight). "Yes, and I'm your witness from now on. No more hitting, ever again, for you or your sister on Fridays, starting this week. I don't want you or your other sisters and brothers to run away, and I don't think your dad relishes that prospect either. Agreed? You are now the acting mommy! O.K.?"

She actually lit up as her father arose and shook her hand. The father appeared to be relieved too.

I sent a copy of my resolution to the Grade Advisor with the stipulation that she was to check on the progress of Clarice's grades and performance throughout the term. I'm happy to say that my efforts were not in vain, because several weeks later Clarice dropped by the office and said that everything was working out great and no one was planning to run away. My system was much better than her father's old one—thank God.

Ten

"Who Loves You?"

The last important case Iron Mike handled just before he retired concerned a bully. I hate bullies. I hated them when I was a kid in grammar school and even in high school. When I became a certified teacher, it was my sworn duty and goal in life to make war on bullies. I would root them out wherever I found them—on J.H.S. lunch lines, in locker areas, boys' bathrooms and more especially, in the classrooms. I showed bullies no mercy because they spent their lives cultivating the image that they were untarnished angels. Their parents were the last to know of the ways they would torment their victims—not only physically, but far more cruelly, psychologically as well.

First off, all bullies are usually good-looking, not physically repulsive at all. They use their good looks and charming ways to beguile their parents, especially their mothers, into believing that all their actions are in the spirit of aiding and assisting the less fortunate. Somehow, people of authority always appear to misinterpret these very same actions. Secondly, all bullies need a side-kick or two to do their bidding. And conversely, these side-kicks are like little gnomes and hard to look at.

Finally, a bully needs a victim. This unfortunate person usually has a weakness or two and the bully takes full advantage of the situation. The next case in point is a classic.

Alberto Rivera was tall, handsome and very charming. He, also, was a bully. Circumstances in his junior year made that fact very clear. When he got his program for the new term, he decided to pick on an English teacher. Miss F. was no ordinary English teacher—she was a kind and gentle creature who was very knowledgeable in her subject area.

She also had a wooden arm.

Not too much was known as to how Miss F. had been maimed. It appeared that it was a result of a traffic accident many years ago. The focal point here was her wooden arm, which was hard not to notice. Although, it had painted nail polish on the tips of the fingers, the naturally nude color of the prosthesis was not well maintained. It looked "old." The other problem was that this artificial limb was tucked up against the body at a very unnatural angle, some ten or fifteen degrees from the elbow at a downward slope. Miss F. may have thought that this wooden limb looked demure, but, unfortunately, it became the target of Alberto's interest.

It would have been bad enough if Alberto had been programmed in her class, because it would have required transferring him to a corresponding but similar English period. However, due to the trade tracking system in Fashion, an entire make-over of his program would have been necessary. The simple truth was that Alberto "programmed" himself into her class for the sole purpose of tormenting this poor woman!

It all began with a simple referral from Miss F. to my office. One, Alberto Rivera, was taunting and disrupting her class. As it was my practice, I checked my student program card file and noticed that Alberto was assigned to a different English class. How on earth could Alberto be disrupting Miss F.'s English class when he had a different class and a different name?—and I wasn't going to waste the time on an "innocent" student for an unproductive interview. So, I sent the referral back to Miss F. "Please give me the correct name. This student is not assigned to your class," I wrote on the bottom of the referral.

"It is the correct name," she wrote back. "Please interview this student at once!"

With some reluctance, I called Alberto to my office, hoping that Miss F. did indeed have the right name. Since Rocky was not to join me for a term or two, I was working my station solo, and the referral business never takes a holiday.

In came this tall, very good-looking Puerto Rican student, with a slight hint of haughtiness about him as he was escorted to his seat next to my desk. I asked him his name, and when I showed him my copy of his program card, I asked him if the classes on it were correct.

"That's wrong!" he said, as he pulled his program card from his book bag. "My English class has been changed, and Miss F. is my teacher now."

"Then, what about this referral?" I asked, somewhat confused. "Your teacher states that you disrupt her class and that you don't even belong there in the first place!"

"Wait a minute," Alberto retorted, slightly offended. "She's wrong on both counts, I showed her my new program card, and the kid who's disrupting the class, must be somebody else. It ain't me!"

"You mean to tell me that someone else is disrupting Miss F.'s class, not you?" I asked. "How many boys are in this class?" I pressed.

"I don't know, two or three others," he answered. "I

just got assigned to her class. You can check."

"I will," I replied. "You can bet on it!" I added. "Something is definitely out of line here, and I can't believe that an experienced teacher like Miss F. can be so wrong. Do you know who she is alluding to?" I asked Alberto.

"I really can't help you, Mr. Manicone," he answered. With that I dismissed him back to his trade class, and went to hunt for some answers. First, I went to the Program Room to check his official program card from which the student retrieves his or her individual program. In those days, everything was written out by hand during our two-week reorganization period after each term. It was an awesome job.

When I began to check his official class stack of cards, I found something very interesting and odd. Alberto had two programs! One looked genuine because it was completed and checked in adult handwriting. The other card looked phony because it was done in an amateur way and it lacked check-offs and side comments in the margins like the others. However, I did notice the change of English class. I took the doctored card to the Program Chairman, and he immediately knew it was a phony.

"How is that possible?" I asked. "Who slipped this phony card in here?" I added.

"I don't know, maybe some kid who works here during her service period. I don't know—maybe his friend works here? We must have a dozen or two kids who are assigned here during the day and do all the petty stuff," Mr. P. said. "I can't check that type of thing. It just happens," he added.

I was smelling a rat. Next, I went down to Miss F.'s English class to verify the referral and its contents. She was absolutely sure that Alberto was the offending party, as she pointed to where he was sitting, and she was also sure that he was not assigned to her class, either officially or unofficially. I called Alberto down to my office again for a chat about this growing problem.

Talk about playing the innocent! Alberto had no idea *how* Miss F. could get him confused with another boy in her class. He didn't know *anything* about the "doctored" program card I let him examine. His counselor might have done it and forgot to remove the original . . . O.K., I called his counselor; she was not in that day, but I left word for her to see me as soon as she could. In the meantime, I ordered Alberto not to return to Miss F.'s class until I sorted everything out. He was to go back to his original program until he was instructed to do otherwise. He agreed.

Guess what was in my mailbox the following morning? You got it! *Another* referral from Miss F. about Alberto's abusive behavior, and in particular, his insulting and ridiculing remarks about her wooden arm! I couldn't believe it!

I immediately called Security and told the guard to pick up Alberto from his first class, and if he wasn't there, to wait for him and do the same for his next class. I wanted Alberto to be personally escorted. As soon as the guard left, I ran over to the Guidance Office and caught Alberto Rivera's counselor just as she entered her office. I showed her the "doctored" program card, and she completely dismissed it.

"Yes. Al said he wanted to change his English class," she started, "but I saw no reason to alter everything on his card, so I told him to forget about the switch and stay with Mr. R. I thought that was the end of it. That was about 2 or 3 weeks ago!" she said.

"Well, it's *not* the end of it. Alberto has an obsession with harassing Miss F., and I'm going to put an end to this thing right now. Thanks, El."

I left her and waited in my office. In came a beaming Alberto Rivera, under escort.

"What did I tell you yesterday?" I began, half shouting and looking right in the boy's eyes.

"Oh, you mean about the English class? I told my mother and she says that I can make out my own program. I don't have to obey your orders because she outranks you! She pays your salary!" he said. The grin never left his face.

"Oh, really?" I stormed back. "And Mr. K. has appointed me Dean and he gave me the authority to *order* you! Mr. Rivera, I am ordering you to stay away from Miss F.'s class regardless of what your mother said. Do you understand?" I thundered.

The arrogance of this kid, the gall of this creature was incredible! He just sat there, and *still did not answer my question.* I added, "And there is still this little matter of your comments to Miss F. Why do you insist on tormenting her, or is that O.K. with your mother too?"

I struck a nerve! "You watch what you say about my mother!" he shot back.

"Well? What about this comment about her being the mother of Pinocchio?" I asked.

He giggled. "Nah, that wasn't me. That was the other kid. Besides, we weren't talking to her! The other guy was talking about someone else!" he said in a mockingly offended tone.

"Mr. Rivera, this referral along with the others written by Miss F. are going into your Dean's folder. One more incident and you will be suspended! Now, did you get that?" I bellowed. "No more acts of disrespect, or following your mother's instructions about changing your program whenever you want. Do you understand that?" I added.

"Ah . . ." he tried to say, but I cut him off.

"You are dismissed, and I don't want to see you again."

He left, but I wasn't sure that he got the message that I meant business. I made it my job to wait outside Miss F.'s class that afternoon, just in case. After lunch I went to her room and I waited in the corridor. The late bell had just rung and I took my position near Miss F.'s back door. I looked in the room and Alberto was not there, but I heard footsteps racing around the corner. I looked up, and there was Mr. Rivera!

"Again?" I said. "What's wrong with you?"

"I called my mother and she said I can go here. You can't stop me!" he said as he reached for the door knob.

"Mr. Rivera, in order for you to touch that door knob, you have to first touch me! And over my dead body are you going into that class!" I yelled. I was hoping he would push my arm, because I badly yearned to deck him.

He retreated and screamed in frustration, "Wait till my mother hears this!" and raced down the staircase.

I never got to suspend him. His mother showed up in the Principal's office the next day.

Early that morning, I had a phone call from Iron Mike's secretary asking me if I knew anything about a student by the name of Alberto Rivera. "He and his mother are here right now and Mr. K. wants you and the boy's folder and all his records up here on the double! The mother's hopping mad at you for some reason. Please hurry."

I picked up all the pertinent materials I could gather

143

in ten minutes, including my file, and I raced up to the 8th floor. As I entered the waiting room, Mr. K. was ushering Alberto and his mother into the Conference Room. As I stepped inside, Mrs. Rivera screamed at me, "Over your dead body, oh? Over your dead body!" shaking her finger in my face. Word for word—what jewels come from the mouths of babes? I wondered.

I took my seat next to the Principal and began to relate the entire story, starting from the first referral, to the doctored program card, to all the denials and finally, the last straw, the incident outside Miss F.'s room yesterday. The mother sat throughout, impassively, even when I got to the part that Mrs. Rivera "outranked" me, but she became visibly upset when I mentioned Miss F.'s handicap.

"Is that true, Alberto?" she asked her son, "that this teacher has a wooden arm? Tell me the truth, now!"

"Yes, momma," he replied, sheepishly. "It's true."

"Why did you do this bad thing, Alberto? You never did this before, did you?" his mother asked.

Before Alberto had a chance to say anything more or incriminate himself further, Mr. K., a non-practicing attorney, jumped in and said, "Of course not, and he won't do it again. Right, Alberto?"

Alberto was slick enough to know when he was offered a chance to extricate himself from further revealing things his mother should not know of, and he quickly nodded his assent. I wanted the whole ball of wax, but the Principal knew better and he thanked me and said something like, "I know Mr. Manicone is very busy. I'll see Mrs. Rivera out.

As I departed from the room, even Mrs. Rivera thanked me for my efforts. Alberto didn't—then.

Several years later, as I was seated at my desk,

going over some reports, I looked up and there stood a U.S. marine. I was struck by the sharp, crisp look of the blue uniform with the white piping down the side of each leg. The Marine had his cap tucked under his arm and he stood at attention. His demeanor was familiar, but I just couldn't place it.

"Yes?" I said, as I rose from my chair. "Can I help you?"

"You don't remember me, do you, sir?" he asked. "I'm Alberto Rivera!"

"You're Alberto?" I stammered. "The same Alberto Rivera connected with Miss F.?" I asked.

"The one and the same, sir!" he said.

"Well, let me look at you," I added. "And a corporal to boot! That's great!" I just couldn't get over the transformation. "How was boot camp?" I asked, hoping that someone beside me had knocked some sense into him.

"It was as they described it, sir. An experience!"

"Well, I see that they made a man out of a boy, if I remember it right," I added.

"No, sir," he said. "You did that first!" I was truly amazed. The kid came around and he made his statement. I was touched. He said he had more people to see and thanked me again. He wasn't living with his mother anymore, he said. I wished him luck and we shook hands. He left my office straight and tall. I certainly didn't want to confront him again. Thank God!

No sooner did one case end when another remarkable one would take its place. Several weeks after the Rivera hearing, I was visited by two plain-clothes undercover cops who were working the streets in and around our school. They came in with four male students and a cutting machine, which was dropped on my desk with the question, "Is this yours?"

145

I turned the tool over and immediately noticed a small red dot painted with nail polish on it.

"Yes, this is our machine, but, who are you?" I asked as I got up from my chair. I recognized two of the four students who were standing by the other officer.

"I'm Detective Owens, and he's my partner, Rich Towers; and we're working undercover from the 10th Precinct," as he displayed his badge in my direction. "Are these students yours too?" he pressed.

"I know two of them," I replied and I then went to the other two students and asked for their program cards. When they produced them, I said, "Yes, all four are ours. Now, what's the problem?"

"They're all under arrest!" he said, matter-of-factly, and then ordered all four to "drop your books and spread them!"

I said, "Wait a minute! You can't *do* that in a school! Tell me what they did or I'll have to ask you to leave."

"Sorry, Dean, but here's the story." As Officer Owens began to tell me this incredible tale, his partner, without stopping or hesitating once, continued to shake the kids down, patted them for weapons and read them their rights.

"About an hour ago, Rich and me were standing in front of your picture windows, looking at all those swell garments and things," he began. "I noticed something in the next window that displayed all the machines and tools the kids use, and I asked Rich here if he saw the same thing on the tools.

" 'Yeah,' he sez, 'each tool has a little red dot either on the side or top. Pretty clever to stop a kid from swiping the thing for himself!' he sez.

"No sooner does he say that, when these four walk out of your building, right in broad daylight, and out the front door, carrying a shopping bag. 'Wait a minute,' I said to Rich, 'Since when do kids walk out carrying things OUT when they should be bringing stiff IN?' So, I tell Rich, 'Let's follow them. If nothing else, we'll nail them for truancy,'" Officer Owens continued.

I let him continue. "So, we follow them up the street, this is 24th Street right? And they go up 7th Avenue. They make a left on 7th and continue to 25th Street. They all crossed the avenue together, and we're right on their tails. They didn't suspect a thing! They marched up the avenue to 26th Street, and when they got to 27th Street, they hang a right and proceed up to 6th Avenue. About half way up the block, on the left side of the street, they spot a store that sells and repairs all kinds of machines and things, you know, and they cross the street and they leave this short guy, that one" (as he pointed to one of the four), "and he's the chicky. The other three guys go into the store with the shopping bag.

"Rich and me have a pretty good idea of what's going down, so we collar the chicky and we move right into the store. On the counter is this here piece, and I immediately see the red dot. I know this belongs to the school because we just saw the same thing in your window. And, this guy is holding a $10 bill in his hand. He just sold the machine for ten bucks! Now, Dean, do you know about this machine, what is it?"

"It's a textile cutting machine. . . ." I interjected.

"Do you know how much this cutting machine costs?" the detective asked.

"I don't know," I said, "but I'll find out for you in a minute. Gladys!" I called to the school aide, "please ask Mr. A., who's next door in the school store, to come in here for a minute. I have to ask him something. You stay in the store, O.K.?"

She left and Mr. A., the school store trade teacher came in. "Al, how much does this machine cost us? The cops want to know."

"That item is $350!"

"Bingo!" I said. "That makes it a felony. Thank you!"

Just about that second, the other police officer, Rich, hands me a set of keys that look like school keys to classroom doors, lockers, and various closets. "Do these look familiar?" he asked, "because I took them from that tall one over there."

"I'm not sure, but they look like ours. Yeah, here's the room number and closet number," I said. "Who's in Room 621, Gladys?" I asked.

Gladys checked the program cards and said, "Oh, that is Mr. H.'s class."

"Gladys, go up to 621 and see if these belong to Mr. H., and ask him if he gave these keys to anyone. We'll wait till you come back," I said.

Detective Owens got up from his seat next to my desk and walked over to the four students who sat gloomily on the other side of the room. "Fellows," he began, "from where I sit you guys are in deep doodoo! If that lady comes down with wrong information, meaning, that those keys *do* belong to the trade teacher, I count four, possibly five felonies because, according to your birth dates on these cards, each one of you is sixteen or better. And two are seventeen. Whoa!"

Gladys came down, all out of breath, with the information. "Mr. H. said that he thought he lost these keys, and he had to get replacements for some of them. In this closet," Gladys said, as she was holding one particular key by its stem, "he's out a cutting machine!"

"Double Bingo, boys!" Officer Owens shouted. "We got breaking and entering, burglary, possession of burglary tools, the keys, theft of an item over $250 and possession of stolen property, to name a few. I hope you guys have good lawyers! Rich, did you read them their rights? I'll call for a van!"

I turned to Gladys and handed her a Dean referral form and told her, "Get back to 621 and have Mr. H. make out his form now! Watch the class as he fills this out! Hurry!"

Then I turned to each of the students and asked them to give me their parents' phone number, either at home or at work. I would call each and inform them what happened.

Officer Owens approached my desk with a silly grin, and asked "You are pressing charges, aren't you?"

"You bet I am!" I said. "I want you to throw the book at them!"

I called the Principal and the A.A. and they both came down. The Principal was filled in on details and he absolutely concurred with everything I had done up to this point. In fact, he said the same thing I did: "Throw the book at them!" as he walked out and the other officers came in.

I wish I could say, "end of story," but I can't. At the arraignment, the four culprits stood before Judge "Turn-Them-Loose" Bruce Wright of the New York City Criminal Court. I was not present at this hearing, but Officer Owens filled me in. When Judge Wright heard the complaint by the officers and that they (the students) had sold the $350 cutting machine for $10, he dismissed all charges, saying that this was an "economic" crime, and that these boys were not stealing for profit, but for something necessary—something like, food!

Food? What food? Donuts for four costs about $10 bucks if you throw in four medium sodas, maybe! An economic crime? Don't make me laugh! What about all the other charges? They're economic, too? I couldn't believe it!

The only satisfaction I and the school got was that all four were suspended and then given a Superintendent's Suspension, meaning, that they were all transferred to a school in their home borough.

Believe it or not, one of the four actually came back to the school and wanted to see me, personally. He was seeking a recommendation by me to let him pursue a basketball eligibility at his new school in Queens. "If you won't give me a recommendation, and the Fashion coach doesn't even want to see me, I can't apply for a basketball scholarship in college! Can't you help me out?" he pleaded.

I really got ticked off at that point. I really wanted him to go see his friend, the judge, for some help on this, but, in my true professional best, I said "I can't do it! Don't ask! Sorry."

In my book, this was not vindictiveness. This was simply justice. People have a distorted sense of values about the things and people they love. They think that compassion is a sign of weakness and that they alone know how to put something over on someone with great cleverness. All I know is this: people steal and people hurt other people. Saying that they didn't really mean to do it, or that society doesn't understand, is not our problem. It's *theirs.*

Eleven

I Need a New Shovel.
This One is Broke.

Since I could remember, The High School of Fashion Industries was called a Special High School, meaning that, in order to get in, a student had to pass the entrance examination, which was given to all 8th and 9th graders who applied. The only stipulation was that the applicant had to be a New York City resident. It didn't matter if the student was from a parochial school, male or female, wealthy or poor. We accepted any student who filled out an application and could make it to our school on the test day, which usually was a cold Saturday morning in January. Normally, we tested anywhere from 3,500 to 4,000 children during three or four weekends but we accepted only about 800. One year, we took in nearly 1,200! We tested one group in the morning, and then another in the afternoon. By the end of the day, our testing committee was quite punchy. But, the system worked and it worked very well. We really believed that we had a special high school.

The candidates who were to be tested fell into one of two categories: Art students with portfolio, and non-Art students. I would say that that on any given test day, approximately 80 percent of the applicants were non-Art students. The Art students were required to submit their artwork for examination by a committee of Art teachers who would give the work a grade, which was compiled in the final score.

It was on one of these occasions when I was called into an examination room to look at some work that had been done by a male student. Normally, I took my place in the large cafeteria to administer and supervise the reading or math portion of the entrance examination. I was not a trained art teacher, but one look at the submitted work clearly reminded me of a statement by a Supreme Court Justice who was asked about pornography. He said, "I know it when I see it!" This work was definitely pornographic. And, what detail!

Well, anyway, the Assistant Principal of the Art Department called the kid into the room and began to question his "line" of work. As she thumbed through the many beautifully graphic pictures, she asked,

"What is this?"

"My work," he said.

"Don't you have any other samples of your work you would like to submit to us?"

"No, not really. What's the problem? Don't you like them?" he asked her, pointing to his portfolio.

"It's not a matter of me liking or disliking anything at this moment," she replied, somewhat annoyed. "It's your taste in art. Don't you draw or paint anything else?"

"I used to," he answered, "but then I found this model and that's all I like to draw now!" he matter-of-factly said.

"You use a model? How old are you?" she asked the applicant.

"Fifteen. That's no big deal. They have live models in college and in art schools all over the country. That's no big deal," he replied.

"Quite unacceptable!" the A.P. said and, handing

back his portfolio, she concluded, "I hope your mother's in that studio, young man!"

As I walked the young man back to the cafeteria to get his coat, he continued to repeat, "It's no big deal!" I wonder what line of work the kid eventually got into.

A very important part of the overall grade a candidate received was for the "Interview." We wanted to know if the applicant was suitable to take on the great load of both trade and academic classes, all of which were required for graduation. Remember, Fashion Industries was not really just a trade school. When the school was first formulated, it was the intention of its founding fathers to have students not only join the work force and the fashion world, but, if the senior wished, he or she could go on to college without taking remediation classes or pre-college courses. It was a novel experiment, and it worked. Normally, we accepted about 800 students, but we only graduated about 225 on any given June.

I had been at Fashion for four or five years before I was invited to join the elite group of Entrance Testers. The pay was very good and, being the Dean, it was to my benefit that I helped with the interview of potential newcomers. The Administration kept a tight lid on who remained and who were invited to test these grammar and junior high school candidates. The Vocational Department wanted a certain image; the Administration didn't want any future problems; and each tester, regardless of what subject they taught, wanted the best kid possible. A candidate could pass the math or reading part of the entrance examination, but if he or she failed the Interview segment, the kid was "out."

The Entrance Exam usually took about 2 to 3 hours to administer; one session in the morning and another in the afternoon. The Art candidates required an extra half hour because they had to take an Art test to prove that their portfolio samples were not the work of someone else. We thought of everything! As I mentioned before, my station was to administer the entrance examination to the non-Art students. We normally gave the reading part first, then a break, then the math section. While the students were taking the second part of the test, the interviewers would start calling the candidates by name to the front of the cafeteria. There, we had arranged the interview tables in such a way that the backs of the students faced the rest of the room while we conducted our interview. In our hands was the questionnaire that the child filled out before taking the reading segment of the test. This information sheet not only included the usual things like name, address, name of school and hobbies and the like, but we also asked the candidate why he or she selected our school. We got varied, but unexpected answers to this one. Most would write, "It was my life-long ambition to come to Fashion!" Many wrote that it was "a safe school." But, the answers we didn't want to see were these: "I want to be a stewardess!" or, "I want to join your basketball team," quoted by a male candidate to a school that had less than 100 male students out of an overall population of 2200; or, "Lots of my friends are here," or, "I heard that we get to keep all the clothes we make."

In a three to five minute interview, on average, we had to make up our minds immediately about what type of student we had here. Was the child shy, or evasive? Was the youngster nervous or hyper? Was the student lying, or bending the truth a little? With each question, a skilled interviewer can be accurate more times than not. For example, I remember one particular interview where

I asked the male student which subject was his best.

"Math," he answered with a little bravado.

"Math?" I said. "What grades do you get in math?"

"Oh, nineties and hundreds."

"Really. 90's and 100's. That's terrific, Jerome."

"Yeah, I always did real good in math. It's my best subject," he added.

"O.K., Jerome, I'm going to ask you a question which includes your best subject, math, with a practical trade problem in men's tailoring. O.K.?"

"Yeah, sure. Go ahead," he said.

"The problem is this: your teacher wants you to make half-inch cuffs on a pair of pants. You know what cuffs are, right?"

"Yeah, on the bottom of the leg. Yeah."

"O.K. Jerome, how many half inches are there to an inch?"

"Thirty-nine!" he said proudly.

Jerome failed the interview. Not because he didn't get the right answer, but because he lied. If he lied about such a small matter as selecting his best subject, he probably would be untruthful about more serious situations. I always asked the candidate to state his preference first before I would pose a question in that subject area. Most students would say math, not because it really was their favorite, as I found out later, but because the student thought it would impress the interviewer. Math! Wow! Science. Really! To my favorite question about the half-inch cuffs, I got these answers, believe me or not. Everything from one to a million. One student informed me, after several minutes of contemplation, "We didn't get to that part in math yet!"

And yet, if I phrased the question a little differently, like, "How many quarters in a half dollar?" the results were better. My job was not to trip up the youngster, but to see if we could acquire a decent and honest kid wherever possible. If a candidate said that English was her favorite subject, you would think that she had read at least a book or two since September. Here too, the liars would say things like, "I lost my library card," or "My teacher didn't assign us any books to read this term." All we wanted was an honest kid. Period.

When children are questioned, you find some typical reactions. Girls would avoid a male teacher's eyes. Male students would have a macho "image" to protect. They would swagger to the interviewer's desk, or would look "down" when they got to the desk, then sit down. Many students wouldn't sit down until asked to, and to me, that was a sign of good manners. A good first impression.

Being the Dean, it was a very strong concern on my part to keep out a possible troublemaker. I would never come right out front and ask a student if he or she had a record at their school. The student could flat out lie and there was no way I could verify the existence of a record on any given Saturday or Sunday morning. I wanted the kid to tell me if a record in fact existed, so I would take the high ground with the question: "Why did you have that last fight?" Because the student thought I was reading about this "fight" from a referral I conveniently held in my hands, many would reply that they indeed had that fight, but "I didn't start it!" As the candidate incriminated himself further with other forays, I knew I would deny his application.

Many civil libertarians might not subscribe to my methods, but neither do these people earn a living by teaching a class full of undisciplined teen-agers. It was a matter of taking in the best candidates for the new school year. It became a matter of determining which was "best" for our school. Do you want a student body made up of more literate, but disruptive, children, or less literate, trade-conscious and better disciplined youngsters? I suppose you may want both, but sooner or later, our three- or four-year trade curriculum would weed out those who couldn't stand the rigid training. Believe it or not, my method, which took only five minutes of intensive questioning, could spare the wise acre a lot of unnecessary trips to my office.

Our method was not foolproof by any means. My filing cabinets gave testimony to that fact, but it boiled down to a simple question. "Why would I need another headache?" Our school was not your average community high school, nor was our building two or three floors high. Our student population ran 20 to 1 in favor of girls and most of the trade classes could consume three to four periods in a row. Our introductory trade class, called "Exploratory Trade," ran one full year, three periods long, every day, divided into eight-week segments. The first eight-week class was devoted exclusively to shop class drill, like placing your trade box under your chair at all times—a violation in which necessitated a Dean's referral to my office to sewing and ripping out stitches around a pot-holder-size piece of cloth. Eight weeks of this! Only a dedicated, honest-to-goodness trade-loving student could do this without going mad. An undisciplined-minded junior high school brat couldn't last two or three weeks.

And, the referrals would pour down like rain water: "student failed to keep trade box closed and stored under her chair as instructed," or, "Melissa came toward me with a pair of scissors in a threatening manner," or, "student opened window more than the two inches allowed," or, "after I told Sharon to rip out the stitches from her sample for the fifth time, she told me to fuck myself," or, "Felix urinated in the class waste paper basket after I refused his request to go to the boy's bathroom." I had a definite obligation to keep out a future problem, not only to spare the trade teachers, but to spare myself as well.

I was a member of this elite panel of entrance examiners for some eighteen years. One day in the mid-eighties, after I left the Dean's office, I happened to run across your typical "wise guy" in my subject class of American History. This male junior had a definite chip on his shoulder and he was as arrogant as he was undisciplined. He was loud-mouthed, carefree about his punctuality in class; he strolled in at will, and when I would challenge his reason for this behavior, he was hostile and insulting. "How did this kid get past our interview?" I asked myself after I found that he had an extensive record in our Dean's office. So, I went to check his personal record, which contained his entrance examination scores along with the grade he had been given by the interviewer. Boy, did I get a jolt! I had been his interviewer! And, I failed him! On the interview sheet, I had indicated that this candidate was unsuitable because of the surly demeanor he had displayed during the interview, and his hostility to authority was visibly apparent. A single red line crossed out my comments, but they could still be easily read by anyone who cared to see this file. However, the strangest development was yet to come, because at the bottom of my interview page, my signature was also crossed out and the Principal's scrawl countermanded my evaluation. I hit the ceiling! I promptly marched into the Principal's office with the thick Dean folder and this kid's personnel file, including the changed Interview Sheet.

I sat in the outer office, cooling my heels, for about five or ten minutes. The Principal called me—and I have to say, he always was gracious when we conferred about anything. Today was no exception, and as he heard my story of woe and disbelief, he agreed that I was right and he was wrong. "The bastard should never have walked into our building, John, I'll admit it! Your evaluation was right on target," he said as he leafed through the many referrals, "and I was wrong!" he admitted.

"But, why did you do that?" I asked, hoping to get additional satisfaction.

"You think this was the only one?" he chimed back. "I countermanded lots of your sheets and the sheets of others as well!"

"Why on God's earth would you deliberately do that?" I yelled back.

"John, for Christ's sake! We needed the numbers!"

"Numbers?" I said. "All this for numbers!"

"John, grow up, will you!" he shouted back at me. "Do you know how many kids applied to our school last year, and how many the year before that?" he asked. "Do you have any idea?"

"I know the numbers have been dropping."

"Dropping, shit! They're down to *nothing.* Last year we had some twelve hundred, this year maybe a thousand. They're not coming here, or Printing, or Music and Art. We have to take what we get, and that from the mouth of our Superintendent. Do you want this school to close?" he demanded.

"This is incredible," I answered. "What you're really asking is, do we maintain our old standards and close down, or, do we accept everybody and anybody with lower expectations and stay open for awhile. The school can't take it, and I'm not the Dean anymore."

"John, that's how it is right now. We have to take whatever we get. The Superintendent says that our selecting days are over. Schools that can't hold on to numbers will be closed. I'm sorry."

As I walked out of his office I knew that I couldn't be party to such a sham. I couldn't receive money for being a rubber stamp. That winter, when I received my formal invitation to be on the Entrance Testing Committee, I threw the form away. Many of my colleagues thought I was crazy and foolish to be so high-minded, but I just couldn't do it anymore. I was content knowing that for some twenty years or so, I had kept Mortimer Ritter's dream alive and had thought that an ideal was more important than money. I suppose it depends on your reference point, because right after the devastating UFT teachers' strike of 1968, which lasted 10 long weeks, I was down to $54.00 in our savings account. In those days, just a year after we bought our home in New Jersey, all I could think about was money. And, right about that time, I entertained the thought of teaching night school. And, I thought Junior High Schools were bad!

As luck would have it, a former student of mine was looking for a job, and after I spoke to my chairman he was offered a position in our department teaching social studies. Al was also moonlighting in Brooklyn and now that he had a permanent position, he wanted to drop the night job. Fortunately for me, another member of our Department was teaching at the very same night school for a couple of years. So, the three of us went to see the director and I got Al's job, with a very strong recommendation by my other buddy. The night school was Prospect Park High School on Eastern Parkway, just off the Brooklyn Botanical Gardens. We three were the only white faces in the whole area. At the next faculty conference held by Mr. Brown, the director, I was happy to see additional white faces.

The problem for me wasn't getting to Brooklyn, it was leaving the high school at 9 o'clock at night and taking my train at the Eastern Parkway station. For almost four years, Curt and I would take the 7th Avenue line to Brooklyn, but whereas I would have to make it all the way back to New Jersey, Curt would stay over at his mother-in-law's somewhere in Brooklyn. I had it down to a system. I would race from the building as fast as my legs would take me, and then would enter the station, with token in hand, and I would wait next to the token booth. The train was scheduled to arrive into the station at about 9:12. If that train came early or I was late, I was a dead duck because I had to catch the last bus, Number 14, on the Red and Tan Line out of the Port Authority, in Manhattan at 10 P.M. sharp. I did this twice a week for almost four years.

But, I'm getting ahead of myself. When I took my place at Prospect Park, I had almost ten years of teaching under my belt, seven of them in Gustave Straubenmueller Junior High School on the Lower East Side. I considered myself a seasoned teacher as things went but nothing prepared me for that first night in Brooklyn.

Al was good enough to come with me to help me adjust, and to meet some key people (like the janitor), and he introduced me to his former class. Al showed me the texts they were using, the materials that were to be duplicated, and the form tests and quizzes I was to prepare. Just as he was going over the class roster, before the class was to begin, we both heard a bang! Then another. Since it was a warm September night, the windows were open so we both ran over to see what had happened.

A young man was sitting, propped up against the front wheel of a car parked in the middle of the street, in front of our building. The young black male was wearing a white shirt and it had blood all over it. "Oh, another shooting." Al said. "You'll get used to it," and with that, he returned to the teacher's desk, leaving me by the window, wondering if I had made the right choice. Seconds later, the classroom filled up with adult students and I never gave it another thought.

By and large, my classes—and all my future classes there—were made up of Haitians, Jamaicans, Dominicans and Puerto Ricans, along with native American blacks. All my adult students were attempting to take the GED High School Equivalency Test to help them get a better life. Soon, I was caught up with their desire to improve themselves by expanding the American history curriculum to include how to fill out forms for bank loans, job applications, and what various expressions meant or implied. They were eager to learn. Near the end of the term, they became anxious and fidgety as their day approached to take the Big Exam. Many passed it, and those who didn't, redoubled their efforts and tried again.

It soon became apparent, each night I was there, that a pattern was developing. Practically all my Caribbean students were seated and ready to go, and suddenly some altercation would break out either in the hall or in the staircase. Usually it would be between an Afro-American and a non-Afro. But what was somewhat disturbing was that for the main part, the audience watching the fracas were almost all native blacks—to a man or woman. The teachers on the floor would have to break up the minor spat, and then the rest of my class

162

would slowly drift in. Unfortunately for them, it was these very students who did the poorest on the GED test. When I left Prospect Park nearly four years later, I still had about six or seven of these original students still in my class, and the others had been processed through.

Those who passed the test were most appreciative. It wasn't easy for many of them who had to work all day; many were married and still attended evening school and completed many of the assignments in a foreign tongue. All this came to a crashing end in the spring of my fourth year of night school. As I would normally do, I would get to Prospect Park about one half-hour early to get the room tidied up, the board erased, and the chairs straightened in proper rows so that I could walk around the room and into the aisles without banging into a chair. I gathered my rex-o-graphed materials and stacked them on my desk, did a little hall gossiping with my buddy, Curt, next door and finished entering some homework grades into my marking book. My class walked into the room just as the bell rang, and I watched and chattered with one or two students as they passed by. A couple of minutes later, the late bell rang. Some seats were empty and I went out into the hall to urge the latecomers to get a move on. Then, I went to my desk and started to take attendance.

Those students who were with me, year after year, had gravitated to the front of the room in their assigned seats. Tonight the seats were empty, but sooner or later, they would make it to class—I hoped. On this night we were about ten minutes into the period, when a female black student came through the front door and deposited her screaming baby on the empty front desk. She was a new student of mine, and her seat was in the middle of the room. I had to stop what I was doing, and I walked over to her and asked her what was the problem. She had never brought her baby to class—ever.

"Mr. Manicone, I had to bring the baby in. No one is home to baby-sit my baby!" she said.

"Fine," I said, "but I have to teach my class. Can't you walk the baby out in the hall until he quiets down?"

"I can't do that! I have to change him first," she replied.

"Fine," I repeated, "but do it in the back of the room so I can continue my lesson."

"Mr. Manicone, I can't do that now! I have to change him right now!" And with that, she popped opened the infant's pants and undid the pins to his diaper. His diaper was full and as she lifted the baby by his legs, the rest of the excrement, stuck to his bottom, was revealed.

I yelled, "Couldn't you do that in the back of the room?"

The room was quickly filling up with the disturbing smell of waste that prompted some of the students to move to the rear. Again, I challenged the young mother on her choice of where to diaper change. All I got was a skittish giggle as she played to her audience. "Haven't you ever had to change a baby before?" she teased.

"Not in a classroom!" I replied. I then excused myself: one, because of the noxious odor, and secondly, I wanted someone on staff to talk to this student. I went down to speak to Mr. Brown.

When I finished talking to the director, he said, "So, what do you want me to do?"

"Do?" I yelled back, "I want you take that girl and her baby out of my room so that I can continue to do what I'm being paid to do!"

"Mr. Manicone," Mr. Brown retorted, "look at this girl's motivation to come to school. She wants to be educated. I admire her efforts!"

"And does that include changing a stinking diaper, right there in the front of the room?" I shot back.

"Mr. Manicone, I'll admit that she could have been more discreet, but I don't think she did anything wrong!"

"Well, I quit, then," I answered. "The next student might bring in twins! I just believe it was a deliberate act of exhibitionism and I want you to support my stance."

"I won't do that, Mr. Manicone," Mr. Brown replied.

"Then, I quit!"

"Mr. Manicone, reflect on what you say. Jobs are hard to get because of all the squeezing by the Board. Remember 1973," the director pointed out.

"I don't care. I quit!" and with that, I wrote and submitted a hasty letter of resignation.

"You're bluffing," he said as he read the letter.

"See if I'm here on Thursday," I said as I left his office, dismissed my class, and left the room with that grinning idiot rocking her baby in the front seat.

Little did I realize then that I would do the same thing, but not in such a dramatic fashion, about fifteen years later. Some people might call it elitism, but I have a better definition for it, and that is "without some integrity, some standard of discipline, you get what you deserve." In the army, we used to have a crude expression which I think sums it all up, and that was: "You can't polish shit!"

Twelve

Scotty, Beam Me Up. Now!

One of Mr. B.'s favorite expressions was, "If God made them, we have to teach them!" I have to honestly say that I sometimes began to question the validity of that statement. In the course of my career, I saw, literally so many dozens of malicious acts of wanton vandalism and total disregard of human welfare that it still boggles my mind to this day.

For example, why would anyone force 3/4 inch steel doorplates, six of them, mind you, at 90° angles? Or, what would possess someone to throw a classroom window pole out of the third floor junior high school window? How do you account for 7th and 8th graders throwing lit matches over an open transom window of a storeroom and simply walking away? In Brooklyn, where I did some summer school remediation work, we apprehended a male student using a Zippo-type cigarette lighter that had a pipe lighting attachment, similar to a miniature blow torch, attempting to burn up a bulletin board right outside of the main office!

Sometimes, the destruction of property, like the work performed by a student in the trade class, may not only be senseless, but also downright premeditated. Once I was called to a senior trade class to be shown a trade box. When it was opened, I saw what was left of a completed garment, now cut in shreds. The female student, whose work was ruined, was inconsolable. She was the star pupil in the class and her work was outstanding. The completed garment was needed to graduate. One of her colleagues, out of jealousy, had seen fit to destroy this girl's work so as not to show up the mediocre efforts of others. Perhaps, it would have been more understandable if one were a freshman—but certainly, not at 18 or 19.

Other malicious acts of unbelievable public destruction were events waiting to happen. Take the case of the girl who dropped down to my office to inform me that she could not get her books and other personal things out of her locker.

"Where's you locker?" I asked her.

"On the second floor; you know, by the gym," she replied.

"So, what happened?" I asked her. "You forgot your combination?"

"No, no!" she said. "I can't get to my locker!"

"What do you mean, 'you can't get to your locker'!" I pressed on. "Is something obstructing your access to the locker, or what?"

"No, that's not it at all!" she said rather helplessly. "I think you should come with me and then you'll know what I'm talking about!"

"You caught me in my less busy time, Miss; I'll go with you and I'll take my handy 'friend' with me, just in case," I said. And with that, I went to my closet and took out a bolt cutter, which doubled as my lock-cutter. "O.K., Miss, show me the way!"

She led me to the second floor and when we approached her area, she stopped and pointed down the aisle of lockers and said, "In there, number 345." I turned into the aisle, and had taken about two steps, when I was hit with the strongest, most offensive stench I ever smelled. I was stopped in my tracks as if an invisible force ray kept me in check. As I quickly retreated back to the student, I yelled, "What the hell is that? I can't believe anything could smell that bad!"

"See?" the girl said, somewhat vindicated. "I told you I couldn't get to my locker. It's down there," she pointed.

"Wow," I said.

I put down the bolt cutter and then asked her, "Do you have any spray cologne or perfume in your handbag, honey?"

"Yeah," she said and took out a small vial. I sprayed the scent on to my handkerchief, and got ready to "go in" a second time. Approximately half the lockers had locks on them, so I decided to quickly open the unlocked ones first to see if I could locate this incredibly offensive odor. So, with my left hand to my face, I proceeded down the aisle of lockers. As trite as it sounds, the stink literally brought tears to my eyes. After I successfully opened 5 or 6 lockers, I had to retreat back to the main corridor where the young woman was waiting.

"Do you mind if I take your spray?" I asked her. "I'll reimburse you for the cost."

"That's O.K.," she said. "You're really helping me to get to my locker. I should thank you!"

I liberally doused my handkerchief with the cologne and tried again. About two-thirds of the way in, I found the problem. I opened this particular locker and I just couldn't believe my eyes. There, sitting on the floor of the locker, was a huge pile of human excrement. Not animal, not fake, but honest-to-God *human*. Littered next to the offensive mound were sheets of composition paper, which had served as toilet paper.

The immediate question that came to mind as I gazed stupidly at this offense was "how in the hell did a kid get his butt into such a narrow space?" Most lockers are no more than 14 or 15 inches wide. Slamming the locker closed, I again retreated to the main aisle and told the student to get down to the custodian's office and get someone up here with a pail, lots of cleaning materials and their best smelling solvent.

After about 10 minutes, Mario showed up and he too froze as he attempted to walk down the row of lockers.

"Holy Christmas!" he yelled. "Who died in here?"

I pointed to the locker and said, "It's number 345. Do what you can. This young lady needs to get her books."

Mario did a very good job, because within several minutes, the locker area was decontaminated. But, I never got my man.

To most people, this incident would be considered a prank—nothing more and nothing less. But to me, with a healthy dose of logic constantly working, this "prank" was an itch that I couldn't reach. Why would *anybody* contort himself (or herself) out of shape to pull a stunt like this? There are bathrooms at either end of the hall. If a parent came with a child to see a basketball game in the next-door gym after school, there were plenty of facilities to accommodate anyone. Why in the *locker*? I came to the same conclusion Sherlock Holmes might have reached if we could have called for his services. When you eliminate all rational causes, you're left with just one. Vandalism. Here was another example of a spiteful act performed by someone who destroys property "to get back at the system."

These angry attempts to destroy or damage public property took another turn when it was discovered one bright Monday morning that someone had literally ripped off the heavy bronze plaques that proudly proclaimed THE HIGH SCHOOL OF FASHION INDUSTRIES from the front of the building! Both plaques were made of solid bronze and each weighed about 150 pounds. During the weekend, according to the police, thieves, using a ladder, made off with their prize. The going rate for bronze, at the time, was about $.80 to $1.00 a pound. It was a nice haul for a drug addict with a serious problem. At least in this case, Mr. B. and I believed that our students could not have been involved because an automobile had to be used to carry off the ill-gotten goods.

Luckily for the school, we had a pair of plaques, which adorned the rear of our building. Mr. B. got the Board of Ed to transfer these plaques and had them bolted to the front very securely. I always reacted very negatively to acts of wanton vandalism. Maybe because I'm a "Depression baby"—I don't know, I just couldn't understand or *want* to understand why someone would deliberately destroy property, whether it was a seat on a public bus or a priceless work of art. But, in my case, I came across this crime repeatedly: in the classroom, the staircases, the cafeteria, locker areas, the gym, and even hall closets, not to mention the lavatories.

Early in my career as Dean, I was confronted with a situation that involved vandalism between two young men that could have exploded into a gang fight. Since each of the major players here represented a competing element in our school, one, Dominican and the other, Puerto Rican, I almost called upon King Solomon for assistance.

It all came about when the Dominican student came into my office to complain about "his shades." At first, I was surprised that he would attempt to use my office to help him in his predicament. So, I was cautious at first when this senior sat down at my desk.

"Mr. Manicone," he began, "do you know Felix Matos?"

I nodded that I did, and he continued.

"Well, he did something to provoke me and I don't want to start any trouble and ruin my chances of graduating. So I come to you to fix the problem, and if you can't, they'll be a war!"

"Hold on, Pedro," I said. "There won't be any war and I don't like threats!"

"Who made any threats, Mr. Manicone?" he replied, slightly affronted. "I meant no disrespect. I like you because you are fair and that's why I'm here!"

"O.K.," I said. "Now, what did Felix do?"

"Well, I got these shades for Christmas from my aunt. They real expensive and they make me look real good. Well, Felix and some of his crowd were ragging me about them and how they made me look like a faggot. I didn't say anything, because I knew that Matos was jealous, so I wore them all the time. Well, today I had gym and put my shades in my gym bag. Somehow, Felix got into my locker—and look what he done!"

With that, he thrust out his right hand. I almost lost it right there and then, but I had to swallow my snicker, because his face was like that of a little boy who was holding his favorite, but broken, toy. I never saw a pair of glasses so twisted and crushed as those. The green glass was almost welded to the frame.

"Well, Mr. Manicone, what are you going to do about it?" he asked in a small, pleading tone.

It's exactly at moments like this that teenagers will accuse the grown-ups of "copping out."

What could I say to the youngster? "Go beat the hell

171

out of Ramos!" or, "Pedro, you have my full permission to get your boys together, and start a gang war in the cafeteria!" Or, "Leave it to me, Pedro; I'll suspend Felix today!"

Here's what I did say: "Pedro, this is a very difficult situation both for you and me. No matter what I do or say, someone is going to feel cheated. Cheated, because either you or Felix will think I was too easy with the other, right?"

Pedro nodded.

I continued. "Now, Pedro, the only two things working for you are those crushed sun glasses and your belief that Felix did it. Did you see him do that?" and I pointed to the metal frame in his hand.

"No, I didn't actually see him do anything. But, I know in my heart that he did it, Mr. Manicone. You got to believe me!" he said.

"It's not whether I believe you or not, Pedro, but I have to follow the rules of law. In law, *thinking* that someone did something and *seeing* someone *do* something are two different things. You don't have a case, it's as simple as that," I replied.

"Na, Na. That don't cut it!" he said, raising his voice.

"Here's what I will do, Pedro," I interrupted. "I'll call Felix down here and see what he says. Maybe he'll admit to the whole thing and you can get a new pair of glasses out of it."

"No way!" he yelled. "He's got a brother in Attica and he'll never cop a plea! Why should he admit to anything? He's a pro."

"Let me have a chance. You never know how things will turn out," I replied.

"It'll be a waste of time. I should have never come here in the first place," he said as he got up from his chair. "You already made up your mind and you won't help me. Sorry to bother you!"

He left in a huff and I sat there like an idiot. People come to you for help and you are powerless to gain them a measure of what they would call justice . . .

I decided to call Felix in anyway to hear his version of this episode and, at the same time, try to head off a possible fight between two ethnic groups right inside the school. As luck would have it, I didn't have a monitor for the remainder of that period, and, I was scheduled to teach the next two periods. Mrs. F., the Girls' Dean, didn't care to settle male student problems of this nature, and the Dean in charge of the cafeteria never took anecdotal notes by precedent anyway, so it would have to hold till the afternoon.

I got back to my office by period six and the fat was already in the fire. There was trouble in the 10th floor gym, involving Felix and Pedro.

The Security Guard and I raced up to the 10th floor. The elevator only went to the 9th and then we had to leg it up the additional flight. The 10th floor at Fashion contained the two banks of machinery for the elevators that serviced the students and faculty on the East and West sides of the building; one small gym used mainly by the boys of our school; their locker area, one or two small classrooms, and one very small lavatory.

The male gym teacher was doing his best to keep the two factions apart as we rushed into the gym area. Mr. P. was holding Felix, while Pedro was taunting him with, "Now, how do you like it, wise face?"

I rushed over to Pedro, and demanded, "What did you do?" Before he could say a word, Felix screamed, "Look in the bathroom. Look in the bathroom and see what he did to my beret!"

As the gym teacher continued to hold on to Felix, Pedro and I went into the bathroom, and there in the middle stall, in the white commode, sat, as pretty as you please, what first appeared to my eye to be a large water lily. But in fact, it was a black beret sporting a huge pom-pom on it. This time, I did lose it. The beret was still spinning ever so slowly in the john. It appeared that Pedro had unsuccessfully attempted to flush the beret away several times. No luck!

I pushed Pedro out of the toilet with a firm shove before I started to roar uncontrollably. I banged the sides of the stalls with my open hand to muffle my laughter and when I was through, I came out pretending to be enraged instead. The boys bought it, but the old sly gym teacher had to suppress his own laughter by feigning coughing and wheezing. I wished I had a camera, as the old saying goes. But we were still not out of the woods. This type of retaliation could spell some real trouble for everyone. I had to put a stop to it now.

I ordered the Security Guard to take Pedro down to my office and tell my aide to start the paperwork for a Parent-Dean Conference. I ushered Felix into one of the small classrooms and closed the door. "Felix," I shouted. "What happened?"

"Hey, man, don't lean on me, man! It's that crazy Dominican who should be tagged. Did you see what he did to my beret?" he asked. "Hey, did you see? My girl gave me that beret! That's a gift from the heart, and you don't mess with that, you understand?" he added.

"Yeah, I understand," I mimed, "but you don't come off this thing smelling like a rose, either. Why did you smash his glasses?"

"That faggot had it coming," Felix admitted. "I wanted to teach him some manners and respect."

"What respect?" I asked. "What the hell does he owe you?"

"Hey, man," he said, "we came to this school together as 9th graders. I never did anything to him. Then, all of a sudden, he comes around with this attitude. Because he's a senior and I'm a super junior, he starts to show me up. Him and those faggot glasses!"

"Well, you owe him a pair of glasses," I said.

"Yeah? What about my beret?" he asked.

During this banter, an idea hit me. What if I could get Felix to think he could get away with not paying for the glasses and at the same time retrieve his beret? It was worth a shot and if it worked, I had Felix in my pocket and Pedro dealing with me to get out of a Dean's Hearing.

This whole thing could rival the best of King Solomon! "Listen," I said to Felix, "if I can help you retrieve your beret from the toilet, and I hold off on pressing payment to Pedro, will you play ball?"

"How you going to get my beret out of the toilet?" he asked with a painful, but puzzled look on his face.

"Let's go back to the can and see what we can do," I said, and with that, we walked across the deserted gym floor into the locker area. After searching through a few vacant lockers, I found a couple of plastic bags and one wire hanger. Then I went into the bathroom with Felix by my side. He appeared to be monumentally depressed. "It won't work," he said, dejectedly.

"Sure it will," I said confidently. "Hold the bag open and we'll fish this thing right out for you!"

After a couple of tries I had the sucker, and as I pulled the beret out, I felt the weight of the urine that was heaped on this "lily pad." I could hardly contain my amusement at this charade. As I deposited the reeking thing in the first plastic bag, Felix continued to protest.

"Hey, man, what am I supposed to do with this thing now?"

"Have it dry cleaned, you idiot!" I answered as I put the mess in the second bag. "And don't tell Pedro anything! You still have your hat and he's got nothing. You come out ahead on all counts. Get it?"

I was praying he would bite.

He not only bit, he swallowed the whole line.

"Man, you're a genius! I see. Yeah, yeah!"

With that, he shook my hand very vigorously and left the 10th floor with his prized package swinging by his side. Now, I had to deal with Pedro.

As I entered my office, I knew I had to earn my Academy Award; so I came in fuming and cursing under my breath.

"O.K. Pedro, how many days do you want? Three? Four? Five? Maybe the whole ten days? Hmm?" I asked him quite loudly.

"What days are you talking about?" he asked, somewhat sheepishly.

"Oh, didn't I tell you? It's the days you'll be suspended for pulling that prank today on the 10th floor!" I screamed. "You wanted to handle it yourself, right? So now be man enough to handle the suspension.

"Marge, where are those papers I have to prepare for the principal?" I asked, still pretending to be angry and in a foul mood.

I winked at Marge and she picked the whole thing right up. "Mr. M. do you want them in triplicate or duplicate?" she asked.

"Marge, the triplicate for five or more days. You know that. Get the necessary information from his personnel card and bring everything back to me. Mr. B. might still be in his office, let me call."

As I reached for the phone, I glanced over at Pedro. He was very distraught.

"You had to piss on his beret, too?" I asked, rather sternly.

I thought that Marge was going to lay an egg. She rushed out of the room. "Don't forget the Guidance folders, Marge!" I screamed out the open door and she disappeared down the hall holding her sides.

I tried to busy myself with bogus paperwork, politely moving Pedro's arm from the top of the desk as if I were looking for a key piece of paper, and, all the while, sneaking a peek at the student to see his reaction. It finally came.

"Mr. Manicone, will this hurt my chances of graduating on time?" he began. "Because all this stuff, it ain't worth it."

"Look, Pedro, you brought all this stuff down on yourself. You just couldn't wait for me to work my magic, could you?" I replied.

"Yeah, but—"

I interrupted him.

"You want to know the real kick in the head? He admitted that he destroyed your glasses!"

"He did?" Pedro asked without blinking. "He really admitted that he whacked my shades?"

"Yes," I said rather disappointedly, "but now you face suspension. All for nothing. I could have had him suspended, had your glasses repaired or restored, and best of all you would still graduate without this all hanging over your head. But, no! You knew better. Terrific!"

"Wait a minute!" he protested, "but you said that he

admitted breaking my frames. Don't I get some money or new shades?"

"You get nothing! You're the one being suspended. Not him! You closed me down! I can't deal anymore. You admitted to destroying his property with all those witnesses?"

He nodded sheepishly.

I continued to press. "You didn't see him do anything. I can't suspend him on what you *believe* he did, so here we are. Destroyed property everywhere, but now you go down, not him!"

I waited while all this began to sink in. Meanwhile, Marge returned to the office. She was composed now. I began.

"Now look, Pedro, you have to admit that this whole thing went too far. Right?"

Again, he nodded. He shuffled his feet.

"If I make a suggestion to you, and mind you, only if the Principal says it's O.K., are you prepared to at least consider it?"

"What do you have in mind?" he asked, with his head still resting on his chest.

"Let's make a swap. Your glasses for his beret! How about it?" I proposed.

I knew down deep in my heart that no kid wants to be suspended. Too much dirty laundry comes up, and students are always hoping to keep as much from their parents as possible.

Pedro looked up. I saw there was hope in his eyes. "You mean, we drop everything right her if I forget my busted-up shades and I don't get suspended, or nothing?"

"Right!" I said, "but the principal has to say it's O.K."

"Yeah, but what about Felix's beret?" he asked.

"Don't worry about Felix. I'll threaten him with suspension if he queers the deal. Now I'm asking you the sixty-four dollar question. Does my suggestion sound good to you?" I pressed.

Now it was Pedro's turn to 'pretend', and while he did that, attempting, to consider the offer, I pretended to be impatient. "What's it going to be? Go, or no go? I want to get Mr. B. before he leaves his office for the day, Pedro!" I snapped.

"O.K., O.K.—it sounds good to me," he replied.

I picked up the telephone and pretended to call the Principal's Office. The dialogue went something like this:

"Mr. B.? John Manicone here. Mr. B. I need an O.K. from you about a deal I made with a senior involving a rather serious matter today. Well, it involves two acts of vandalism. Yes, vandalism. Uh uh. Well each of the two boys destroyed the other's valuables. In this case, a pair of sunglasses and a man's beret. Yes, a beret. Yes, I know how you fell about sunglasses in school, but, nonetheless, that's what we have."

Pause. A deliberate three-minute pause.

It was working. Pedro was on the edge of his seat listening to every word. My only concern was that Mr. B would waltz into my office, unannounced, and blow the whole deal. "Yes, Mr. B. I understand. Yes, I know," I continued. "The deal? Well, here it is in a nutshell. I believe I have both parties agreeing to drop everything pending. Yes, yes; I'll get it in writing, and both boys will forget the whole thing. No. No. I haven't informed the parents. That's also part of the deal. I thought that since both fellows are seniors" (I lied here), "I can take that chance. I see. That's right. I'll take full responsibility.

Yes, Mr. B. Yes, yes, I understand fully. I'll get everything in writing to cover all eventualities. I understand. Thank you. Thank you."

"There! We got a deal." I exclaimed. "Now, will you live up to your end so I don't look stupid to Mr. B.?"

"Mr. Manicone, I promise you full cooperation. You can count on it," Pedro said, as he held out his hand for me to shake.

"Done," I said.

Little did Pedro realize as he left my office that day what a huge laugh he missed sharing with me. Somewhere, deep in the subway underground, a teenager was carrying a plastic bag containing a urine-soaked beret, thinking he got the better of a deal that was nonexistent from the beginning. I'm sure that Felix thought that he was the proverbial cat that swallowed the canary. At the same time, Pedro might have thought that *he* got the deal of the century. "Wow, I pissed on a guy's hat and I got away with it! How many times does that happen to someone in his or her lifetime?" I'm sure that Pedro would have given one of his eyeteeth to roar with me as his antagonist took his dripping prize home to be "dry cleaned." Sure. Right.

The school won that day. I seized on an opportunity and ran with it. If I failed, I failed. But, I didn't. The school won and that was what counted. Vandalism, nonetheless, reared its ugly head again several more times during my watch, but, unfortunately, never as good as this, or this satisfying.

Thirteen

Now They Tell Me!

A close friend of my wife worked as Assistant Dean at Newtown High School in Queens. She and I were always at the opposite end of the spectrum, but no more so than when it came to discipline in the city schools. She, somewhat of a liberal, believed that children needed to be allowed to grow in "their space." Rigid rules were counter-productive, and an open-ended classroom, where everybody learned at their own speed, was paramount to the development of the child.

I, on the other hand, tended to favor the conservative approach: the harder, the better. I believed in separate classes for boys and girls, the use of uniforms (this was way back in the 1960's, mind you!) and tougher standards. To me, schools were not supposed to be day camps. I also frowned on jewelry, which always caused trouble. My wife's friend disagreed, saying jewelry represented individualism. So, it came to me as a very pleasant surprise to hear that she took the position. I wanted to see if anything could make her "illiberal." She was on the firing line a couple of months when this event occurred.

A female student was referred to her for using excessive profanity in class, and all of it was directed at the teacher. The student called her everything in the book and then some. The referral contained nearly a sheet and a half of the most foul and filthy things one person could say to another. It was horrendous. Being new to the game of discipline, this gal went slowly as she first read the referral, conferred with the teacher over a cup of coffee, and then called the offending student to the office. It was a remarkable interview. The student was vulgar; coarse in her language and not in the least repentant for what had transpired. It became all too evident that she had to abort the interview and call in a parent.

Our family friend typed up the usual form requesting the parent to see the Dean along with child, on such-and-such a date and time, and placed the form letter in an envelope, sealed it and gave it to the student, who then departed.

This young lady was no mere high school delinquent without some resources of her own. If the new Assistant Dean had no clue as to what her parent looked like, why not shop around for one? And that is exactly what the kid did! She met a man, the right age, type, et cetera, and promised to pay him if he showed up on the appointed day at the appointed time on the steps of the high school. He was to pretend to be her father during the required conference with the Dean. He agreed. To him, this was going to be a real gas!

Sure enough, the young lady shows up with her "father." They sit down, and the Assistant Dean relates the incident to the "father." He is shocked. So much so, that he gets up from his chair and wallops that teenager.

"What did you do that for?" screams the kid. "You're not even my real father!"

"I never heard such filth, not even when I was in the army," he yelled back. "And from a girl!"

"Did I hear right?" interrupted the Dean. "You're not her *father?*" pointing to the girl still on the floor.

"That's right, Dean," replied the stranger, and then he related the whole shameful tale that had taken place. He appeared to be truly remorseful, apologized, and left the room, with his prostrate "daughter" still on the floor rubbing her jaw.

I relate this incident because I was impressed with the fact that strangers to the day-by-day operations within a school system don't have a clue to what goes on behind pedagogical walls. This is doubly shocking because all these "strangers" are, or were, products of this same system. How can they forget so easily? Don't they remember what it was like to be in a classroom?

As for my wife's friend, she became less and less tolerant and more and more conservative. Today, she too believes in uniforms, more controls and less "understanding of the needs of the child." Well, given the time, we'll convert them all!

Unfortunately for me, I didn't want to be proven right or wrong—just to support my instincts about discipline. I had evidence enough, daily, to remind myself to do the job as objectively as I could. For example, take the time when I happened to be patrolling the west side staircase a floor or two above the students' cafeteria. The period was only a few minutes old and I wanted to move those students along who were straggling to class. The fire alarm sounded.

I raced to the next floor, opened the staircase door and poked my head out to locate fire or smoke. Instead, not three feet down the hall stood a female student with her hand in the firebox, pulling the alarm. I grabbed her arm and asked (brilliantly), "Where's the fire?"

She looked at me with a vacant gaze, and I repeated, still holding her arm, "Why are you pulling the alarm?"

"I'm not pulling any alarm," she replied.

"You're not pulling an alarm?" I asked incredulously. "You're not pulling an alarm? What's your hand doing in the firebox?" I persisted.

She looked at me with an angry stare. Here, I caught the culprit in the act, with the lie already in her throat! How can we expect adults to behave responsibly if a mere teenager has been able to master a behavior we're trying to stamp out?

The attitude of "I didn't do anything unless you catch me" is pervasive within our society in general, but it seems to fester in our school system, in particular. A case in point: An English teacher, for an infraction, refers a female student to me during a class outing to see a play that was staged at F.I.T. Since our school was only a two-block walk to the Institute, the students had made it to the play and were now on their way back to our building via 7th Avenue. Being upper classmen, the students were given permission to buy salted pretzels from a street vendor, which they could munch on at their leisure, as they strolled back to Fashion. The girl who was seated by my desk as I read the referral decided to "lift" her pretzel.

"Why did you steal the pretzel?" I asked.

"I didn't steal no pretzel," she shot back.

"The teacher saw you take the pretzel, and you didn't pay for it! That's not stealing?"

"I took it from the man, not from her! I didn't steal nothing from *her*. Why is she so hot and bothered?" she replied.

"Ownership is not the problem here," I tried to reason. "You took something that wasn't yours and you didn't pay for it!"

Then she hit me with this line I'll remember forever. She said, "Anyways, he didn't see me take it, and that's not considered 'stealing'!"

"What?" I shot back. "He didn't see you take the pretzel, and therefore, according to the Law of Miss Williams, it's not considered 'stealing'? Where the hell did you get that idea from?"

"That's what I've been told, since way back: if a person doesn't see you take something, it's yours, legally," she answered, nodding her head, as if reading from a Book of Statutes. "And anyway, I didn't take the pretzel from Mrs. Gordon, why is she writing me up?"

I sat in my chair with all the restraint I could muster. I really wanted to slap this kid silly. Where the hell did she get the gall? This convoluted crap, typical of today's logic, was almost too much to bear.

"First off, it's stealing, whether a hundred people see it or no one sees it. But how can a private citizen write out a referral of something he didn't see. My dear, that kind of legal bunk may someday get you into a heap of trouble. Young lady, have you ever heard of the crime of burglary?"

She frowned, inferring a "no."

I continued, "Burglary is a crime in which the criminal enters a premise with the intention of taking something without being observed. It's still called stealing. Do you understand?"

"No, I don't understand. If somebody doesn't see you take something, how does he know I took it?" she said proudly. "He didn't see me take nothing, so I didn't steal his pretzel!"

I couldn't take much more of this, but in an attempt to make her see the legitimacy of my reasoning I happened to notice that she had placed her handbag on the floor, by her foot, and against the leg of my desk.

I shouted, "Look at that spider!" and I pointed over

her shoulder toward the ceiling. As she turned to look, I quickly swiped her handbag from the floor and put it in my desk drawer. "Oh, I though it was a spider," I said slightly apologetically. "By the way, are you missing anything, Miss Williams?"

She looked down at her lap, and then by her leg. "Yes, yes," she said with a start, "My bag's missing! I know I brought with me and put it down by my foot. It's gone!"

I placed my hand on her arm to reassure her.

"Calm down," I said. "I have it and it's mine. According to you, I didn't steal it because you didn't see me take it, so, using your own words, Miss Williams, I didn't steal it if you didn't see me take it! Right?"

She sat mute.

"Right?" I pressed her.

I had her. She made no more protestations. As I handed her bag back to her, she wore that smirk of defeat.

"Remember," I told her as we concluded our interview, "this referral stays in your folder until the day you leave this building to remind you of the valuable lesson you learned today. Stealing is stealing; no matter what limitations you want to place on it. Right?" She nodded and left.

And then, there is *stealing:* not just swiping. Not just taking, but out-and-out robbery. Like the time in the spring of 1976 or 1977, when some of our male students decided to act in a cavalier manner at dismissal time as it started to pour cats and dogs. Our young ladies had neglected to bring umbrellas, but that did not find our young lads without resources. They decided to take matters into their own hands and supply each and every lady in distress. The corner of 8th Avenue and 24th Street, right down our little block, held the answer. A Woolworth Five-and-Ten Cent Store! The boys helped themselves to arms full of umbrellas, neglecting the little formality of payment, and raced up the block with their ill-gotten goods. Unfortunately for them, the manager of the store was a star football player and raced up the block with the best of them. Some girls were lucky, but most of the items were soon retrieved, with the help of our security staff and this ex-footballer.

I was now holding court in my office with five or six umbrella-snatchers and their accusers. After I was apprised of the rain-induced caper, I yelled at the assemblage before me.

"What the hell were you guys thinking with? Are you Asses? I never heard of anything so stupid. You steal something in broad daylight so that you score some points with the girls. Now, the girls are dry and you dopes go to jail. And, for what? So, you can act like big shots and give out things that were not yours to give? Why don't you give sand to the Arabs, or ice to the Eskimos while you're at it?"

My little speech really satisfied the manager because he nodded with each pronouncement. The young men, however, could only stare at the floor and shuffle their feet. Two or three were seated; the rest were standing next to the security guards and the manager. I walked over to one of the culprits whom I knew by name and confronted him with, "Nestor, is your girl worth up to a year in jail for this?"

By now, the Assistant Principal had arrived and he placed himself in one corner of my room.

Nestor replied with a subdued "No, I—"

I walked over to the manager and asked, "How many umbrellas are missing?" as I pointed with my head

187

toward the stack of umbrellas in the outer office.

"I don't really know. Maybe six. Maybe ten. No more than that, Dean," he replied.

"And, how much for each?"

"The price is right on the handle. See? $5.99 each."

"O.K., boys. What's it going to be?" I shouted. "A night in jail, if we get all the paperwork in on time, or a money package settlement? Let's go! The manager hasn't got all day. He has a store to run."

I looked over to the A.P. who was grinning but keeping his composure.

I added, "Also, remember, any deal we make has to be approved by the school, and that's why Mr. Daniel is here—to either give his O.K. or not. What's it going to be?"

It was Nestor who asked, "Mr. Manicone, if we agree on money, how much each?"

"Now, let's see," I answered. "If we round off, six dollars times ten it $60.00. That'll be $10.00 each, on my desk, tomorrow morning, or you're going to eat meatloaf at lunchtime tomorrow. Is that O.K., with you, Mr. Daniel?"

"It sounds fair to me, Mr. Manicone, if it's O.K. with the manager of the store," he replied.

The manager nodded. He seemed quite pleased that the wheels of justice worked so well. He turned to leave. "Remember, boys," I added. "Every dime on my desk by 9:00 A.M. tomorrow, or there will be hell to pay. I mean it!"

"Mr. Manicone, please also inform these young men that a record will remain in their files until they graduate or are transferred," Mr. Daniel soberly stated. "I want all parents to receive letters and I will want a copy of everything in writing." He was standing in front of my desk, winking all the time, out of eyesight of the young men.

The manager was just frozen by the doorway. He really was pleased. He picked up the umbrellas with some help from the guards, and left.

By 8:45 the next morning, all the money was on my desk. As I counted the singles and quarters at the 5 & 10, the manager was appreciative. "You know, Dean, you really helped me out quite a bit. I couldn't press charges because we can't waste a whole day in court. My boss would have hit the ceiling if the kids didn't come up with the money."

"It would never have happened," I replied. "It's all in the way you say something. You get the desired effect. I didn't want to go to court either, so I got the boys to see it our way. And, it works. Nice doing business with you."

As I was leaving, he insisted I take something. I did. It was an umbrella for our office staff. You know, for that rainy day. Right on!

And then there is mugging.

Several months before, we had another outright theft. Not from a store, but from a disabled veteran. Again, it involved a student of ours who was in need. During a change of period that morning, two fellows were running down a flight of stairs. As things sometimes happen, one of the boys fell and twisted his ankle. When he tried to get back on his feet, he found that walking was difficult because of the pain. For a period or two, the young man attempted to walk it off. Instead of going to the Nurse's office as he was supposed to do, the wounded chap complained to he friend, saying that what really would help him was a cane. "Get me a cane!"

A cane? No problem. There's a Veteran's Administration Building right up the street. There are plenty of canes there. Sure. Be right back.

So, his friend leaves the building without permission, goes up to the corner of 7th Avenue and 24th, and waits. Sure enough, a veteran wounded in Vietnam comes hobbling out and our resourceful Fashion Industries student jumps him and appropriates the cane. True to his word, he returns to the building. As luck would have it, the A.P. happens to be in the lobby supervising a display installation in one of our show windows. Mr. Daniel, like myself, always questions those little odd incidents. *Why is a male student, without books, and without a pass, entering our building at 10:13 A.M. with a cane?*

As he begins to question the young man, the victim comes hobbling in. "That's him! That's him. He stole my cane!" the veteran screams.

"Well, well. What do we have here?" Mr. Daniel exclaims. "Maybe, we all have to go to the Dean's office, right down the hall here, and sort this out."

Thirty seconds later, a small parade marched into my office, headed by the A.P. It included Mickey (the alleged perpetrator); the screaming, hobbling victim; and one or two security guards.

Mickey sat down, the A.P. handed me the cane, and I asked the veteran to take the other chair. Mickey spoke up. "It all started when . . . "

When Mickey finished, the A.P. and I exchanged glances.

"Mr. Manicone, I thought that the Age of the Good Samaritan was dead. I was wrong!"

"Mickey," I began, "did you ever hear of the Good Samaritan?"

"No," he said. "Who was he?"

"It wasn't a he, it was a "she," I said. "A Good Samaritan is an expression which is used today to refer to a person who takes the trouble to do good things for his fellow man—but not at the expense of another person, like you did," as I pointed over to the seated veteran.

"Hey, I didn't do nothing bad," the culprit said. "My friend needed a cane, and anyway," pointing to the disabled man, "he was walking good!"

"Oh, he was walking good, so therefore, according to your logic, the cane belongs to anyone who needs it? I see. So, according to you, if a man has a car and happens to be walking, it's your right to take it from him because he doesn't need it anymore. According to you, right? Are you crazy?"

I turned to the veteran and, handing him his cane, I said, "You don't have to listen to this. You can go. Thank you, and I'm sorry for what happened." The security person walked him out.

"Now, let's get back to the beginning. Where's you friend now?"

"He's got lunch now," Mickey replied.

I called security back and gave these instructions: "Take Mickey with you to the lunchroom. He'll point out his friend who's limping, and you take them both to the Nurse's office. Drop off the limper and you escort Mickey back here. Got it? Good-bye, and don't lose anybody."

I then called the Nurse's office to expect a patient and do what was necessary. I waited with the A.P. until the guard returned with Mickey. When Mickey was seated I started my harangue. With my right thumb and index fingers right under his nose I began. "Do you know how close you came to becoming our newest felon in the great State of New York, young man?" I said. "*This far.*" I was flexing my fingers for effect. "Do you know the name of the crime you committed because you thought you were helping your friend? Take a wild guess!"

"What crime are you talking about?" he asked.

"My friend, the crime you committed is called robbery and in the state of New York, it is a felony punishable by at least 4–7 years in prison if you were tried as an adult. You are 16, aren't you?"

"Yeah. But, I didn't use no gun or nothing."

"In the case of robbery, you don't have to have a gun. You have fists, don't you? You forcibly grabbed that cane, and that man was incapable of defending himself. It's what is called mugging. You are a mugger!"

"I ain't no mugger! I was only trying to help my friend," he protested.

"And, the professional muggers you read about in the papers were only trying to support their drug habit, or buy the baby new shoes," I shot back. "The reason is not important. The crime is a fact, and if that crippled veteran, who limped his way out of here, wanted to press charges, there wouldn't be a jury in America that wouldn't have nailed your hide! You are one lucky dude, dude."

Mickey just sat there. I wanted it to sink in. The A.P. nodded his approval, and left the room.

The ring of the telephone interrupted the silence. It was the nurse. She had spoken to a parent and someone was coming up to get the injured student. Mickey just continued to sit there, lost in his thoughts. I finished by saying, "Mickey, I have to keep this incident on file for the record. God forbid if that vet comes back and wants to press charges, I have to be ready for him and the police, who will come to investigate. For the moment, just reflect on what you did, and go and sin no more. One important lesson should remain with you forever, and that's the old saying that the end never justifies the means. Remember that!"

With young people, they get mixed up so easily because they can never believe that their reasoning is not flawed. "It felt good for the moment," or, "I thought it was the right thing to do at the time." They never look in their rear view mirror to see what is in their wake. It's just too easy to always look straight ahead, and being restricted with blinders, the horizon appears to be unencumbered. They need to turn around once in a while!

There would be times when I just sat my desk mulling over the farcical incidents that involved the Nestors or the Mickeys and I wanted to be the fly on the wall to witness their actions after they left my office. Did it do any good? Did they learn anything? Were the values all gone, and were they just pulling my chain to keep me in my ignorance? Was I wasting my breath?

It was just in such a moment of reflection when I was rudely interrupted by an art teacher who stormed into my office, screaming, "You have to come up to my room at once! There's a boy sitting at his desk with an axe in his lap. *Right now!*" As she was demanding my presence to her room, she kept jabbing the air with her index finger pointed towards the ceiling to stress the gravity of the situation.

A kid with an axe? This I have to see!

Sure enough, when I reached the room and passed the kid's desk, there he was, drawing a figure. On his lap was a paper bag, and protruding from said bag, the unmistakable handle of an axe!

I ventured down one aisle, and proceeded up another until I came upon the rear of his desk. Then I bent over to his ear and whispered that I wanted to see him outside the room for a moment. All the while, I quietly slipped my hand over to the brown bag, picked it up and, using the contents as bait, lured my "catch" out of the room. There was no screaming, no hysteria, no confrontation—and no one got hurt. With the axe in my possession, the class and the teacher were out of harm's way. I escorted the young man down to my office. We did not stop at "Go" and we certainly did not collect "two hundred dollars."

As he sat down, I wrote out a receipt for "one green-handled axe" and gave it to him. He appeared startled. "What's this for?" he asked.

"Very simple, Wesley. I have in my custody one axe and you have one receipt describing the property that I just confiscated—a perfectly legal transaction. It will stand up in any court of law."

He sat there, stunned.

"Now, to the matter at hand. Why would you bring an axe to a school of fashion? This school does not have a wood-shop class; we don't make furniture and we certainly don't have any lumberjacks that I know of. Why the axe?"

Wesley quickly picked up on my cynicism; he smiled and said that the girls were teasing him.

"All the girls, or just one in particular?" I asked.

"It's this one called Doreen. She's always got something to say. I told her to stop, but, no, she keeps talking trash, so I got mad and told her to stop or I would give her a fat lip. So, yesterday, she had her boyfriend come to me at lunchtime, and he said that if I touched Doreen, he would kick my ass."

"And you brought the axe in to even the odds?" I finished.

"That's right!" he said, raising his voice. "They were

going to mess with me, so I decided to mess with them. First she would get it, then I would get him and mess him outside."

"You know," I said, pointing to the axe, "you certainly could mess someone with that, and that's called 'murder' or 'attempted murder'. You could go to prison for a long time for that. Is it worth it?"

Wesley was in a snit. "Yes, it would be worth it, but now I can't do nothing. You got my axe!"

"Yes, Wesley, but I can do something. As of today, you are suspended from school for five days, until your parents come for a Principal's Hearing, which I will schedule. Your 'messing days' are over!"

I then called in security and we all went upstairs to make it official. We had our hearing, and to this day, I still have the axe, as a souvenir. It's a Boy Scout Axe!

Every day is New Year's Eve.

Fourteen

I Should Have Stayed Home!

There were times when I was involved in "school things" that were really not part of my job description. The Dean's job was enormous. I mean, there were the time-consuming "investigations," interviews of both students and parents; "hallway interviews" of teachers (when they were available); principal and assistant principal conferences, and write-ups of EVERYTHING! So, to say that I was "busy" was an understatement when Mr. B. called me to come to his office, pronto!

What was this emergency?

As I walked into the Principal's inner office, an exasperated Mr. B. and a sobbing student greeted me. "Take her to your office and see if you can make sense of her story," he requested, as he pointed to the door with his right hand. "Now!"

I took the young lady to the elevators and I pushed the button. As we rode down, she never looked up and she never stopped sobbing. I wanted to speak with her in the privacy of my office, so I waved everybody out, closed the door, and asked her, "Why are you so unhappy?"

"It's my science class," she began. "I don't understand what my science teacher is saying."

"Who's your science teacher?" I asked.

"It's Mr. L. You know, he teaches biology," she added.

The name was not familiar, so I asked, "Is he new?"

"Yes, yes," she said. "He took over Mr. J.'s classes when he retired."

"Oh," I said, "but from what you've told me up to now, I still don't see this as a Dean's Office matter. Maybe you should take this up with the chairman of the science department?"

"I did," she replied. "I told him everything. He told me to meet him in the Principal's office this morning and repeat everything to the Principal. But, he must be late or something, and the Principal told me to go ahead without him. I told Mr. B. the same thing, and that's when he called you!" She started to cry again.

Just at that moment, there was a rap on my door, and in walked the department chairman. "I told you to wait for me," he said, as he pointed to the girl.

"I did!" the young lady shot back, "but Mr. B. said he was very busy this morning, and ordered me to start without you."

"It would be nice if someone would let me in on all of this; Mr. B. just dropped this mess in my lap," I said with a little sarcasm.

"O.K., O.K.," Mr. D began. "Vanessa came to me last Friday and said that Mr. L., who was starting a new unit in Bio, was saying things she couldn't understand. She gave me her notebook, and I tried to see if I could help her understand the new terms. I couldn't make out what she had written."

And, all of a sudden, Vanessa blurted out, ". . . and I'm not going to Virginia!"

"Who said that?" we both asked at once.

"I don't care if he fails me, I ain't going!" she added.

"What the heck are you talking about?" I yelled. I could see that Mr. D. was really concerned and motioned me to step outside the office. We left Vanessa, hunched over in the chair, and we talked in the hallway, right outside my door.

"Bill, what is going on?" I asked.

"I really don't know, John," he answered. "This Mr. L. was transferred into the department from another school with good recommendations. You know how hard it is to find a good science teacher, so I grabbed him. I haven't had time for a full classroom observation, but I dropped in a couple of times unannounced, and I liked what I saw. All this," he said as he pointed to my door, "all this is new to me. But, what disturbed me was what the kid said to me in my office and what was in her notes, and that was the report by Dr. Kinsey. Now Kinsey is not in the science curriculum that I know of! That's why I told her to wait in the Principal's office."

"The Kinsey Report?" I said. "Holy Cow!"

Just then, my phone rang. I answered it. It was Mr. B. He wanted to know if Bill was with me, and if the girl was still in my office.

"Sure they are, Mr. B." I replied.

"Good, then all of you come here now," he barked.

"But, Mr. B." I began, "this is not discipline-related and I think . . . "

"All of you, *now!*"

We all took our places in the Principal's office but I remained standing. "Now, young lady, what's this all about? Start from the beginning," Mr. B. demanded.

She repeated everything again, pointed to her notebook several times, and indicating the direction of the chairman, she again repeated her statement about "not going to Virginia."

"Virginia? What about Virginia? Bill, fill us in,

O.K.?" The Principal was really annoyed.

I asked Mr. B. if it was acceptable for the young lady to remain in the waiting room and offered to wait with her. He said "Fine," but then added, "No. I want you here. We could use you."

As I returned, Bill was just mentioning *The Kinsey Report.*

"Jesus H. Christ!" screamed Mr. B. *"The Kinsey Report!* What the hell is going on in this school? Bill, I'm directing you to get a hold of Mr. L.'s ass and his lesson plans and find out what this shit-head is doing! John, I want you to interview a few kids out of this science class and see if you can make sense of what has been going on in this unit. Hop to it!" Then he added, "John, find out about Virginia!"

Inside of two days, we had everything, including Virginia.

At the appointed hour, Bill and I journeyed into Mr. B.'s office—sans Vanessa. "It's the unit on reproduction," began Bill. "The son-of-a-bitch has been on this unit for 3 weeks! Three whole weeks, and he's nowhere near finished with it! At most, one week; not *three!"*

"So, what about *The Kinsey Report,* the steel something or other, and Virginia?" Mr. B. yelled back.

This was when Bill and I lost it. We both began to laugh so hard, we couldn't get anything out intelligibly. The more we tried to explain, the more we laughed. Mr. B. attempted to laugh, too, but he was showing frustration. All he got was bits and pieces. Finally he ordered, "Hey, you two. I'm not paying you to be comedians. I want the whole story, right now!"

"It's not Virginia. It's *vagina!* Mr. L. told the class that they could heighten their sexual pleasure by putting ball bearings in their *vagina!* Not Virginia!" Bill screamed out.

Now we were gasping for air. Mr. B. just sat there and kept repeating, "Where do they come from? The bottom of the barrel?"

Then Mr. B. turned to stone. Bill and I quickly composed ourselves. Here it came!

"Bill, I want that bastard in this office in the next thirty minutes. Now! He is going to explain to me how this garbage is high school material. Now, Bill. *Now!"*

I waited in the outer office. Mr. B. was not a man to fool around with in matters of morality, educational accountability or professional ethics. Mr. L. was in a lot of trouble.

About fifteen minutes later, I saw Bill and a fortyish-year-old man walk past me. As the chairman was about to close the door, I could hear Mr. B. yell, "I want Mr. Manicone in here as well!"

We all sat around a conference table. It was big. I always admired it. Mr. B. sat at one end and the accused, Mr. L., at the other. Bill and I sat opposite each other.

Mr. B. began, "Mr. L., I'm not going to beat about the bush. I . . ."

Mr. L. interrupted, "What's going on? Did I do something wrong? I didn't do anything wrong!"

"If you would just wait a while longer, I'll tell you why we are here," Mr. B. continued.

"Are these your lesson plans?" Mr. B. asked.

Mr. L. nodded, "Yes, they are my lesson plans. We are on the new unit, Reproduction. Yes. But, I didn't do anything wrong."

"Wait a minute, Mr. L. We're just getting some background information, O.K.?"

Mr. B. asked, "Now, how long have you been on this

Reproduction Unit?"

"Oh, a couple of weeks, but it might have gone a week longer, I think. I'm almost through with it. I didn't do anything wrong." Mr. L. insisted.

"Isn't this unit supposed to be only one week in duration?" Mr. B. asked as he leaned over the table, looking Mr. L. right in the eye.

"Well, I added a few things to make it more interesting, but I didn't do anything wrong," Mr. L. said. I noted that he was smiling throughout the questioning, never losing his composure.

"Well, what about this *Kinsey Report*? Is this what you would call 'making it interesting'?" Mr. B. said, as he started to raise his voice.

"*The Kinsey Report* is factual and responsible reporting," said Mr. L., still smiling. "I did nothing wrong." Then he added, "*The Kinsey Report* is world famous and accepted scientific data, and . . ."

"I'm not interested in *The Kinsey Report,* Mr. L.—it's all these other things. Mr. Manicone, give me those statements by his students about ball bearings, oral sex and 'other interesting' practices discussed in your class, Mr. L." Mr. B. continued sarcastically, as he flipped through the sheets of paper I had given him. "What about these notes, Mr. L.?"

"I did nothing wrong!" Mr. L. repeated. "Where's the crime?"

"The crime?" repeated Mr. B. "The only crime that was committed here was that we hired you!" he shouted as he stood up, flushed with anger. "Where do you come off discussing these adult matters with our students? Who gave you that authority?" he yelled.

Mr. L. just sat there, composed as ever, and said, "You would be surprised to learn what our students already know and don't know. It's my job to instruct them—and anyway, what crime did I commit? I didn't do anything wrong," he said.

"Mr. Manicone," Mr. B. said, "escort the waiting young lady back to her regular assigned class. She's in the other conference room. We won't need her at this time, and you are free to go about your business; Mr. D. and I will finish up here. Thank you."

I never got to see the axe fall, but I did get to hear about Mr. L.'s "obituary." It seems that as soon as I left, Mr. B. really tore into the science teacher. Without calling him any names, he mentioned how unprofessional Mr. L.'s conduct was, how he was derelict in not clearing these "additions" to his lessons without chairman approval, and how lucky Mr. L. was that he didn't face a lawsuit or two from any one of the many parents who disapproved of this material. Mr. B. reminded Mr. L. that since he was not a regular teacher, but only a regular substitute teacher, he did not enjoy the privileges of the former. The principal fired him on the spot and instructed Mr. D. to see that he was escorted out of the building by Security.

Believe it or not, I was told, that at every possible junction, Mr. L. continued to remain poised and self-confident, and constantly defended himself with the phrases, "What crime did I commit?" or "I didn't do anything wrong!"

I have to tell you that we laughed about this one for years. The girl had written in her notes about placing "her ball bearings" or "steel balls" or "steel bells in Virginia." We thought that Mr. L. was really teaching more about metallurgy than about reproduction. The school was never hit with a lawsuit and Mr. L. was seen no more. However, science teachers, good science teachers, are still hard to find. Ask Mr. D.! So what did Mr. B. tell me to do? "Go back to your duties." My day was filled with "duties" and, like I said before, many of them were in that gray area, like this little gem.

A fairly attractive freshman student came into my office with a problem. She didn't know who to speak to and thought that I could be of help. "What is your problem, little girl? This is the office where we store all of them, big and small," I teased.

"Well, it's this man," she began. "I noticed him down in the subway, always looking at me."

"In the morning or in the afternoon?' I asked.

"Well, he's always there when I leave here, and he's already on the platform at 23rd Street, going downtown. I live in Brooklyn," she added.

"O.K." I said. "Did this man start watching you back in September, or did this 'watching' start recently?"

"Oh no, it started about a week or so ago," she replied. "But now, he came up to talk to me yesterday. He said he was an undercover cop or something for the Transit Authority. He showed me a badge and everything," she said confidently. "I said 'Wow,' and then he took the train with me, but he got off at West 4th because he was working on another case."

"So, you think that he's a phony or something?" I said.

"No," she replied, "but before he left the train, he said he would be waiting for me again at the 23rd Street stop. He said I could be working with him on this other case. Should I help him or not? I'm only fourteen."

"Wait a minute!" I shot back. "You don't do anything with anybody unless you get your parents involved. By the way, did you get this cop's name or badge number?" I asked as I grabbed a piece of paper. "I want your name, and your parents' names and phone number, so that every thing is on the up and up."

She wrote our her name, "Blanca T." with her parents' names and phone number. Then she said, "I spoke to my mother, and she told me to speak to someone in school. What should I do?"

"First, did this guy give you a name of a badge number?" I asked again.

"He said only his first name, 'Ramon'. But, he flashed his badge so quickly, I didn't see any number, but I think it was gold," she replied.

The more I listened, the more I knew this was a phony. I was going to call the Transit Authority anyway to find out if they had any men assigned to the 23rd Street stop at Eighth Avenue, just to make sure.

"O.K., Blanca," I told her. "You take the same walk to the train like you always do, the same platform. Everything like before, with one exception. You go on the platform with some girl friends. You do not go alone! Do you understand? *Not alone.* If you can't find somebody, stop by the office, and I'll get all the girls you want! Do you understand? Say 'Yes, I understand,'" I told her.

"I understand," she repeated.

"Now, the next part. When you see him, if you should see him, let him do the talking, but under no circumstance, you do not leave the group of girls you came down with. He might want to talk to you in private, take a step or two, but no more than that. See what he wants you to do. O.K.?"

"O.K." she said. "Don't worry, you gave me some very good advice, Mr. Manicone. I'll tell you what happened tomorrow. O.K.?"

"You are a very brave girl. But remember, you never

leave the group and you never, under any circumstances, go with him anywhere," I warned.

"My mother said the same thing!" she replied, and then she left.

I called her home, no answer.

I called the Transit Authority and they said they would check and get back to me. I have to tell you that my heart was heavy all that afternoon and evening. Did I do the right thing, sending the kid to that platform? Had I led myself to believe that Blanca was "street smart" enough to avoid trouble with this character, 'Ramon'? Should I have sent my aide, Roberta, down to the station just to be on the safe side? And am I authorized to send a school aide to perform a non-school task?

All I did know was that I could not send the City police to what appeared to be a Transit police problem. But, that still was all conjecture. What if Ramon was legit? Anything was possible. I had to wait.

The next morning I was on the phone talking to a Transit Police lieutenant about this undercover situation at 23rd Street. My heart dropped out of my mouth when he informed me that no such operation was taking place. They had no 'Ramon' working that detail, and anyway that the Transit Authority would never use a 14-year-old for anything. The Transit Department had its own departmental young-looking people for that situation. The lieutenant said that he was sending over two men from his department to ferret out this impostor. He asked me if that was possible on such short notice. As we were talking, Blanca rushed into my office all out of breath.

"Mr. Manicone, you'll never believe what happened!" she gasped.

I held up my index finger and indicated that she sit down quickly as I continued the conversation.

"Dean, my people will be in your office before lunch, O.K.? You're on 24th Street, right?" he asked.

"Officer, the young girl in question just popped in this second. Let me talk with her first and get back to you in ten minutes or so," I suggested.

"Sure, sure," he replied. "The more information we can get, the easier it will be for us to nab this guy, maybe as early as this afternoon, Dean. O.K.?"

As I hung up, I let out a sigh of relief. Turning toward Blanca, I asked, "So, what happened?"

"Well, I went down to the platform with a couple of girls, like you told me," she started, "and, he was waiting on the downtown side just like before. I pretended I was busy talking with the girls, and he walked up to us real casual like. 'Who're your friends?' he asked me. 'Oh,' I said, 'Friends of mine. We have to study for a big test tomorrow. They're coming home with me.' I saw he was annoyed!"

"So, what happened next?" I prompted.

"You know, Mr. Manicone, there's no test. I made that all up!" she said, beaming. I could see that Blanca was enjoying this tremendously. "Then, he goes, 'I got to talk to you alone!' 'I can't,' I said. 'This test is very important!'

"He takes my arm and we move about a couple of feet away from the pole, and he says, 'I need you in this case I'm working on!' 'What do you want me to do,' I ask him? He says, 'I want you to pretend that you're my girlfriend, and we pretend to hug and neck while I keep my eye on this guy I'm following!'

" 'What,' I said, 'on the platform here, here in front of all these kids?'

" 'No,' he said. 'No, on the train. I'm following this guy who's goosing girls on the train!'

"So, I go and say, 'Is this guy here right now on the platform?"

"No, no. He's always on the train you take. I want to nail him in the act. We have to look like a real boyfriend and girlfriend to fool him. We might have to take this train all week before I catch him.'

"I must of looked at him real weird-like, but then the train started to come into the station and he started to walk away, saying, 'I'll see you tomorrow to fill you in. And, no girl friends! O.K.?'"

"Wow," I said. "What a load of nonsense! You didn't believe him, did you?" I asked.

"Are you kidding, Mr. Manicone? I saw him up close this time. He's too young to be a cop. He probably goes to high school, or he's a drop-out. He's no cop," she answered.

"O.K.," I said. "Now, I have things to tell you. I just got off the phone with the Transit Authority, and guess what? You are right. Ramon's no cop. He's a phony. And, they're sending over a couple of men here today to nail this guy. I need to speak to your mother. Where is she right now?" I asked.

"She's probably at the store with my father. Here's the number."

I called the parents and told them what had transpired. They were so supportive and said whatever I decided was all right with them. About an hour later, two Transit Officers in civilian dress came into my office. One looked German or Irish and the other was Hispanic. The non-Hispanic did all the talking, while the other officer just stood by my desk and took everything in.

"You're the Dean, right?" he began. "I'm Officer Dunn and this is Officer Cruz. Here are our shields." He held his out proudly, as did his partner. "We want to get this creep, so if you got anything we can use, we would really appreciate it. Also, if we can talk to the girl, it would be very helpful in making the collar!"

I asked both officers to sit down while I sent for Blanca. We waited and they listened very intently while I related what had been told to me. Officer Cruz took out his pad as Blanca showed up.

"Is this the girl?" Dunn asked.

I nodded. "Blanca, these are Officers Cruz and Dunn. They want to speak to you about 'Ramon'. O.K.?"

"I understand," she said.

Officer Dunn took a chair and sat right next to the girl, never taking his eyes from her face. Meanwhile, Officer Cruz stood directly over her chair and scribbled into his notepad from time to time. "Alright, Blanca, give us a description of this guy first. Is he fat, short, tall? Anything you can remember, O.K.?"

Blanca gave a general description of the suspect. He wasn't tall or fat. He was "average." He was Spanish, shorter than Dunn's partner. He wore jeans and his shirts were always dark. Also, she remembered, he always wore a black beret and had some facial hair.

"When you saw him close up yesterday, did he carry a holster, or a knife holder on his belt? It's important," added Dunn.

"I saw nothing like that," she replied. For the first time, I noticed that Blanca was becoming uneasy, and kept looking at me for help. Maybe she realized, also for the first time, this was not TV.

"It's O.K.," I reassured her.

Then Dunn motioned for me to step outside while Cruz stayed with the girl.

"We need her to come with us to the station and

finger this shit. She won't be in any danger, I promise you."

"Well, Officer Dunn, you should reassure her. Her parents said that if I thought it was O.K., it was all right with them as well."

We returned to the office and both officers promised and reassured Blanca that she would never be in any danger. They told us both that they had to arrange some back-up on both platforms and have everything ready when Blanca walked to the train station. She was to pretend that she was going home as normally, and when the suspect approached her, they would collar Ramon and no one would even notice that an arrest had taken place. Blanca left my office after I spoke to her parents again and told them what was decided. They reluctantly consented. It was on!

At 2:45 P.M. that afternoon, Ramon's career in the Transit Authority came to an abrupt halt. He was in custody and I thought it was all over. It wasn't. Officers Dunn and Cruz came back to my office. There was a small detail to complete. It was called "identifying the suspect at a police line-up," at transit headquarters at the Union Square station. Oh, my God!

I was on the horn to the parents again and told them that a positive ID at a police line-up was required.

"Will Blanca be in any danger?" they asked.

I gave them my word that I would be with Blanca the whole way and no harm would come to their girl. Again they reluctantly agreed.

The next afternoon, Blanca and I were sitting at the transit headquarters. We waited and we waited. Then we waited some more. The lieutenant I spoke with earlier reassured us that the line-up was just moments away. Meanwhile, he regaled us with the items that Ramon had in his possession, such as his phony badge, a "doctored" Transit ID card, and a small penknife.

"What's the problem?" I finally asked after waiting about 2 hours on a hard bench. I could see that with every passing half hour, Blanca was getting more and more nervous, like someone visiting a dentist for root canal work.

"Dean, I'm sorry about this delay," the lieutenant said, "but we're having a hell of a time getting the right sunglasses. And, the beret wasn't black, it was a dark maroon!" he added.

"What the hell are you saying?" I asked. "What sunglasses, and what about the color of the beret?"

"Don't you see," he said, very patiently. "When we set the line-up in place, all the 'suspects' must be wearing as close to what the real suspect was wearing when he was collared. Otherwise, the identification is not objective enough for legal counsel and cannot be used as evidence. Now we had no problem with the facial hairs, or the dark shirt and jeans. But those sunglasses have a greenish tint to them and it took us almost an hour to get the right colored beret."

"My God, what an ordeal this is. All this just to please the A.C.L.U." I yelled.

"Hey, Dean—I didn't make the rules. We can't parade people in a line-up if one stands out. They must all look exactly the same, as is humanly possible, or no go. That's the law."

We waited another twenty minutes or so. We could hear the trains roaring into the station with more and more frequency. The rush hour was in earnest. At long last, the lieutenant motioned us into this room.

He said, "Now, remember, you can see *them*, but

210

they cannot, I repeat, they cannot see *you*. Do you understand? It's dark in the viewing room at first, but your eyes will get accustomed very quickly. Then, at a signal, we open the shade and you will see the room where we conduct the line-up. The suspects will march in from the left, stop and face forward. Did you get all of that?" he asked.

We both nodded. Blanca was shaking.

"Please don't be nervous, Blanca. I'll be with you every step of the way. You are one heck of a good little soldier. You are very brave," I confidently told her. With that, we went in. It was dark!

As we faced this long glass panel, I held Blanca's trembling hand. The shade zipped opened, and within several seconds, the men marched into the room. They stopped at a certain point, and then turned to their right.

"My God, they all looked exactly the same!" I said to myself. In front of us were seven or eight Latin types, wearing shades, dark berets; and all had facial hair, one description or another.

She'll never I.D. anybody! I thought.

"It's number three!" Blanca shouted. "Number three!"

All I could see was trying to identify one Santa from another and there was this kid pointing to the real one. "Are you sure?" I asked quietly.

"Yes, yes, it's him. Number three!" she repeated.

"That's all. We're through, and again, we're sorry for the delay, but it couldn't be avoided. Thank you again," said the lieutenant, and we left.

That afternoon, as I headed home, I reflected on some weighty subjects. I was impressed—I was truly impressed with the law and with a brave young girl. Lessons are learned all the time, but the ones that are

211

most meaningful are those by people who place trust in others. That young lady trusted the system and me. I hope she never stops believing in Santa.

Fifteen

It's Just a Bad Dream

Back in the late sixties, when I had been at Fashion just a couple of years, a very close friend of our chairman joined the department. He was about sixty and a veteran of World War II. I learned many instructional things from Walter, not only relating to the classroom in particular, but about the world in general. Walter had nothing to prove, and his worldly experiences were very helpful when I went on to the Dean's office. However, Walter was not immune from learning a thing or two from our students, as this little slice of pedagogical life illustrates.

Walter was teaching a freshman class in World Geography I at the time. He was attempting to differentiate the various disciplines within the curriculum in areas such as geology, topography, paleontology, and the like, as a basic understanding to the subject. He came from a business background, so the going was somewhat difficult for him. He finally got to the point where he was leading a discussion on the three basic elements of nature: animal, mineral and plant life. "Everything on this planet must belong to one of these groups. There is no exception!" he declared.

"*Everything?*" some kids yelled out. "Including people?"

"Yes," said Walter, "even people. People are classified as animals."

"I'm no animal," yelled a student from the front row.

"No?" answered Walter. "Then, there are only two things left. Either you're mineral or a vegetable. Take your pick!"

The student reflected on the choices, and then, shooting her hand into the air, exclaimed, "I know! I know! I'm a vegetable!"

I too, although a veteran of the U.S. Army (and combat duty at J.H.S. 22M), had many things to learn from our dear students! In the early seventies, the drug problem was really serious. The Board of Education had to admit to it by mandating a new category on the budget: Drug Coordinator. This person and I worked on the problem almost daily. Somebody, or something, was always tying the use and the possession of drugs to a disruption in class or poor schoolwork.

Many times, we came up empty after weeks of attempting to find the offending student in possession of the drug or drug paraphernalia. These kids were not easy to nail down, either through a convenient, constant absence or stony silence. Don't rat out your friends! But then again, we were lucky sometimes, like in the case of Jimmy.

Barbara, the drug coordinator, was given some real hot stuff on Jimmy. He was in school, in class and he was high. "I've been after this kid a long time, John. Get him now! He's in his trade class right now!" she pleaded.

Always ready to help a damsel in distress, I sent Roberta, my aide, up to the room with Security just in case, to bring Jimmy down and see what would develop. A few minutes later, we had our suspect; somewhat edgy, nose running and couldn't sit still for a second. I cleared the room so that only Barbara and I would interview our client.

"So, Jimmy, how are you doing?" I began. "What's shaking?"

Nothing. All Jimmy could do was wipe his nose repeatedly and slump down and back up again in his chair. He kept twitching one leg or another. He was obviously very uncomfortable.

Now Barbara tried. "So, Jimmy, how are you doing in trade? Are you passing?"

"It's O.K.," he said, as he attempted to straighten himself in the wooden chair. "I'm doing O.K."

"Really?" Barbara replied. "Then, this first marking period, with all these failing grades, must be a mistake!"

"I *almost* passed!" he replied.

"Fifty is not 'almost passing' in this school," Barbara shot back. "You need to be closer to 65 to be 'almost passing', brother!"

"The work's hard, man," he said, defensively. At least the coordinator had Jimmy talking, so I stayed on the same street.

"Jimmy, what about these other grades? 40 in English, 55 in Social Studies—and so forth and so on? Hm?"

"Hey, this stuff is harder than last year! I'm *trying*. Really, I'm trying!"

Looking right into his face, Barbara wagged her finger and said, "Don't give us that crap, 'you're trying'. You did it last year. You passed everything. This year, everything's in the toilet! Can you tell us why?"

"Hey, get off my back! You sound just like my mother! I told you, the work is harder now!"

"Other people are passing their classes," I chimed in. "If your logic was correct, everybody would be failing—and that is not happening. Our system takes all that into account; we assign the more difficult work as you mature. Jimmy, either you're not maturing, or

215

you're lying. Which is it?"

He sat there, fidgety as ever, and continued to wipe his nose.

"Do you have a cold?" Barbara asked.

"No, er, yes," he replied.

"Well, which is it?" she asked. "You either have a cold or you don't."

"I think I have a cold," he replied, straightening himself again for the umpteenth time.

"Are you taking anything for it?" she inquired, "like Vicks, or Bayer's, or pills?"

"Yeah, yeah, pills," he said.

"May I see what you're taking?" Barbara pushed.

"I don't have them with me," he said, squirming in his chair.

While we were grilling Jimmy, Roberta signaled to me to step outside for a minute. There, she told me that Jimmy had passed something to a friend as they exited the trade room. I returned and shouted, "Let's cut all this crap, right now! Either he has a cold, or he doesn't! Either he's taking something, or he left it home! Which is it, Jimmy? What did you pass to your friend, Jimmy? Some nose drops? Huh? Huh?"

"I'll bet he gave those pills to Hector! Can Roberta go up and get Hector?" asked Barbara.

"Sure, sure!" I said, "but don't bet the ranch that Hector is still up there!"

Roberta came back empty-handed.

"That's it, Barbara! What do you want to do with him? Odyssey House or the hospital? Pick your poison!"

"I ain't going to no hospital!" screamed Jimmy, as he tried to get out of his chair.

"My friend," I said, as I placed my hand on his shoulder, "that's not your decision to make! She is calling the play!" as I pointed to Barbara.

The Drug Coordinator was wasting no time. She was already on the phone, talking to Jimmy's mother. A couple of "yeses," a few "nos," and Barbara ended the conversation with a "thank you." Then she called Odyssey House. Exact conversation, brief and with the same ending. I asked Roberta to get Security to hail us a cab. Jimmy never stopped protesting, "No way. You can't do this to me! I got my rights!"

While we headed uptown, he still screamed, "I'm getting a lawyer! You can't do this to me!"

For just a second, I started to doubt my decision. Was I too premature? Had Barbara really done her homework? What the hell was my neck doing out on this limb? I'm the ranking man here, and I'll have to do all the explaining if the spit hits the fan. I had my doubts as we walked into Odyssey House.

I said, sotto voce, "Barbara, I hope you know what you're doing?"

"Relax. I got this one in the bag!"

The three of us walked into a room crammed with books, stuffed furniture and wall decorations. Behind a desk loaded with magazines and stacks of folders six inches high sat a bearded gentleman busily engaged in a phone conversation. With his right index finger, he motioned to us to sit down, and kept nodding and pointing all the while he was talking. He got up from his chair and, clearing off some papers and magazines with one hand, he signaled with the phone in the other hand for us to sit down. He never took his eyes off Jimmy, and he never stopped talking. I observed that he wore a thick set of brown beads around his neck that contrasted vividly against his black and white beard. The phone conversation lasted about ten minutes. Then, hanging up the phone, he walked smartly over to Jimmy and said, "Son, you've tried Ludes, you're currently on Red Devils and some Bennies!"

I thought he read it right off Jimmy's shirt!

Jimmy started to protest by attempting to stand, by posturing, by arm movements, and yelling out, "Man, you're crazy! You're . . . "

The kid never got to finish the second sentence. The bearded gentleman slammed Jimmy back into the stuffed chair, and retorted, "Hey, kid, a pothead can't fool an old ex-pothead! I swiped everything from the toaster to my old lady's shorts, but I never had to wipe my nose like you've been doing since you sat there. Now shut up and listen! Hey, Mark!" he called out to the next room. "Take this Twinkie to Paul and get him ready for his initiation. I know Barbara here has a folder chocked with good information."

After Jimmy and Mark left the room, I asked, "How were you so certain?"

"Should we let him in on my little secret, Babs?" replied the *charge d'affaires.* "When I saw you coming up the walk, I picked up my phone and called 'Dial-a-Prayer' and pretended to have a lengthy and engaging conversation with some important cat. Meanwhile, I'm eyeballing your student. Get it?"

He never stopped stroking his beard all the while he gleefully outlined his prescription for success. I perceived those thick beads around his neck like trophies to his success.

"So," he continued, "when I know whether your boy is on uppers or downers, I lay him out. Tell him what he's using, not the other way around! I ain't got time to dance and weave for hours with 40 Questions. Once I know, his counselor, Paul, will know, and then we start on him today! Jimmy will be on the road of rehabilitation this very afternoon. Right, Babs?" (Barbara hated to be called Babs!)

After Barbara finished turning over all the necessary folders on Jimmy, we left. I was in the company of a genius! And that doesn't happen everyday. And, true to his word, the perceptive head honcho went one step further. He permitted us to see his "graduates" during one of our faculty conferences, about two or three months later. There they were, some six or seven of these ex-junkies sitting at a panel table in front of about 100 teachers and administrators, telling us about their experiences before and after treatment. They told us about taking out the garbage, going to the supermarket to do the weekly shopping, cleaning and washing the dishes, and taking responsibility for all those things they'd never done in their own homes. And, guess what they entrusted Jimmy to do? There he sat, with his plastic disposable gloves on, looking like an intern, telling us that he was in charge of distributing aspirin to his comrades! In other words, the drug dispenser! How do you like that!

Several years ago, there was a commercial on TV promoting the Volkswagen, the little German supercar which always included remarkable, but true accounts about the car taken from police records, attesting to the desirability or reliability of the vehicle. The commercial always ended with the line, "We just can't make this stuff up!" Enough said.

In the same vein, I remember, one day, patrolling through the student cafeteria during lunchtime, looking for a particular individual. In the hustle and bustle of food service for six or seven hundred students at a time, the atmosphere was filled with activity of all sorts. Some students were yelling, some were moving from place to place in a hurry, and others, were actually eating. Caught up in all this hypertension, I distinctly heard my name being called out, "Mr. Manicone! Mr. Manicone! A girl is in trouble!"

Trying to avoid a large following of students tailing us, I gently grabbed the young girl's hand, and whispered, "Just lead the way!" I then closely followed her. We hurried to the other wing of the cafeteria, dodging and bobbing all the way. Near the window side, a rather large group of students had already formed around a youngster who was thrashing and writhing on the floor. The lunchroom teacher arrived there just as we showed up. It was obvious the girl was having a fit, probably an epileptic seizure. I immediately bent over the poor kid, and taking my wallet from my back pocket, I inserted it into her mouth. She bit on it hard. "Get the nurse, or a doctor!" I ordered.

"Already called down," said the lunchroom teacher. "She should be up here in a couple of minutes, if the elevator cooperates. I just was on the phone and the doctor is coming up, thank God!"

All we could do was wait. We attempted to keep the size of the crowd to a manageable level. A friend of the stricken victim was holding her hand, trying to comfort her. Again it was obvious that the girl, thrashing as she was, could hardly understand what was going on around her. I kept my eye on my wallet, just in case she was to affect a miraculous cure before the doctor appeared. Soon, we noticed some activity near the entrance of the lunchroom. The doctor was worming her way in the direction of the finger-pointers. "Over there! Over there!" they cried.

Our diminutive physician, known as "Doctor Doctor," sauntered in wearing her ever-present white lab coat, her hands buried deeply in her pockets, she strolled to her patient. The young girl had spit out the wallet and was screaming, rolling her eyes and writhing uncontrollably. The doctor leaned over the victim and said, in a raised tone, "Why are you yelling?"

"*Why are you yelling?*" I said to myself.

"Are you serious, Doctor?" I said aloud in complete disbelief. "This girl is having a fit! Can't you see that?"

Turning toward me, she said, "I have to see her chart. Take her down to the office so I can examine her." And with that, she turned on her heels, leaving the lunchroom and the poor creature still going through the last segment of her seizure. We were finally able to get the girl seated, and after a glass of water and a respectable period of time elapsed, several of us escorted her down to the nurse's office.

I couldn't make this stuff up!

When I started to write this memoir, I promised myself that I would tell as much as I could recall, warts and all. This next story is still painful to this day. It's about Nora W., a pretty black girl, about 15 years old, who wanted to be a fashion designer. She did fairly well as a freshmen, but in her second year, when she had to devote at least three periods a day to her major, she went downhill. First, she started failing her quizzes; her homework was erratic, she started to cut classes, and for the first time in her school life (that I knew of), she took home a failing report card. That was in October.

Her first Dean's referral came across my desk in early November. I interviewed the student, reviewed her cut classes and her poor grades. I referred her to her counselor, and when the second Dean's referral showed up, I believed some type of conference was necessary.

In mid-November, without the parents or the student, the guidance counselor and I held a brief meeting to discuss Nora's case in the Guidance Conference Room. Since I had only the two referrals to deal with, I thought that her counselor should handle the first parent interview; she could review the poor grades and counter-productive attitude demonstrated up to this point.

The counselor disagreed. She believed the problem was more serious than that. "Look at all this cutting!" she reminded me, and since the position of "cutting Dean" had been abolished a couple of terms back, it appeared that I was to hold the first parent conference, and I scheduled it before Thanksgiving.

Mrs. W. was a lovely woman. She and her daughter were almost like twins. During that conference, I mentioned the Attendance Card.

"Attendance Card?" she asked. "What's an Attendance Card?"

I explained to Mrs. W. and Nora how the card worked. It was the closest thing to a foolproof system we had ever developed. I would issue the card, weekly, every Monday morning. There were boxes already drawn on the card where the youngster would write in all her subject classes on the left, and the top columns indicated each of the five days of the week. At the end of each period, the subject teacher would initial his or her name and the youngster would go on to the next class and do the same. Each evening, the parent would sign the bottom of the column for that particular day to give witness that she had seen the card, and then I would countersign under the parent's signature each morning to validate that all the subject teacher's initials were genuine. The child could not attend class without the card. Duplicates were given out by me, and indicated as such, so that the parents would be aware that something had happened to the primary card. Mrs. W. loved it!

Nora was very attentive as I filled out her first card. She had lots of questions. I answered them carefully and to her satisfaction. She asked things like, "What if I leave home without the card and get a duplicate; do I go back to the first one again?" or "Do only Regular teachers sign the card? What about Subs? Do you recognize their signatures as well?" Or, "What if I get sick?" I explained each situation. The mother didn't miss a beat. She had taken out a pad, and was writing everything down.

Now, why couldn't all the parents I interviewed do the same thing? Mrs. W. and I were becoming fast friends. After the conference was over, Nora took her card, kissed her mother's cheek and went off to class. Both Mrs. W. and I were very satisfied with our little talk.

In the beginning, Nora was as good as gold. Her attendance and class work improved greatly during the first two weeks of December. Mrs. W. saw the card at night, and I checked it the following morning. The parent and I spoke several times by phone congratulating each other over the turn-around. I found out that Mrs. W., being a single parent, raising her only child, could relax somewhat now that a crisis with her teenager was averted.

Then, a small blemish appeared. On her third card, a teacher's initial didn't look kosher. When I questioned Nora about it that morning, she admitted that a sub had "forgotten" to sign the card, and rather than go back and locate the sub, Nora "signed off" for her. I told Nora that was a "no-no" and now I had to call Mom at work and tell her. Nora became upset for a moment, relented, and sat there, in my office, while I called Mrs. W. I later found out that the sub was really not certain that Nora had attended her class that day, but I didn't tell that to the parent. I gave Nora the benefit of the doubt, and let it go at that.

That Friday something similar happened, but I didn't pick it up until the following Monday. This time, it involved a three-period trade class. The signature was a definite forgery. When I confronted Nora that morning, she vehemently denied doing anything to the card. "I dropped the card in trade, and when I found it at the end of the session, it was already signed. I though the teacher had to sign it quickly because it was the beginning of lunch, and I ran out of the room," Nora explained. It wasn't the first time that a convenient "friend" signed for a teacher. I checked it out, and found that Nora was not in her trade class at all on Friday.

"Where could she have been?" asked Mrs. W. when I revealed all the doings to Mom.

"She probably was in the lunchroom, or sneaked out of the building," I said. "I don't know."

"I'll be up there tomorrow, Mr. Manicone. And, I'll bring Nora with me to tell you herself!"

A different Nora sat in my office that Tuesday morning. She wasn't eager to please, she didn't smile or sparkle, and she sat somewhat defiant and quite subdued. She admitted to Mom and me that she had cut class and sat all three periods in the lunchroom, changing her seat frequently so that she wouldn't get caught.

"Is that why I put clean clothes and shoes on you so that you can sit, smell, and watch people eat, what? For an hour and a half or two hours, Nora?" her mother pleaded.

Nora said she was sorry and that she could be trusted again. I wasn't so sure. She wasn't angry enough, she didn't want to transfer to her local high school as others had done in the past, and it appeared that she might be biding her time. I just couldn't put my finger on the problem, but there it was. Christmas was around the corner, and maybe the New Year would give Nora and her mother a second chance. If only she could show her mother some improvement on that second report card when it came out at the end of January . . .

Nora never gave her mother that gift, or even a little bit of relief. After the holidays, Nora was on her fourth or fifth card, and to my surprise, the phone was ringing as I entered my office that cold January morning. It wasn't even eight o'clock yet, and Mrs. W. was on the other end of the line. "Mr. Manicone, she did it again! This time, it's so obvious; I saw the forgery last night when I asked Nora for her Attendance Card. We'll be there about 10 o'clock. Is that alright with you?"

"Sure, sure!" I said. (What could I have said? "No?") I made some minor changes in my schedule, and waited for Nora and her mother.

Mrs. W. looked terrible. It seemed like Nora had given her the silent treatment all the way down from Upper Manhattan. She hardly glanced once or twice at her mom as Mrs. W. outlined all the hopes and dreams she had for her daughter. She brought up the struggle of her divorce and how difficult it was to raise a teenager "in this day and age" with all its temptations and problems. She went on about the sacrifices she made to give Nora a decent home—and on, and on, and on.

I realized that Mrs. W. had to voice her frustrations,

but being a stranger to the family on a personal level, I felt uncomfortable listening to this harangue; so at a convenient pause, I interrupted the discourse with, "Mrs. W., let's give it another try. O.K.?" She nodded approvingly, and I sent Nora back to class with a brand new Attendance Card.

A couple of mornings later, my phone rang again at 7:55 A.M. as I was removing my coat. It was a very subdued Mrs. W. on the line.

"Mr. Manicone," she began. "Nora is dead. She threw herself out the balcony window of my apartment early this morning. I thought she was getting ready for school."

I collapsed in my chair, holding the phone in one hand, and a scarf in the other. "Oh my God! Mrs. W., I'm so sorry. I'm so sorry," I heard myself say. "Do you know how it happened?"

"Oh, yes," she replied. "She jumped right in front of my eyes!"

"Dear God, no!" I stammered. "Did you two fight?"

"Not really," she said, almost automatically. "I went into her room, holding the Attendance Card to confront her about another irregularity, and she wasn't even dressed!" She paused, and then continued in a monotone. "She saw that I was holding the card."

She paused again. "Then, Nora walked into the living room, and she slid back the balcony window and said, 'Damn you, and damn Mr. Manicone!' and she jumped! Right in front of my eyes!"

"I'm so very sorry, Mrs. W. What can I say? I'm totally speechless!" I was ready to cry.

"I know you are, Mr. Manicone. You're a good man and you tried, but I've got to live with this for the rest of my life. There's nothing more to say. I have to take care of the arrangements. Goodbye."

"Goodbye," I repeated and sat there in the dark for some fifteen or twenty minutes until Roberta turned on the lights. "Oh!" she said. "You startled me!"

In my lifetime, I've had other terrible phone calls, but none have or will ever affect me like the one I got on that particular January morning. Ever.

Sixteen

Warm Up the Relief Pitcher!

I was either in my eighth or ninth year in the Dean's office when I experienced the worst act of violence that occurred at Fashion. We though we had seen it all, but that one day in March remained with me for a very long time. Basically, it was the end result of a fight between two seniors in the lunchroom—involving two girls.

I indicated earlier, that in order to feed nearly 2,000 students at lunch, we had to program three lunch periods within the school day, with the first seating at about 11:20 A.M. Usually, the first lunch period went by without too many hitches. For whatever reasons, it was during the second and the last period of lunch when Security or my office could be expected to call me. A substantial problem was the cutters. The addition of some fifty or eighty more people in an already crowded space reserved for the scheduled 700 assigned diners heightened the already prevailing tension. It was a serious dilemma.

The bell rang for the third period of lunch, around 12:50 P.M. I was in my office on the first floor doing what Deans are supposed to do—interviewing a student about a classroom infraction. I was just about to close the interview with my standard admonition when someone from Security literally burst into my office. "Mr. Manicone! Mr. Manicone! Emergency! Two kids in the lunchroom . . . they went crazy!"

I had learned from past experience that not all "emergencies" were really emergencies. Nine times out of ten, what was initially described as a "huge fight" later turned out to be nothing but a pushing and shoving incident. So, I tried not to be swayed by the hysterical Security person when I asked, as I rose from my chair, "O.K., O.K.! What happened?"

"Blood, everywhere! Two girls! I never saw such a fight!"

"Where are they now?" I yelled back. "Did anybody call the medical office?"

I attempted to leave with the Security person, but we didn't even reach the outer office when another Security guard appeared, escorting a girl toward my open door. The youngster was holding a blood-smeared hankie to her mouth, and she had blood all over her blouse.

I yelled at the escorting guard, "Why the hell are you taking her here? She has to go to the Nurse's office! Right now!" as I pointed in the direction of Room 343.

"We can't!" screamed the guard. "The other one is already in there! She will kill her!"

"Holy cow!" was the only thing I could say, as students and other Security started to mill around. "Take her into my office, and dismiss the student sitting at my desk," I ordered.

"How bad off is the other girl?" I asked of the first guard.

"Bad, Mr. Manicone. Really bad!"

"O.K., Henry," I said. "Do you know what happened? What started this?"

"Mr. Manicone, all I know is this: I was walking around my post outside the lunchroom, near the boys' bathroom. You know, near Room 421, opposite that open door of the lunchroom? It was real crowded and real noisy?"

"Yes, yes," I said, encouraging him to get to the point.

"Then I heard a terrible scream," he continued.

"Wait, Henry, wait," I said, interrupting him. I realized that the other guard was signaling to me to re-enter my office to see to the needs of the stricken student. The injured senior was seated on a stool facing the door of my office. To this day I've always wondered how that stool, typical of the type that are universally found in shop classes throughout our building, ever wound up in my office that day. Maybe it was brought in earlier that day by one of the assigned teachers who covered the Dean's office during the morning shift? I really can't explain it any other way, except it was in the office this particular day.

I returned into the office and asked Henry, the attending guard, "What's her name?"

Holding the student's program card, she said, "Tiffany Baker."

"Tiffany, can you tell me what happened?" I asked cautiously.

Still holding the bloodied hankie to her mouth, Tiffany could only shake her head from side to side, indicating either that she was unable to speak or that it was too painful for her to do so. So, I volunteered to help by pointing to Henry; I instructed Henry to continue with his description of the fight and told Tiffany to either shake her head for "no" or nod her head for "yes" as he told the story. "Do you understand, Tiffany?"

She nodded and Henry continued. "Well, Mr. Manicone, after I heard the scream, I ran into the lunchroom.

Boy, was it crowded! I looked around, and pulled out my walkie-talkie and called for backup."

Looking at Tiffany at first, my impression was that she appeared to be disinterested, because she was stealing glances out the office window while Henry spoke. But, looking at her again, she appeared dejected and restless, like someone who is about to hear a story for the second time.

The telephone rang. It was Frank, my security chief, who said, "Mr. Manicone, I'm here with the other girl in the Nurse's office. We called 911 and the ambulance is on its way!"

"Frank, stay there until they arrive. Then call me again as they walk through the door. Got it?" I ordered.

"Got it!" repeated Frank.

I turned toward Tiffany and, with the aid of the female guard, suggested, "Tiffany, I'm sure you'll be a lot more comfortable in a chair than on that stool. Please sit here," and we helped her sit at the other desk in my room.

"O.K., Henry—then what happened?" I asked the guard.

"The kids, the tables, the chairs—were flying every which way. A couple of assistants, I don't know their names, came from the other wing and we tried to get to this one and the other one. There was milk, and trays of food, all over the place, on the floor and everywhere. I almost slipped a couple of times trying to break them up!"

"I got the picture, Henry. It was a war zone! Right?"

"Right, a war zone, that's what it was. Gee!" Henry repeated and continued, "This one," pointing to Tiffany, "was on the bottom, and the other girl was on top of her. They were rolling and screaming, and each one of them was clawing and pulling hair and everything! I waited for the right moment," he added, "and with the help of the other teachers, we tried to pull them apart.

"When we managed to separate them, that's when I noticed all that blood! This one," still pointing at Tiffany, "had blood all over her face and blouse! The other girl had some blood on her, but not much, But, she was screaming and cursing to beat the band!"

At this moment my door flew open. Barbara, our Drug Coordinator, came charging in, demanding, "What happened? *What happened?*"

"Mrs. Miller, glad you could drop in," I said facetiously. "Is Tiffany one of yours?"

"Yes, she is!" she yelled back. "I want to know what happened here!"

As I looked over Barbara's shoulder toward the opened door, I could see quite a large group of students, and some teachers milling about. I picked up Henry's walkie-talkie and barked, "I need either S-4 or S-5 in my office, on the double! Ten-four!"

"S-5 responding; will be there in two minutes. Ten-four!"

"O.K., S-5. When you get here, I want you to police the area and clear out any students who do not belong on the first floor. Ten-four?" I shot back.

"That's a Ten-four," was the reply.

I closed my door and asked Mrs. Miller, who had first-aid training, to look at Tiffany. As Tiffany removed the red hanky, Barbara gave out a definite "Holy shit!"

"Let me see!" I said, and as I approached the injured senior, I thought the same thing. "Oh, my God!" I said, sotto voce. Tiffany had her mouth closed, *but we could see her bottom teeth*!

I ran over to the phone and called the Nurse's office.

"Frank, did the paramedics get there yet?" I yelled.

"No, Mr. Manicone. We're still waiting!"

"How's the other girl?" I asked. "And did anybody contact a parent?"

"She's holding her own. We got her in bed and S-4 is looking for her lip!"

"What?" I screamed. "Her *lip's* gone, too?"

"Yeah," said Frank, matter-of-factly. "I thought you knew that from Henry."

"No, I didn't know and I'll get back to you in a couple of minutes!" Then I remembered. "Did you get hold of the parent of the kid you got up there in 343 yet?"

"We're working on it now. The kid can't talk, so we had to get the information from her program card. Her books were hard to find in all that mess upstairs. How are you doing?"

"Fine, just fine, Frank. Call me when the stretcher gets here. Ten-four?"

In all the confusion, we still didn't get Tiffany's phone number or reach her parent, either.

"Barbara, get me Miss Baker's program card from the file!" I ordered. "I must call her mother and tell her about this!"

"John, let me do it," said Mrs. Miller. "I've had dealings with Mrs. Baker a couple of times already. She knows me!"

"O.K." I said, and relinquished the phone.

While Barbara was calling Tiffany's parent, I returned to Henry and Tiffany. "O.K., Henry! Let's get back to the description of the fight!"

Tiffany had put her head down on the desk.

Henry continued. "O.K.! We pull them apart, and I get Tiffany by the waist and sit her down in a chair. She was a mess!"

I interrupted with, "Now, Henry, what's this about another lip?"

"I'm getting to it, Mr. Manicone. Give me a second, O.K.!"

"Alright, alright, Henry! You were there, and I wasn't. Go ahead," I said.

"O.K. Then, when the other girl is pulled away, we got them about ten feet apart or so. That's when Tiffany realizes that her lip was bit off, and all her friends were screaming, 'Tiffany! Tiffany! Your lip's gone! Your lip's gone!' She runs her finger up to her mouth, and screamed a lotta curse words, and charges the other girl who was still being held by the other teachers. I tried to grab this one, but she flew right past me!"

"Holy cow!" I gasped.

Just at that second, the door flew open again, and this time, it was the principal, Mr. B. standing in the entrance way. He must have loved what he saw; the drug coordinator at my desk talking to someone on the phone; Henry, the security guard, disheveled, standing by a student resting her head on the second desk; and his Dean, standing there somewhat confused and completely harried.

"Hi, Mr. B. We are just coming to the interesting part!" I confessed.

"Indulge me!" Mr. B. said. "I want you to give me a quick recap, and make it as short as possible," he continued, as he pointed to me.

I gave the Principal his recap, and while I did so, I would turn toward Henry from time to time, to get his necessary corroboration. As I got to the part where Tiffany lunged at the first biter, I paused and pointed toward the security man to pick up the thread. Henry pointed at the student—still with her head down on the desk—and said, "She jumped right past me like a shot and fell on the same girl, like someone possessed! I mean it! Before we could do anything, she was all over that girl's face!"

"Wait a minute!" interrupted the principal. "You mean there was a *second* fight? A *second* lip biting?" he screamed.

Before Henry or I could answer, Barbara chimed in. "Hey, guys! Did the EMS get here yet? I have Tiffany's mom on the phone, and she said to take her daughter to Emergency, pronto! John, John, which hospital? Do you know?"

I held up my index finger in Mr. B.'s direction, hoping he would be a little patient, as I attempted to field Barbara's multiple questions.

"Barbara!" I said. "The EMS is still not here, and they're going to go upstairs first to treat the other one who's in worse condition than Tiffany!" I continued. "And as for a hospital, the EMS guys tell us where they're from. It can be St. Vincent's, or Bellevue, or where ever. Got it?"

Barbara nodded and returned to her phone conversation with the parent.

Mr. B. inched up toward me, and said, sotto voce, "You telling me that the girl in the Nurse's office is in *worse condition* than *this* one? Is that what you are telling me, Mr. Manicone?"

"Mr. B." I responded, "that is the story line that was told to me. Yes. I feel like Captain Pierce of MASH, to tell you the truth—and we haven't even found out yet what caused this terrible fight."

"Forget the cause, Mr. Manicone! I want the police here, now!" yelled the Principal. "That girl," he said, as he pointed in the direction of Tiffany, "is a criminal! She deliberately maimed a student in an act of revenge! What kind of school am I running here, anyway?" he shouted even louder.

"Mrs. M., please get off the phone," the principal directed. "The Dean needs it!"

For a second or so, I felt like Chester A. Riley ("What a revolting development this is!") We have here two maimed seniors; a Principal who's taking over my duties; a drug coordinator who's trying to calm down a hysterical parent; our security staff scattered all over the building, with one or two of them trying to find lip pieces amidst all the garbage on the lunchroom floor—and for all intents and purposes, a school in paralysis. What a predicament!

Mr. B." I started. "What will we gain by arresting Miss Baker? She was attacked first," I protested, "and she retaliated. There's no disputing the fact that it was pre-meditated, but, she was attacked first!"

"Mr. Manicone, the second fight was separate! You know the law," he said. "She was *separated*. The first fight was finished. *She* started the second one. The sequence was broken, and she deliberately maimed the student upstairs. No! I want her arrested." Turning toward Barbara, who had just finished her call, "Give John the phone. Call the 10th Precinct."

The drug coordinator appeared to be in a fog, and clearly had missed the entire conversation between the Principal and me.

"Who's getting arrested?" she said, as she eyed the two of us.

"The Principal wants Tiffany arrested, Barbara," I replied.

"She's a criminal, and I want her charged!" Mr. B. added.

"Wait a minute! Hold the phone!" Barbara shot back. "That's not fair!"

"Babs," I said to myself, "this female logic won't cut the mustard this time." I tried to place myself between the Principal and Barbara, to keep the dialogue from overheating. But Mr. B. wouldn't buy any of it.

"I'm sorry, Mrs. M., but I'm going to stand firm on this one," the Principal said. "Let the Dean make the call, please!"

Just as I reached for the receiver, Henry's walkie-talkie crackled. "We found it! We found it. S-2! Tell the Dean we found one of the lip pieces! Ten-four?"

"That's a Ten-four!" responded Henry.

I seized the moment, and hoping to re-establish my weight again, I said, "Mr. B., maybe they can save the tissue. I think we should go upstairs and evaluate the situation!"

"Good call, Dean! Let's see the other student while we're at it!" the Principal replied.

"Barbara, can you mind the store here, with Henry and his trusted walkie-talkie?" I asked. "If the EMS ever gets here, I'll call down," I promised.

As I left the office, I reminded the female guard to relieve Henry in ten minutes or so. He really needed the break!

Now that I had the Principal alone in the elevator as we moved up to the third floor, I gave him my best argument for not calling in the police. "Mr. B., do you realize that if we do go ahead and arrest Tiffany, we might open a can of worms that will be hard to control?"

"What can of worms?" he asked.

"Publicity. Publicity that would be very negative and hard to cover or gloss over! *That* can of worms!" I replied.

"John, that's an excellent point you make. What do you think we should do, then?" the Principal asked, as we arrived on the third floor.

"I think . . . " I said, as we neared the Nurse's office, "we should . . . " At that exact second, Frank (my S-1), opened the door for us from the inside and excitedly announced that the other security officer was holding the "missing" lip piece. "He's got it!"

The S-3 held out his hand, and in his palm, he cradled a dried brown object that resembled a potato peel lying exposed on top of a piece of white tissue paper.

"My God," I exclaimed, "it's all dried out! They can't use that!" The S-3 backed up some and, looking a little sheepish, handed the tissue and its contents to Frank.

"Where's the other girl?" I asked.

"In here, Dean, said the nurse. Both the principal and I entered the room where the other student lay.

"How bad is she?" I asked.

"You can look for yourself," the nurse replied as she removed the blood-soaked gauze from the senior's mouth.

Mr. B. and I simply froze in place. Half the top lip was gone! Just *gone!* You could plainly see at least two or three teeth, nothing covering them. I know that I stepped back a pace, but the picture was still vivid in my mind. The girl was disfigured. They could never sew that piece back on now. There was just too much damage.

"They're here," Frank yelled, as the EMS team pushed through the door.

"It's about time!" I heard the Principal say. "In here! Guys, in here!"

I couldn't help but feel a sense of revulsion as the Principal and I left the nurse's treatment room. A beautiful girl scarred for life—and so was the other one! I was sure I had lost my argument about calling the police.

The Principal interrupted my thoughts when he said, "John, no way this gets out more than it has to! Do you understand? *No way!* I knew I picked the right man for this job, and you handle this as you see fit. I'm right behind you, O.K.?"

He knew I was right about the adverse publicity, but I really wanted to nail that bitch downstairs, lip or no lip! This was about as savage an act as a Hollywood vampire movie could ever make it. In this day and age, how could a person deliberately bite off a piece of *human flesh* like that? How could they do it?

I walked over to Frank and asked him, "Frank, did you ever find out what started all this?" as I waved my arms outward.

"Yes, Mr. Manicone. But, you won't believe it when I tell you," he replied.

"Try me!"

He took a deep breath and slowly uttered one word. "Milk!"

"*Milk?*" I asked, half in jest. "What about it, this milk?"

"The student downstairs, Tiffany? She wanted chocolate milk, and asked this one, Naomi, to get it when she went to the line for her lunch. Naomi came back with plain milk, not the chocolate one. When Tiffany said, 'Where's my chocolate milk?' Naomi must have 'dissed' her and pushed the container towards her and told her to get it herself!"

"I don't believe this! Over *milk?*" I asked, again.

"I'm sure there were other things thrown into it, but, yeah, it started over milk. Isn't that a kick?" Frank said.

I went over to the Principal and told him what Frank had related to me. He heard what I said, but it didn't faze him in the least. Turning, I told Frank to escort the EMS team to my office to tend to the other victim. I had to fill Barbara in without Mr. B. present. Also, I wanted Barbara to see Naomi before she left for the hospital. "Frank, make sure you get the name of the hospital before they leave!" I reminded him.

"St. Vincent's!" Frank yelled out as the door closed behind me.

In a couple of minutes, I was back and I started to give Barbara all the details, including my personal feelings as well. We were well out of earshot of Tiffany. Barbara didn't say a word. She nodded a few times and then did what I asked her to do. She went out toward the lobby and asked the EMS fellows if she could look at Naomi.

I heard Barbara gasp as I was watching the whole episode from some 30 or 40 yards away. And, interestingly, Barbara stepped back a pace or two at the same time as I did. The EMS team came to my office, and I ushered them in. I heard one of the attendants give out a low whistle while he treated Tiffany.

"Hey, Dean!" one of them yelled over his shoulder, "was there a fire sale here, or something? This isn't a school for gladiators, is it?"

I just couldn't come up with a clever retort, because I kept watching Barbara, literally staggering toward me.

"I would never have believed this in a million years!" she finally said. "I've got to get out of here for an hour or so. Please, John. Cover for me! O.K.?"

"Sure, Barbara. Walk it off! It'll do your soul a world of good," I said. "You really look pale."

"Thanks. I'll be right back." She left for her office, and I went back to mine. The female guard had relieved Henry. She and the EMS team were ready to wheel Tiffany out.

"I'll call her mother. St. Vincent's, right?"

"Right! By the way," I said, "was that piece of lip that the guard found usable at all?"

"Sorry, Dean. Too dirty and too dried out. We got it in a plastic bag, but I don't think it can be used at all. Anyway, it's up to the emergency doctor, not us." The attendants then wheeled Tiffany toward the ambulance.

I walked over to the remaining guard and thanked her personally with a kiss. "Well done!" I added. "And tell the others, 'well done,' from me. I'll thank them individually but only you get the kiss."

She laughed a little—more to relieve the tension than finding anything amusing. As if anything that day could be called, by any stretch of the imagination, "amusing."

I closed the door behind her and gave out a sigh. It wasn't enough. I was totally drained. I locked the door behind me and went up to see the Principal.

"You look like shit!" he began and, reaching inside a desk drawer, he pulled out a bottle of scotch and two glasses.

"I thought it was illegal to have liquor in a school building!" I said—but accepted the glass.

"Only exception is if you have lip-biters," he replied. He poured out a couple of fingers of Scotland's best and indicated his directive. "As commanding officer, I am ordering you to drink!"

Not wanting to disobey my superiors, I downed the scotch.

Then Mr. B. asked, "Do you want to take the rest of the afternoon off?"

"No," I answered. "I'll walk around the building and try to see some new faces. Thanks for the drink. I may come up again for another!"

"Anytime," he replied. "Anytime. You do good work."

I left the office, and at 2:30 left the building. As I drove, the picture of those gaping facial wounds haunted me all the way home. I tried to raise the music on the car radio, but it didn't help. The wounds were frightfully real—as they are to this very day.

Both girls were suspended for five days. At the hearings, each held separately, the stupidity of the fight became all too evident. Two seniors had been acting out a bar-room brawl, but, in fact, the wounds—and later, the scars—would not go away. Each girl sued the other. Each demanded some ridiculous monetary amount, to no avail. The more seriously injured girl, Naomi, did have several operations, but she must have gone to some butcher. He did a lousy job. Tiffany opted for the natural cure. She let Mother Nature do her best. And that wasn't a good choice, either.

From time to time, a spark would ignite between the two girls, but I always believed that it was the doing of the mothers involved. They would look at their girls, say something, and words were later exchanged.

Barbara really took the whole episode rather traumatically, and within two years or so, she quit teaching altogether. I couldn't say that incident was the one that did it, but I can say for myself that this particular even shook me right down to my foundation. How many traumatic experiences in a person's lifetime could still be recalled with such detail after all these years? Not many, I bet.

Anyway, all these things began to take their toll on me physically. In early spring of 1981, I started to feel poorly. I was exhausted, had flagging energy levels, and it became harder and harder to act as Dean and teach my two classes each day. Then in the first week of June, I passed out a couple of times at home, and after a comprehensive series of tests for sixteen days at Columbia-Presbyterian Hospital, it was determined that a pacemaker would do the trick. It did—and the replacements that followed are still humming away.

When I returned to Fashion in September, Mr. B. indicated that my days as Dean should be over. He had already assigned the position to a woman in my social studies department. He said I could take my old position back anytime I wanted; but in reality, he felt I had given him my best eleven years in the office, and that a new person should have a go at it. I agreed. Then, practically in the same breath, he said, "John, I'm still not going to give you a full load of five classes, so how about becoming my Immunization Dean?"

"Is there a budget line for this position?" I asked, thinking that he was kidding me.

"John, I'm serious! This may be your most challenging job in this building yet! Will you take it?"

"Sure. Why not? It can't get any worse!" I remember saying.

Boy—was I wrong! This job was a dilly. He told me all I had to do was to make sure everybody in our school was fully immunized. Ha!

Seventeen

"Calling Dr. Kildare. Calling Dr. Kildare."

During the spring of 1981, the New York City Board of Education saw fit to enforce an order, long supported and endorsed by the City Health Department, that every child in a public school prove he had all the necessary medical vaccinations as required by N.Y. State law. These shots, mandated by the Board prior to registration into any elementary grade school, were three; the Three-in-One, which included diphtheria, whooping cough and typhoid protection; German measles (or rubella), and polio. In addition, the child had to show that he or she had received a smallpox vaccination and a booster for rubella. In a nut-shell, all students (numbering over one million for New York City, but only 2,200 at Fashion High) had to produce a written record to prove inoculations of all five shots by September 1981 in order to remain in the school system. The Chancellor of the New York City Board of Education signed the order. I went from the frying pan into the fire!

So, after I settled into my new office on the third floor, I rolled up my sleeves and began my new job as the Immunization Dean that first week in September. Being a good administrator, my first task (I told my tiny staff), was to separate the "wheat" from the "chaff," meaning to remove all the dead-wood from the thousands of medical records stored in dozens of filing cabinets and cardboard boxes scattered in the suite of rooms that made up the "Nurse's office." Using the most up-to-date lists of our current official class rosters, we immediately found our first huge headache. Dozens and dozens of medical files were so antiquated that we had a serious problem of just storing all this "chaff." We had medical records that went back into the early 50s, *believe it or not!* Were any of these students even still alive?

Our second problem was that our files were in no way complete. In each class (and we had about seventy-five official classes), as many as one-half of the students were missing folders. There were seniors who did not have a medical file. How could an upper classman *not* have a medical file? When I reported this to the Principal, when he asked how I was progressing, he literally hit the roof!

"What?" he screamed at me. "What are you talking about? There *has* to be a medical file for each student in this building! That's the law!" he bellowed.

"You can yell all you like, Mr. B., but that's the story," I shot back. "There's no way I can comply with the directive of the Chancellor by September 30th. There are too many records missing!"

"How can that be?" Mr. B. demanded. "The Nurse's office is full of filing cabinets! I ought to know because I approved the requisitions for all of them!" he pressed.

"Mr. B., try to follow my lips!" I said in reply. "The files were never cleaned out. I've got medical records going back to the early 1950s," I said, as I pointed down to the third floor Nurse's office. "*The early 50s,* for God's sake!"

"That's it! That's it!" he said. "John, you meet us down in the Nurse's office. I'll be there shortly. There's going to be hell to pay today, I swear to God! *Today!*"

As Mr. B. escorted me out of his office, he stopped at his secretary's desk, and ordered Florence to call down to Room 201 and page Miss H. over the P.A. to meet the principal in Room 343. He added, "And John, pull those 1950 folders so I have some ammunition to hit her with before I drop her like a lead balloon!" he commanded as I walked over to the elevators.

"Miss H.! You are to report to the Nurse's office right away! Miss H., you are requested to . . . " the P.A. blared as the elevator doors slowly closed.

Miss H. was the Physical Ed chairman in all things— except she wasn't on the budget line as such. The position never materialized and the department "floated" from one unofficial chairman to another. She had all the perks; the shortened program, and she could come and go as she pleased. No one in the building knew how or why Miss H. could flout all authority, but she could and did. However, on this particular September morning, all was about to change. I never even had a chance to warn her, because, as I waited, the posse came into Room 343 in tandem.

"Mr. Manicone, where are those folders?" Mr. B. barked.

I smiled at Miss H., and then, Mr. B. walked her to one side of the room as I pretended to continue working on the folders. He was not a happy Principal. He was raising his voice.

"What do you mean, you didn't have enough time to keep up with the record work?" Mr. B. questioned her. "Not enough time? Is that some kind of joke, or what?" he demanded. "And, and, what about these?" he continued. "These records go back to 1952, 1954, 1955! They're over twenty-five years old! You didn't have time to get rid of these? What the hell are you talking about here?"

Mr. B. was fuming and Miss H. just kept staring at the floor.

After an incredibly long silence, Mr. B. finally said, "It's over! You're through here!" Then, turning toward the filing cabinets, he handed me the incriminating folders and escorted her out of Room 343. My little staff looked at each other for a brief second to record the historic moment; then we resumed our work. "Class 202 goes over there!" I said, as I pointed in the direction of the window.

Little by little, we made our daily and weekly goals. I wanted this grade finished by Friday "or you don't eat on Monday" routine. It appeared that almost every school in the city was experiencing the same type of headache and frustration, so the Chancellor's office gave all of us a reprieve. The deadline was re-set for February first. No child could be admitted without the necessary shots after that date. Thank God!

Speaking just for Fashion, we had only about 85 percent of our medical records. Or to put it another way, about 300 student medical records were either incomplete or missing. I still hadn't had time to go through each existing folder to determine if the student had all his five shots. Luckily I had two things working for me— the telephone, and an inexhaustible supply of monitors. Our gym was right next door!

Because of this "inoculation emergency," all the NYC elementary and junior high schools were inundated with requests for medical health records. A typical response (if I got through to the school at all) was, "You want the health records of Albert Jones? But, he graduated three years ago! Why didn't you ask for them in 1978 or '79?" or, "We mailed those out to you two years ago!" or, "We don't have them!" or, "Sandra never graduated from J.H.S. 64. She transferred to another school." And so on and so forth.

That's when I used my second weapon, the "health excused from gym" monitors, and they were more than happy to help. I gave them carte blanche to roam the building and "bring me Maria Sanchez! Even if she's in the toilet! NOW!!!!"

The line outside 343 snaked down the hall. All through September and the early part of October, I demanded information like, "Yeah, but where did you go after you left I.S. 188?" or, "When you came back from Puerto Rico, do you remember what school you attended before you came here?" Or, "In what city or town in South Carolina did you attend school?"

I sent letters to obtain duplicate files, and by hook or crook, we got there. All the "dead wood" was packed in cartons and sent down to our vault. At last, the files were complete! Now, the hard work would begin.

Mr. B. assigned a terrific Health Ed. teacher, Nina, to my staff. She was simply superb. She and I did the bulk of the screening and reading of all those 2,000-plus medical folders. A scrawl here on this line meant one thing; something written over a dozen years could mean this or that. Was this a date? Did "3/1" mean March first, or the three-in-one shot? What does this look like to you? Did she get the booster? "I don't know" was the common reply. Many long afternoons turned into longer evenings, but eventually we got the bulk of the work done.

Still being a compulsive organizer, I started to compile lists. In each class, we had lists of completed, nearly completed and in some cases, no records of students receiving any shots at all! We concentrated on the middle group, or the ones who needed at least one or more shots. We had almost 700 of these, or nearly one-third of the student staff. We made duplicates of everything on the outside chance something was misplaced. Each official teacher got his or her list with the names of their students and what was missing.

Most of the students complied, but, we expected the worst and we weren't disappointed. That coming Monday was like a bargain basement sale outside 343. I had already gotten my trusted security staff to keep order and we took on each case, one at a time.

"But, Mr. Manicone, I got all those shots! I swear to God!"

"Yeah, I believe you, Rhonda, but the Chancellor doesn't know you like I do. He wants it in writing. I'm sorry. Next!"

"But Mr. Manicone, I'm allergic to shots! I break out!"

"Really, Melissa, but that don't cut any mustard with the headman. Take an aspirin, and then take the rest of these shots. O.K.? Next!"

The problems and the excuses were endless, but our patience wasn't. We handed out Kleenex for those who thought crying would help, and we yelled at times when we thought that technique was better. The list grew smaller and smaller. However, the group at the top of my list, the students who were not vaccinated at all (or who could not furnish any proof of it) was my worst nightmare. It numbered about 56 or 65. How could a child and the mother get past "King Kong" who interviewed every child coming into the New York

City school system? Unbelievable!

I was working late, around Election Day, when the boss, with hat and coat on, dropped by. "How are you doing?" he asked.

"O.K.," I replied. Nina had gone home and the office looked dreary with only a light or two on, and files everywhere.

"What's the matter?" he asked, as he walked slowly toward my desk. "You O.K.?"

"Yeah, I'm O.K., but my wife isn't," I replied.

"What is it? Will she be alright?" he continued.

"She's got cancer, boss, and she's going to be operated on next week," I replied.

"Holy shit!" he cried. "First you with the pacemaker, now Jo with cancer! I don't believe it! I don't believe it!"

"The doctor is first class, and the hospital is Columbia-Presbyterian. I think we got this one covered."

"Well, John, if you need some time off or anything, just take it. You don't even have to ask! It's yours. My God, *anything*. It's yours," he said very genuinely.

"Thanks, I might take you up on that."

He walked out of the room shaking his head.

Our prayers were answered and Jo got through the surgery very well. Not only that, she didn't need chemo or radiation and, by the end of the year, she was her old self again. I did take a few days off, now and then, to take my wife for check-ups, but believe me, we were very thankful for all the good wishes and prayers that Thanksgiving holiday.

Meanwhile, back at the ranch, we had whittled our initial list of 750 down to under 400. Believe it or not, about a dozen students left the city and transferred outside the state to avoid the shots!

Time was getting short and by the end of November, the rate of moving the kids into the "completed" column was slowing down to a trickle. Nina and I bluffed, and badgered, and threatened the students with everything we could, but a definite pattern was emerging. In almost every class, with the exceptions of the seniors, we were running into a 15 percent non-compliance rate. In actual numbers, we were talking about 375 students who would not meet the health code by February 1st. I went up to see the Principal in early December with the news.

"O.K., kiddo, what do you have for me?" he began.

"Well, Mr. B., Nina and I have reduced the list of under-inoculated from about 750 down to 375, and we're running into . . ."

"Hold it right there!" he interrupted. "You're saying that 375 of our charges will be out in the cold on the first of February? Is that what you are saying?"

"Yes, Mr. B.; while I'm hoping to cut that number further, the kids aren't cooperating!" I replied.

"John, let's take this down to the worst case scenario. Are you prepared to keep about 12 to 15 percent of the students out of the building until they do cooperate?"

"Mr. B. I've started to work on a plan that would do exactly what you're suggesting," I answered. "I should have the whole thing ready for you in a couple of weeks."

"Not a minute later," he shot back. "I want to see the whole enchilada before the holidays, because we have the city-wide exams and reading tests right after we get back! *Comprende?*"

"No sweat, Mr. B., you'll have it by the 17th or 18th. O.K.?"

"O.K., now get back to work. I want those numbers to get to as close to 10 percent as you can make it, or even lower." He didn't scream or anything, that was good, but how was I going to keep almost three hundred kids from sneaking into the building? I had to devise a near-perfect scheme that was practical, simple to implement—and would work. . . .

I told Nina, when I got back, that the Principal was up to speed and that he wanted to see my plan in a couple of weeks. She was to continue to move the "incompletes" into the "completed" columns, and I would try to reduce the number of "absolutely nothing completed" category to a manageable figure. I then went around from classroom to classroom, to buttonhole these characters and bring them downstairs for a one-on-one interview.

"So, Manuel, I've got your medical folder in my hands, but there's nothing in it! Can you explain this fact for me?" I began.

"Hey, man, I took all them shots! I don't know what happened to my records! You must of lost them!" he said.

"I lost your records? Why would I do such a dirty thing to such a nice young man like you," I said. "Maybe you know where they are. Where did you attend school before you were accepted at Fashion?" I asked.

"I went to a Catholic school, but they kicked me out! I was supposed to go to my neighborhood school after, but I didn't like it. Too many gangs, you know."

"O.K.," I replied. "Let's review the record that your counselor handed me. You went to P.S. 76 in the Bronx?"

"Right," he replied.

"Then you moved to the Lower East Side to P.S. 188, right?" I asked.

"Right," he repeated.

"Then, it looks like you went to P.R. Right?"

"Yeah, in the third grade."

"O.K." I continued. "You went back to 188; then what happened?"

"My mother put me in Joan of Arc."

"Alright," I said. "There's the gap! We have nothing after the 8th grade at 188. Now, I'll call Joan of Arc and see if they still have your records. Meanwhile, you can help out by getting your mom to stop by the school and see the Sister Superior to speed things along. You want to stay here, right, Manuel?"

"Yeah, yeah. I don't want to get kicked out of here. This is a nice school!" he answered.

"Good. Help us out and we'll help you, O.K.?"

Then there were the follow-up calls; a sick baby; the excuse that the records were mailed to another school. "Oh, I forgot!" was very common. Many times the kid would lie straight out and then be absent for days on end before you caught him again.

I looked at the calendar and it read December 16th. Holy Cow! My *plan!* The plan *had* to be ready!

I realized that a complicated plan, like meeting the entire student body in the auditorium on February first and calling out names would not work. Too many problems: One, why embarrass anyone? Two, everybody was already inside the building. How can you locate the "unwashed" if he or she is hiding somewhere in the school? Third, who's going to be responsible for having a possible confrontation? Me? Security?

No. No. I wanted something I could sell to Mr. B. that would isolate the problem *outside* the building, not in the building.

The most important factor had to be the accuracy of our lists. The Board announced that we could admit any child so long as they were receiving their shots, or waiting for the time period to get the boosters. A simple doctor's note was sufficient. Well, that would be O.K.

My next consideration had to be a foolproof method to admit a qualified student. There could be no tampering or counterfeiting of the passes I planned to issue to our students. So, I made the passes myself; ran them on the mimeo machines and numbered and marked each one—all 2500 passes. On the 17th of December, I went up to the Principal's office with my up-to-date lists and my passes with a one-page instruction sheet for each homeroom teacher. Mr. B. was flabbergasted.

"It's going to work! Your plan is going to work!" he said quite proudly. "I can't see anything wrong with it!" he continued. "Do you see any problem, Bill?" he asked of the Science Department chairman.

"O.K. John," he replied. "About how many kids are not getting these passes?"

"Right now, we're hoping to keep it down to about 280. Less than 300, for sure!"

"Wow, that's just about 10 percent!" said the Principal.

"We might get down to that number!" I said confidently.

"Many of our problem kids said that they were going to see their doctors over the holidays. I'm hoping to knock off another 50 or so," I added.

"I sincerely hope so," the Principal said. "The smaller the crowd outside our building for our security to handle, the better for us!"

Both administrators were looking and inspecting my array of materials, included the numbered passes. They appeared satisfied.

"O.K., John!" the Principal said. "The ball is in your

court. We'll give you an afternoon sometime during the last week of January, like the cafeteria or the auditorium where you address all the official teachers and give all this stuff out in envelopes. After January 31st, you'll be running the school. Only you will have the final word on who's in and who's out! You got it?"

My God! I never thought about things in just that way, but yeah, I'm the last word. Holy Cow! Is this how megalomania begins?

"Oh, by the way, John, don't forget Security," the principal added, waking me out of my fantasy.

"Already way ahead of you, boss. I gave Frank and the rest of the guards their stations."

"Good man!" he replied. "Let's keep that crowd as small as possible, O.K.?"

"We'll see after the holidays," I replied. "My fingers are crossed!"

On the last day of the term, everything was set. The official teachers had the latest lists, with the names of the excluded and the included. Inside the envelope was a packet of passes, each 3x5 card with a name and a number. That number corresponded with the one next to the student's name on the master list. Any excluded child was NOT to be admitted into Homeroom. Security was to call down to the Dean's office in the event of trouble. It never happened.

Downstairs, in my office, I gave the security staff their last set of instructions. Three guards would be posted at the front door, and only those who had passes (which had been distributed with the final report card) could be admitted. The security guards had been alerted to check for phony passes and if anything looked suspicious, the guards were to direct any student to join the "unwashed" at the 25th Street entrance where another guard would admit students, a couple at a time.

The fifth guard would rove, check all the other doors, mind the front desk and check the Dean's office from time to time. Me? I would be stationed, with my tiny staff, and all the necessary records and files, at a desk, positioned in the hallway facing the 25th Street entrance. Lunch might be a little late tomorrow!

Like most important dates, this one started with premonitions but thankfully remained remarkably uneventful. My desk and several chairs blocked passageway down the hall to the elevators. Everybody, including custodial staff, maintenance people, cafeteria staff, teachers and administrators alike, appeared to use that 25th Street entrance. A number of students had already lined up outside the building facing east. I also remember that it was a very cold February 1st. (As I get older, the colder it gets.) Anyway, it was a bright, crisp, cold day. I know because I had to wear my coat most of that day in that breezy hallway. Others were wearing their gloves. That day, we had about 240 applicants who didn't believe that we meant business. "No shots, no admittance!"

Of course, not all 240 were outside that morning, because we processed only about 100 that day. Word of mouth worked very well, and in the ensuing days, we kept handling smaller and smaller crowds. The main thing, however, was that we were getting quality results. Most kids who had been refused admittance were definitely showing up with medical proof of shots, along with very vocal parents. There was a great deal of anger, stomping of feet because of the cold, and plenty of warnings. "Now remember, Clarissa, you must complete all your shots, including the boosters, by such and such date—or out you go again! Is that clear?"

Each day, it was the same thing. The three guards were posted to admit youngsters with my passes, official teachers were given updates and corrections of their lists. I relieved the outside guard with the desk person, and the parade of staff passed by my desk with all kinds of approval. Even the Principal used the 25th Street entrance!

By the end of the second week, it became quite apparent that I could cut back on this emergency staff. People were relieved by the third week, and only Nina and I held the fortress by the door. I had borrowed a walkie-talkie just in case and by the end of the month, the emergency was declared "over"!

The reason? Our excluded had boiled down to 22! Less than 1 percent!

Either these kids had died, left the country or vanished; we couldn't get it any lower. At the end of the term, Nina inherited the position of 'Immunization Czar' or 'Czarina' (whichever), getting a very nice "well done" for our efforts.

The Principal had mentioned another "Dean" job that coming September and I was eager to see what was in store for me as I rode off into the sunset.

I knew that I had done a very good job despite those early difficulties. I was left with some bittersweet memories though, because Miss H., who was an institution at Fashion, left us at the end of that academic year. I just couldn't help wonder why she had let things "go to pot." Didn't she believe that someone would somehow pick up on her incompetent record keeping? She had been very lucky in all that time that someone didn't call her short on her paperwork sooner than we did. It would have been nice to give her a chicken dinner when she left.

Eighteen

The Saddle Is a Little Smaller Now

"John, how does Cutting Dean sound to you?" asked Mr. B. on the first school day in September 1983. "You would teach three periods like before and you'll have a desk in the Attendance office with Bill," he added.

I knew that my old job as Dean of Discipline was already locked up, so I said, "Sure, why not?"

I was subtly aware that the Principal still had lots of reservations about my health because of the pacemaker. The original one, implanted in June of 1981 gave out in March of 1983, and I needed a replacement. This problem did not go unnoticed and it didn't help me to regain access to my former job.

"Let's see how it goes, John, and we can talk later, O.K.?"

I left his office and made my way to the Attendance office, which was located on the first floor. Mr. R. was a trade teacher, with many years of experience in his field, and now he would be my boss indirectly. His field was not Attendance and I had no intention of making a play for his job. He was very amiable and very easy to get along with. However, he did have one major problem. He was slightly deaf—and should I say, "plenty" deaf. His phone conversations lasted forever because everything had to be repeated or asked three or four times, at the least. Many times, the office would be packed with students who had come down to clear up an attendance problem, and he would no sooner end one call, when the phone would ring another time, and the process would begin again, and the lines got that much longer.

To compound the problem further, my desk was up against the wall near the only door to the office, and I had to see and interview the students I had called down. There was absolutely no privacy in that office at all. Practically all the major offices on the first and second floors had been switched around in one way or another; some were doubled switched and, in some cases, tripled switched. Originally, when I became a Dean of discipline in 1970, my office was on the second floor. We shared our quarters with the chairlady of the Art department, and then, in 1973, the Dean's office was returned to the first floor where it was located originally. It was by far a better place for so many reasons. First off, we were more accessible to the elevators that always came down to the ground level when returning from the upper floors. Getting an elevator to stop on the second floor, especially during an emergency, was almost impossible. Secondly, the poor Art chairperson went home with a headache daily because of the activity generated in the Dean's side of the office. And, lastly, the Principal found it a "damn nuisance" to get to my office when I needed his presence.

Back in the 40s, the Attendance Office was located somewhere else in the building. When I got to Fashion, it was located on the first floor opposite to the Guidance Office. Good location, but hardly a place to make into an Attendance Office. This room was adjacent to our auditorium and stage. In fact, a duplicate room existed on the other side. They were used as changing rooms for the student models. Each room was covered with mirrors to assist the young ladies and gentlemen with grooming and last minute alterations before and during fashion shows.

The room also had a bathroom that was a terrible nuisance and an irritant for us because every secretary, teacher, guidance counselor and visitor who came in the area preferred to use it rather than to avail themselves of facilities further down the hall. This constant parade into our room was distracting and nonproductive, to say the least.

The room in question was about forty feet long, had three desks in a row to each other, and two sides of the room had countertops which were used for the 60 or so attendance books that were picked up daily. The side of the room opposite to the doorway contained two doors, one to the stage and the other to the bathroom. This made the third wall absolutely useless respecting the placement of desks or tables. Therefore, our work station, located in the middle of the floor, was totally impractical. Some might have considered it cozy, but I didn't, especially if someone was on the phone, not five feet away, and someone else was attempting to interview a student.

My job, as Cutting Dean, was to discover patterns of absence, or cutting behavior, of the offending students. I did this with a cutting print-out which was furnished by the Bureau of Attendance daily and placed on my desk each morning. This print-out was never less than 100 to 150 pages long, with the names of all offending students and the accumulated number of cuts and absences these students had incurred. In place, we also had an automatic calling system, approved and paid for by the Board, which rang up the students' homes. This automated system kept calling the house until someone answered, at which time the number of absences or cuts was revealed to the parents. This system was terrific—except for one thing. If the student got to the phone first, the problem was usually not addressed until the first report card was issued. This could be some five or six weeks later and by that time, the damage was done, and a failure in that particular subject area was inevitable.

It then became my job to locate those parents who didn't respond to our automated system, apprise them of the situation and arrange some type of conference with the attendance teacher, the guidance counselor, and/or me. Being at my desk only two periods a day and attempting to reach these parents, and set up interviews with the delinquent student made solving the overall problem of class cutting almost an impossible task. Some improvements were noted in individual cases, but cutting in general was difficult to eliminate. The sprawling physical size of our high school, being 10 floors high, worked against us. In addition, we had three programmed lunch periods in our schedule to accommodate the feeding of some 2,000 students every day.

Our security staff was scheduled to monitor the lunchroom each lunch period and sort out students who were caught there two or more periods at any given time. But being the simultaneous lunchtime for them as well, our security had to monitor the lobby desk, check the locker areas, police the hallways, and the bathrooms on each floor, and find cutters as well—this was asking a great deal. By the time we made some headway with one group, another was ready to take their place and the identification process had to start from the beginning again.

The printout was very useful to keep statistics and we could spot trends with no difficulty. However, the lunch periods killed us and we simply did not have the necessary person-power to remedy the situation, if cutting, for example, was on the increase during periods one or two rather than the middle of the school day. At best, we could count on only three or four security people during that time, out of the five or six who were assigned to the building. This situation only got worse if we had one call in sick, because substitute security simply did not exist.

I stayed with this cutting position for two years. Then, in June of 1985, I asked Mr. B. if I could be relieved of the assignment and return to the classroom full time. He agreed, and in September I was back in the mainstream with five classes and an official class to boot. The run of 17 years with a "plum" job came to an end for me. Being the ex-Dean and having senior ranking within the Social Studies Department gave me a great deal of clout. I could ask for, and get, the classes I wanted. For about eight years or so, I was the only instructor of our elective, Law, which was reserved exclusively for seniors who didn't want to take Economics. All our students had to take one year of geography, one year of World History and one year of American History. In order to complete the three-and-a-half years of Social Studies, and Board of Education in the mid 70s decided to give graduating seniors an option to take either Law or psychology. I had three full classes of Law each term, with kids on a waiting list, from that time.

I had some Law background. I attended Brooklyn Law School for a year after I was discharged from the Army, and I took the necessary courses prepared by the Board as a prerequisite. The only stipulation that the Board made was that the person who was picked to teach the class had to develop a curriculum for new subjects, with the approval of the chairperson and the Board, which I did. I prepared twenty weeks of lesson plans, homework assignments, and a number of quizzes and tests, including a final to satisfy the powers that be.

It was a tremendous success, right from the beginning. I enjoyed teaching the class and I found great satisfaction from the daily high attendance and enthusiastic responses that I received. The textbook was equal to the challenge, with an interesting format and examples of the new terms under discussion. We handled subjects including criminal law, civil law, family law, protections under the Bill of Rights, property law, and contracts.

In the ensuing years while teaching Law, it became quite apparent that my teenage students, some as old as twenty years of age, had a very poor grasp of family law in particular. It became a startling revelation to them that what was being said in class was directly impacting their relationship with their families. Over two-thirds of my students came from broken homes, common-law arrangements, or single-parent situations. It was shocking for them to learn that their mothers had no property rights in a common-law marriage because the State of New York does not recognize it as legal or binding. Neither do the children, for that matter. And, I further pointed out, that if their mother was in fact living with a man, and not legally married to him or, if the man never bothered to get a divorce from his first wife, and their mother was waiting on this gentleman hand and foot for thirty years, she and the children would get absolutely nothing when he died. The first wife had legal claim to all the man's property, period.

Wow!

These valuable bits of information, like rental agreements, leases, property rights and the sanctity of a contract were the drawing cards to my class. We never had a dull lesson. In fact, the new chairman, who was to replace Mr. B. in 1990, later observed me and critiqued my lesson. As he was leaving the classroom he stated, "It's impossible to sleep in Mr. Manicone's class!"

On the other side of the coin, however, was the fact that these young men and women were not in my class to become future lawyers or even paralegals. It was a subject class, and, if what we were discussing that day should conflict with one of their personal experiences back in the Bronx or Brooklyn, then the lesson might possibly generate some fireworks.

For example, take the time when we were involved with a discussion in which we were comparing the marriage and engagement process between a man and a woman, then and now. I related the experience in my lifetime about courting, long engagements, asking the father of the girl for her hand in marriage, getting a blood test, meeting the family and the like, and how the business of "tying the knot" was conducted in the world of today. The class sat there in complete disbelief. It was as if I was describing the mating ritual of an alien from Mars. Their comments ran like, "Really?" "Go way!" "No kidding!" and "Why did they do things like that?"

So, in this setting, when I compared those archaic practices with the sexual freedoms that my students were enjoying and practicing today, I voiced my concerns about the great number of divorces, the absence of courting and realistic engagement periods, and contrasted that with the dangers of hopping in bed with every stranger they meet without any check-ups at all. I told them to always practice safe sex just to be sure, regardless.

Then this young senior jumps from her chair and

yells, "Mr. Manicone, I don't have time to wait for a condom!"

"Oh?" I shot back, "but you do have time for a venereal disease or now, this new thing, called AIDS! Is that what you're telling me?" I yelled at her.

As luck would have it, the bell rang just at that critical moment, with all the eyes of everyone in that room riveted on both of us, and the girl gathered her things and left. I never got a reply.

Aside from family law, I believe I was equally instructive and helpful for my students in assisting them and their families with situations like what to do when you receive something in the mail, free, and then the harassing letters and phone calls follow. I told them to save the merchandise, but that they were not legally responsible for paying anything that they had not ordered; that the next time their parents got a phone call or letter, to please advise the sender that the item would be available for collection at your address at your convenience. Not theirs. I got plenty of "thank yous" for that one.

Another area of help was a remedy sought by their parents in which money was either lost or due them through some accident or claim to property. We discussed the value and importance of the Small Claims Court system and how it works. The students became aware of the fact, that without a lawyer, and at only a nominal cost to their parents, a successful judgment could be achieved with good preparation for starters. This preparation involved lots of documentation, like sales slips, bill of sales, accident reports by the police if warranted, and lots of pictures. In fact, I even came to the assistance of a colleague of mine, a trade teacher, who had learned about the process required in Small Claims

Court through one of her students who happened to be taking my law class at the time. In her case, she was frustrated and quite upset about getting satisfaction with a problem she was having with a local neighborhood dry cleaner. She had just recently brought in very expensive drapes to have professionally dried cleaned. They came back ruined; in shrunken condition and completely unusable. She had returned to the cleaners several times, but the cleaners maintained they were not responsible. I advised her to take plenty of pictures of before and after.

She actually went back to the store that had sold her the drapes and she found an exact match on display. She still retained a copy of the sales slip, the dry cleaners' slip, a statement from the seller of the drapes, and a copy of her credit card receipt. I advised her to take all this documentation to the courthouse in Rockland County in New York (where she lived), fill out the proper forms, pay the service fee, and the courthouse would do the rest. She did, and she won because she "buried" the defendant with the preponderance of evidence as required by law. I was very happy to help with this case as well.

In the more serious cases, students would see me after class or "find" me in the hallways to discuss a criminal matter that might be pending with a relative or friend. In class, we read about and discussed the subject of criminal law in New York State. The text clearly pointed out the differences between felonies and misdemeanors, the various categories of felonies, and the punishment for each. Where I was able to, I would discuss their individual problem with information I had at hand or I would call a lawyer friend for some simple assistance. In more cases than not, I told the student to have

266

their parents call the A.C.L.U. office in Manhattan, or talk to the court-appointed lawyer who was handling the case. These two sets of lawyers had a world of experience in matters dealing with plea bargaining, how to plead the case, and get the charges reduced or dismissed, if some arrangement could be worked out.

For other students, who asked my opinion about automobile accidents, whether to sue a landlord or not, or how to get help with child support, I strongly recommended that they use the Yellow Pages or look through the blue or green sections of the telephone book. I could point the way, but they had to do the "walking" with their fingers.

Anyway, after ten years, the New York City Board of Education, in its infinite wisdom, decided to pull the plug on all electives in Social Studies. My law class was history. It was a lovely run and I was sorry to see it end. In September 1986, my class load was back to American History and World History. I still only wanted juniors and seniors.

Nineteen

When in Doubt, Punt

In my nearly 20 years at Fashion, I made some great friendships and developed strong feelings of affection with people in and out of the Social Studies Department. There was Joe R., who was one of the many personal secretaries of General George Patton. (Yes, THE George Patton.) Joe was a wonderful English teacher, a great raconteur, and a very good friend. Then, there was Curt S., who was just about the best there was in all the areas of History, and especially knowledgeable about the kingdoms of England and Germany. He was the only child of a middle-aged German couple who had fled the Nazis in the 30s with practically nothing in their pockets and made a life for themselves in the United States. Bill D. was a gifted science teacher with a terrific sense of humor, who loved to stop by the Dean's office, whenever he could, to follow up on my adventures there. He later became the chairman of his department, and still later, assistant principal.

Speaking of assistant principals, there was Max S. who had a fatal heart attack while vacationing in Europe. He started out as a trade teacher with extensive experience in his field of producing all types of leather and fur outerwear, moved on to the Attendance Office, and later was promoted to the position of A.P. of Fashion H.S. He was very conscientious, a hard worker and wonderfully supportive in my desire to rid the building of drugs, bad eggs and malcontents in general. I once witnessed seeing him, in the lobby of our school during a protest, actually kicking an outsider and rioter, right in the buns with such force that the man literally was propelled into the outside door and on to the sidewalk like a rocket. I can't ever forget his grin of satisfaction when he turned around after this serious "confrontation." His sudden death was a great personal loss for me.

Bobby F. was another Fur teacher. He and I taught on the same third floor during my first couple of years at Fashion. He was a terrific golfer, a very good friend, and also very supportive. I could share ideas with him and ask his advice on everything from teaching methods, to whom I could trust and whom to avoid. However, he made one serious judgmental call about the timing of taking a sabbatical.

In order to take a sabbatical, a teacher had to be tenured for at least 20 years in his license, which meant one had to be on the school payroll for 23 years. In addition, if a teacher took the sabbatical and wanted to return to the same school, he or she had to have been with that school for at least 20 years. Bobby asked for a sabbatical with only 19 years at Fashion and the Principal told him that he would not approve his request. Bob went to the Union and was told that he didn't need the approval of the Principal to take the sabbatical. He then submitted his papers to the Board and took his sabbatical, thinking that nothing would or could happen. He was wrong. Mr. B. closed out the Fur department and when Bob returned, he had no job. It was all perfectly legal, and Bob had to transfer to another trade school in Queens to finish out his career so that he could be eligible for his pension.

I waited until 1987 to go on my sabbatical. I not only had 20 years at Fashion, but I was tenured for 24 years, and I was in the system twenty-seven years. And, I didn't need anybody's approval. My wife and I had planned on this paid leave for some time because we were going to go to Europe. It was my very first trip abroad. I was 53, and I was quite excited because I was about to see the very things I had read about all my life: The Eiffel Tower, Notre Dame, the London Tower, the Hôtel des Invalides, the Coliseum, and Vatican City. I filled two photo albums and with pictures and mementos that I still hold very dear. It was like learning about all these things and events for the first time, but on another dimension. In addition, I took Art history, computer and economic geography classes to satisfy the requirements of the sabbatical.

When I returned in September 1988, I was introduced to the new acting chairman of our department; but my very good friend, Ed, had left to chair at Murray Bertram H.S. in downtown Manhattan. If you remember, Ed and I began Fashion together in 1967. I regard him as my closest and dearest friend till this day. He had his ups and downs like everybody else, but for some reason we drew on each other whenever we encountered those pitfalls in life, those professional frustrations and difficult situations we all have to solve. He left Fashion for one year after getting an MBA, only to return to teaching because he was disillusioned with the researching end of stocks and bonds, and because he had a great affection for the subject matter of History. He was an excellent teacher. While he was the senior G.O. moderator, he would invite me many times to escort the students on "dude trip" weekends, proms, and special fashion show events for seniors.

For Ed's part, he seemed to appreciate my company, my support, my sense of humor and my ability to see both sides of an argument. He was so impressed by my strong religious faith that he, one day, out of nowhere, asked me, "How does one become a Catholic?" He forthwith did so, and I was his godfather in a simple ceremony conducted at my parish. I was very moved by the whole event because I had never evangelized or preached to him in any way, but just conducted myself as morally as possible. I've always considered Ed to be like a second brother, a true friend with no strings attached.

When I returned from my sabbatical, I was "renewed," as the phrase goes. I attempted new things in class. I created new lessons; I relied less on the "big" test after each unit, and I opted for more quizzes. One of the concepts I brought into my American and World History classes was to have each student present a visual display of their choice, like dioramas, instead of typing up a term paper as part of the final grade. Since I had a class full of marvelously talented individuals in the arts and trade specialties, I believed that I could combine two subject areas into one and the kids would get a kick out of it at the same time. A mixed bag was not what I wanted. Some youngsters were very creative with beautiful maps, but they just happened to misspell the name of countries or geographic places, like cities or rivers. Other students made large or impractical displays with plastic soldiers or fortifications that were either not properly suitable or completely ridiculous, like having an American Indian toy figure, holding a hatchet, standing on a parapet, during the storming of the Bastille.

The following term, a student brought in a diorama depicting a scene during the Battle of Midway. It showed an American aircraft carrier with a string of pennants from stem to stern. Among these pennants was—honest to God—a German flag, swastika and all. When Bill, the Science chairman, came to visit my room that afternoon, I showed him the diorama, and he roared in complete disbelief, "How can a kid be so stupid?" I thought he was going to have a stroke that day.

The following year, I dropped the visual display idea and returned to the term paper. At least with the term paper, I didn't have to entertain the whole school. My gain was Bill's loss. After the end of the Vietnam War, many South Vietnamese people, along with their families, who were loyal and supportive of the Americans and very much anti-Communist, were permitted to immigrate to the United States. Our school did not get impacted with Vietnamese students until the early and mid 80s, to any significant degree. They were very good students, quite talented and very much to themselves because they appeared to be uncomfortable with our free and easy ways and our differences in cultural values.

I relate the following story because, for the first time in my experience as a teacher, I was halted in my tracks:

As it was the custom for many New York City students during the Christmas season to exchange greeting cards and to wish their teachers glad tidings, a feeling of well-being permeated the building. Back at J.H.S. 22M one year a parent had sent a casserole of paella to me, via her daughter, that was placed on my desk and all wrapped up. It was delicious!

On this particular afternoon, on the last teaching day in December, as the students were clearing out of the room, a sizeable number of enveloped cards were piled on my desk, including one from my Vietnamese student who sat in the first row. She was very quiet, did passing work and was very attentive in class. She wrote everything down in her notebook, and always handed in the required written assignments, but when it came to classroom participation she was mute. I knew very little about her, and if I remember correctly, I didn't see any parent with her during Open School Night.

Anyway, when the final bell rang, I gathered all the cards together, and it usually was my custom to leave all the cards unopened, take them home, and read them at my leisure. For some strange reason, there in the solitude of my classroom, I decided to read each card. Most of the greeting cards had a simple phrase like, "Have a wonderful holiday" and then a signature. Others were very flattering, and then signed.

However, when I unsealed my Vietnamese student's envelope, I was amazed that there was so much written inside the card.

First, it said how much she appreciated my lessons, and how much she had learned from me in those three or four short months we were together. Then she concluded the paragraph with a brief phrase that said, "And, I want to thank you for being the father I never knew!" What a bombshell! It was as if I was hit in the chest with a sledgehammer, and with the card still in my hand, I bawled like a baby. I never knew that one person could affect another with such intensity as I felt that day. I still well up with tears when I recall the moment. I know I was never the same man after that experience.

And so, to quote from "September Song," the days began to get short for me as well. My lower back began to really bother me a lot, and, it was later diagnosed as arthritis in the lumbar region. To me, it sounded like the name of a forest in Canada. I had great difficulty standing, sitting or stretching. I endured prescribed steroid shots, which helped for a while, but then, the pulsating pain would return with a vengeance. In early 1990, I got a call from my surgeon. It was necessary for me to see him immediately because the pacemaker, implanted seven years before, was not up to speed. It had to be replaced, pronto. I decided, in the spring of that year, that retirement was becoming a strong possibility. My chairman said that I should give it another year, and then see what happens. I agreed.

When I returned that September, I knew the handwriting was on the wall. I had given up my positions in summer school, night school, after-school tutoring, and entrance exam monitoring over the years to stretch out my time, but now I couldn't maintain it anymore. I wasn't burned out or tired. It was really something closer to not enjoying my job as I did before. I was reminded of something Joe DiMaggio said to the press when he announced his retirement: "It isn't fun anymore." Exactly.

I scheduled my retirement meetings with one of the excellent staff people to whom we were assigned at the UFT headquarters at Park Avenue South. I collected all the necessary handouts and forms to study and began to talk, discreetly, to some of my retired colleagues by phone during this period. It all came down to this: I had to make the final decision. Not my wife, not my priest, not my union rep. I alone had to decide.

While all this was going on in my head, with my family and my closest friends, I get a call to see Mr. B. in his office. Now what?

Mr. B. was not happy with the acting chairman of Social Studies, who was still on probation and not tenured at all. Was I interested in the job?

Interested in the job?

You son-of-a-bitch! Why didn't you make this offer

five years ago? Now that I was considering retirement, he wants to know if I wanted the Chair!

I listened and told him that I wanted to speak about the offer with my wife first, and then I'd give him my answer tomorrow. "Is that O.K.?" I asked.

"Sure. Sure. Absolutely, John. Yes, by all means. See you tomorrow."

I left the office in a small panic. What's going on here?

I knew the answer before I reached the house. I couldn't teach anymore. How could I chair a department? When I came back the next day, I went straight up to the Principal's office, unannounced.

I said, "Mr. B., before I give you an answer to your offer, can I ask something first?"

"Sure," he replied.

"I suppose you want me to chair for at least three years or so, right?" I asked.

"Absolutely!" he replied. "It takes that long just to learn the job!"

"Then, I have to say 'No,' Mr. B."

We stood up, shook hands and I left his office. A month or so later, he retired unexpectedly.

I stayed until January 1991, and with my retirement papers all in order, put the chalk back in the tray for the last time, and left the building. The week before, I had been surprised with a beautiful send-off dinner by a very large number of my associates, both retired and active members of the various departments with which I had worked. Administrators and even secretaries came to toast my retirement. The acknowledgments simply floored me. Everything after that was anti-climatic. I never looked back.

Twenty

The Price: Do You Have to Ask?

The phrase I detest the most is one that proclaims, "Those who can, do, and those who can't, teach." I have a corollary for that which says, "Smart-asses don't learn, therefore they *can't* teach."

The path in life that led me to teaching was based on a very simple principle I support very highly. In order to keep and maintain a vibrant and working democracy, we must have literate people. Second-generation immigrants have proven this point millions of times over with the obvious fact that they not only enjoy better living conditions because of education, but our democracy remains strong and is the envy of the world. The author of that phrase that I hate so passionately can live with the luxury of being a snob and boast about his condemnation of the very people to whom he is beholden. Many people, including top management, founders of blue chip companies and social elitists perpetuate this myth about teachers. I vividly remember on one special occasion in my hometown of Old Tappan, N.J., how one individual referred to all teachers as "those people who suck at the public tit" with such an air of superiority and smugness.

Teachers come from all walks of life, as do all other professionals and tradespeople. The good and the bad, the well-trained and the slacker, are found everywhere. I'm reminded of an old joke in medical circles, which asks "What do you call a person who graduates at the bottom of his class in medical school? A doctor!"

Fortunately—or unfortunately—the image of the public school teacher has not changed much in the last 30 or 40 years. I have found that recent immigrants to America, especially Asians, Latinos and Middle Easterners, have high regard for teachers in general. They seem to appreciate the difficulties of teaching and the long training involved in order to successfully perform before a class. They literally hang on every word you utter at parent-teacher conferences and they verbally agree with your criticism and statement of support.

My father was very high on education, even though he never finished the third grade in Italy. He realized very early in his life that here, in the United States, education was the key to success. On many occasions, when he attempted to comprehend the written materials sent by his firm he would feel humiliated and frustrated that he needed the help of us children, to complete the necessary forms and pieces of correspondences with his office. However, he had three great strengths, and they were his love for his country, and the telling and retelling of parables and accounts of people in his childhood, about the Roman Empire and the events that impressed him most about his newly adopted country. I was a better teacher because of my father's influence and by his stories, which I incorporated into my lessons.

Our public educational system has evolved many times since the colonial period when teachers were expected to fire up the furnace, distribute slates and chalk, place "bad" children in corners with dunce hats, help with janitorial tasks about the school house, assist with home instruction, and visit the homes of those who were sick and needy. Every school has its liberals and conservatives, its well-prepared and its clock-watchers, its young and old. Some folks are in teaching for the money (second income), some because they are attracted to the "ten-month year," some to avoid the military draft, and then, there are those we call the "dedicated" teachers. I remember on one occasion, over a lunch table to be precise, how one particular teacher announced to me that he would join the Communist party if it helped him get more money in his envelope.

Then, of course, you had the radicals. These teachers always had a cause to champion, a message to push, and never missed an opportunity to express it. To them, education wasn't an avenue for economic improvement, but a reason to rebel within the limits of social reform, whether it was about Attica, abortion or affirmative action. I've always believed that issues causing civil unrest, dissension among faculty members or diversion from our educational responsibilities only make our schools dysfunctional, and they give the public a misconception of our role as educators. The issue of evolution, and the creation theory in the biology class is a prime example. The uses of religion instruction in public schools would be another. Children should not be made scapegoats by adults who have their own personal agenda. New ideas should be integrated and absorbed slowly into the curriculum, so that nutty concepts can be weeded out. As the ancient Greeks often repeated, "moderation in all things" applies here. We should always avoid rash extremes like in the case back in the 60s when a school board in the Midwest, attempting to remove all politically incorrect materials and books from a school library, banned *Black Beauty!*

The Teachers' Union has made great strides in addressing the many problems in our profession in the last 40 years or so. Salary, of course, is one, and the other is reducing class size. In the many contractual arrangements since the 1960s in New York City, the union demanded and got pay scales, the creation of arbitration boards, the elimination of many abuses by individual administrators, and the funds for improvement of managing a classroom.

However, the union has also been perceived in a negative manner when it came to the situation of protecting and delaying the extraction of incompetent teachers from the classroom. It's not a matter of "siding" with the administration; it's really a matter of "siding" with the children. Dozens and dozens of teachers who can't do their jobs are protected by the union, remaining on the payroll as they occupy a desk at the Board of Ed building. This procedure can literally take years. This is unprofessional and intolerable. The job of a teacher is to instruct, not to be used as a pawn or a bargaining chip in some labor-management trade-off. A person in need of medical help should no more be willingly treated by an incompetent doctor than to permit this farce. Why then, should we support our union at the expense of those who do a great job in the first place?

At Columbia College, we had a professor who would refer to the uneducated as the "great unwashed." Teaching, in a figurative sense, is the removal of the "dirt" of ignorance from those in our charge. I believe that those who profess to want improvements in this noble effort should seriously consider some of my observations and possible remedies I list for your approval.

1) All teachers should teach in at least two of the three grade schools to remain in the system.

By grade schools, I mean elementary (1–6), junior high (7–9) and high school (9–12). If this plan were adopted, a significant number of positions in the least desirable areas would immediately be filled and could be staffed by experienced teachers without having expensive recruiting drives to accommodate these vacancies. In my experience as a high school administrator, I found that people who taught on the junior high school level were always a notch or two better than those who exclusively taught on the high school level. These teachers to whom I refer handled their classes better and had a greater appreciation of leaving a "hell hole" to come into a better situation because they were teaching at last. I also believe that by getting high school and elementary school teachers in the junior high schools and middle schools, the latter can only be improved by the infusion of experienced people with novel approaches in their new settings.

At present, many junior high schools are just one step above a reform school. In the seven years I was associated with J.H.S. 22M, I can honestly state that I did very little actual teaching with the exception of the SPE classes and the music major class to which I was assigned. Most of my time there was spent in a custodial capacity in which I was given difficult classes because I was considered able to "handle those kids." Teachers would not be regarded by the administration simply as "warm bodies" in front of a classroom. We're better than that and, besides, such a perception is demeaning and tremendously resource-wasteful. This proposal would entail that the rotating teachers remain a least two or three years in their new assignment, and then return from whence they came.

2) Teachers—all teachers—should be re-certified every 5 years.

What's the point of preaching "professionalism" if we permit teachers to use the same lesson plans, year after year, simply because he or she is "senior," or "respected," or be allowed to retire "on board"?

In addition, teachers, as the true professionals they are, must keep up to speed, just like doctors and lawyers, by continually acquainting themselves with new techniques and becoming familiar with publications and material conducive to better teaching. It's very important that teachers remain "young" in the eyes of their students. No one wants to have an old crab in front of a classroom. Be positive and well informed about new trends!

But, at the same time, we should avoid impractical or unapproved methods of instructing. I recall one teacher, in a very disruptive junior high school with a serious problem retaining teachers, who "taught" his social studies class while strumming on a guitar. For 6 months, one day a week, during my student teaching days, I witnessed this teacher playing his guitar each time I observed his class. To me, this was one glaring example of a supervisor who just wanted a warm body and a "teacher" who indulged himself in the make-believe world of entertainment.

3) All chairpersons, once selected by their principal

or transferred from another school, should stop teaching completely.

A chairperson cannot adequately or professionally supervise a department of 12 to 20 people if he or she has to teach as well. It's unfair to the department, and more importantly, to the students. The responsibility of ordering new books, supplies, checking inventories, reviewing examinations, and assigning substitutes, is overwhelming. And, if that isn't enough, the chairperson has to observe new teachers two or three times a year to be eligible for tenure along with his annual observations of his or her tenured people. A supervisor would be serving the students much better if he or she were allowed more time to train, assist and develop better teaching skills for all his teachers. He or she could spend more time by acquainting new people with the curriculum, test procedures, and better lesson planning. He or she could spot problem areas almost immediately and work on the "weak sisters." All this takes time—and if supervisors have to teach as well, somebody is going to get short-changed.

4) Bring back the I.Q. Test.

For the life of me, I can't understand how a proven method of evaluating the potential of a child could be cast out simply because someone called it biased. In simple terms, a valid I.Q. test, properly administered, be it verbal or non-verbal, could easily tell a counselor if a student is lazy, unmotivated or not capable of doing the work. An I.Q. test is not a lie-detecting test, which can be highly subjective. An intelligence test accurately and objectively measures the problem-solving abilities of the test-taker. Why would anybody jettison this valuable tool? In other words, we have people who still say, "if I don't like the results, throw it out!" Well, I hope these individuals never take an X-ray to see if they have pneumonia.

For example, if I applied for the position of center on the New York Knicks and I was cut because I only stand 5' 8½" tall, would I immediately cry "discrimination" because no ethnic Italian-American, in my memory, had held that position, ever? Or, would I accept the greater fact that the Knicks could never win another game with such a physical disadvantage—me? For some illogical reasons, people have no difficulty accepting physical disqualifications when they come in the field of athletics, but they will go absolutely crazy if these same qualifying standards are used to measure mental skills. Every civil reformer and liberal will come out of the woodwork to voice his or her bitter opposition to the I.Q. test. "Unfair! Discriminating! You're holding down the minorities!" How ridiculous! Perhaps we should abandon tests for Sickle Cell, or Mediterranean Anemia, or Tay-Sachs disease because they, too, have a similar capacity to single out Afro-Americans, Italians, and Jews respectively.

Tests and test scores can only help and inform us how to better understand our students. We should never be afraid or reluctant to accept what tests reveal to us. Maybe parents don't want to hear that their Johnny, or Hector, or Tyrone, can't be a nuclear scientist, but we, the educators and the evaluators—not the bigots—have the duty to mainstream each student in our care so that each can reach and fulfill their individual potential as we were trained to do. If a doctor told you to avoid a certain food from your diet, why is it politically correct to accept his evaluation and not accept that of a teacher? I believe the reason that we, as teachers, have this problem is two-fold. One, our union; and two, the New York politicians, who want to win elections at any price.

Our union has never had the courage of its convictions when it came to assisting teachers, when shovel hits metal. Our union would rather report in its newspaper the struggles of the lettuce pickers in California than to support its membership with tools regardless if they were politically acceptable or not. We are not lettuce pickers or chicken-feather pluckers. We are *teachers,* and we deserve to have our union concentrate on improving our image as true professionals. We should make the hard decisions about education. Not politicians. Nor should we sleep with them.

As for politicians, they are constantly surrounded by P.R. people out on the sidewalks, ready to pounce on any topic as long as it brings in the votes. They are not in the classrooms, and they haven't a clue about how to teach students who might hate all schools in general and have many critical family problems in particular. We are now experiencing a medical dilemma in our country because pencil-pushers in an insurance office are telling a doctor which procedure is allowed and which is not. We find this unacceptable. Why, then, do we tolerate political input in implementing a particular educational method?

5) Restore the multi-diploma concept in our high schools.

Right now, every—and I mean every—student who finishes high school in New York City has not only the right, but already has a *promise* from the city colleges that they must accept his application regardless of his or her grades and his or her course of study. Prior to this poorly thought-out revision in the 60s, a student who wanted to attend college was far better prepared for the grueling four years awaiting him or her. This student had to take 4 years of English, 4 years of math, 2 years of science, $3^1/_2$ years of social studies, and 3 years of a foreign language, and pass all subjects to accumulate the needed $16^1/_2$ Regents credits to get an "Academic Diploma" necessary to apply for any college in the country.

If a student wanted to eliminate foreign language or science, and substitute something less demanding, he or she would receive a "General Diploma" upon graduation; no college. However, if this same student wanted to go on to college, he or she would have to return to night school, get the necessary credits and then apply to the college of his or her choice. I repeat, an education—not politics—was the essential factor here. Nonetheless, it was found to be politically incorrect and discriminatory to have someone accept the non-college track leading to either a vocational or a commercial diploma. So they were abolished as demeaning, and the "one-diploma" rule was adopted. Not one word of protest by the Teachers' Union.

The message was clear. It was as if no other graduate, except the one receiving the academic diploma, could ever be gainfully employed and earn a decent living. People including junior high school advisors and high school counselors jumped on the bandwagon and made the point that anyone who wanted to become a plumber or secretary or a mechanic was comparable to a social leper. The politicians and the civil libertarians had a field day. It's interesting to note, at this juncture, that

285

since the adoption of the "one-diploma" rule, high school principals now have to take out an insurance policy, as recommendation by the association, of up to $1,000,000—that's *one million* dollars—to protect any principal from a lawsuit by a graduating senior who can't read! No principal ever had to be insured like that before 1960.

Back in 1970, I was taking a class at Hunter College to complete a requirement, Economic Geography, to keep my high school license. I arrived there early one night to go over some notes I had taken the week before when I ran into another student. He was about to leave the student lounge, and I noticed that he had no books. But had a rather large guitar strapped to his back. I commented on the beauty of the instrument and from there we struck up a conversation about attending Hunter. He noticed that I wasn't the typical college student he came to see; I was nearly 35, so he asked me about the courses I was taking. I told him, and then, I inquired about his regimen as an upper classman.

"Oh," he said. "I'm not even a matriculated freshman yet." He added, "I'm in the process of completing my high school education so that I can become a college freshman next year!"

"How long have you been here already?" I asked, somewhat in disbelief.

"About three years now, but I'm almost finished and then I can matriculate next year, my counselor said!" he said proudly.

"You're about 21 now, and you'll be finished with Hunter four years after that? Who's paying you to stay in college?" I pressed.

"I'm in the S.E.E.K. Program and the government pays for my schooling, plus I receive $75.00 a week to remain in college. I'm hoping to be through with schools when I'm around 27!"

"Holy cow!" I said. "This program supports you, pays you to finish high school, and then, college too? What a deal! Good luck!"

"Thanks," he said as he put on his coat to leave, and readjusted the guitar. I was in complete disbelief. This kid is *college material*? No way!

You know, there was a time, once, when Hunter College wouldn't even look at an application if the student didn't have a 90 average. Excellence was rewarded then.

6) Junior high school students, in particular, should be uniformed.

These uniforms should be inexpensive to buy and easy to maintain, and essential to stay in school. Give each youngster some type of reward. It could be in the form of a monthly deposit into their student bank account as an incentive to keep their attendance up. The balance of this account would only be paid out upon completion and graduation from the 9th grade. I found that J.H.S. students are very sensitive to any indiscriminate remark passed on by their fellow students regarding choice of clothing, taste in jewelry or how they wear their hair. All this could be easily moderated by some practical standard of hair length, removal of all ostentatious wearing of jewelry and the selection of wearing a simple, but pleasant-looking, school garment. Each year would be different. For example, dark blue for the 7th graders, tan for the 8th graders, and so on. In this way, security people would easily identify each student by grade, and fights and misunderstandings could be cut down considerably. Schools are institutions of learning and not places to make fashion statements that could embarrass some, develop ostracism for others and resentments by still another group. The wearing of uniforms should be made mandatory throughout the school.

These suggestions should be given serious consideration for the sake of our students, and to give the public a justifiable accounting of our actions. We owe these parents who supply the tax dollars more than just platitudes and the "easy fix." We can never avoid our responsibility to them and the children, be it as chaperones on a class trip, be it as models of propriety of behavior, or be it the person with the red pen.

In closing, I must relate my last impression as an educator on a crystal cold day in January of 1991. I had just finished monitoring a citywide English examination for sophomores. As it was my custom, I would dismiss each student as he/she completed the exam. I only had about five or six students remaining when the bell rang, ending the exam. I collected the remaining test papers and pencils, stuffed them into the large brown envelope and began to exit the room along with these students as they struggled with their outer garments. A poster, in color, near the door caught my eye, and as I stopped to read what it said, I was horrified, because it looked like some type of high school prank I had seen before. This one was a well-drawn penis and scrotum in pink or light purple and a message about avoiding AIDS. At the top of this 8½ by 11 paper poster, was the heading "NYC Board of Education" and its logo. The tiny parade of students who were departing the class didn't even look up, gave it not so much as a glance, as I, the proctor, gawked in complete disbelief.

It had come down to this. Thirty-one years of devotion to my students; thirty-one years of trying to reach a higher plane, and this is my "gold watch." The image of male genitalia, in living color, which would have been absolutely inappropriate to display anywhere in Academia back in 1960, when this all began. This was my parting salute from the NYC Board of Education.

We've come full circle. Where do you go now, Johnny?